WENDY PERRIN'S

secrets

EVERY SMART
TRAVELER
SHOULD KNOW

Fodor's Travel Publications, Inc.
New York • Toronto • London • Sydney • Auckland
http://www.fodors.com/

WENDY PERRIN'S SECRETS EVERY SMART TRAVELER SHOULD KNOW
BY WENDY PERRIN

EDITOR: Michael Shnayerson

CONDÉ NAST TRAVELER CONTRIBUTORS: Carol Plum, Ombudsman Editor; Heidi Turner, Chief Researcher; David Jefferys, Sherrie Liu, John Rand, Research Associates; Ben Morse, Assistant

FODOR'S CONTRIBUTORS: Guido Caroti, Associate Art Director; Fabrizio La Rocca, Creative Director; Linda K. Schmidt, Copy Chief; Karen Cure, Editorial Director

COVER DESIGN: Fabrizio La Rocca

COVER PHOTO: Joyce Ravid

TEXT DESIGN: Guido Caroti, Fabrizio La Rocca

ILLUSTRATIONS: Christina Sun

First Edition

ISBN 0–679–03351–3

PRINTED IN THE UNITED STATES OF AMERICA

10 9 8 7 6 5 4 3 2 1

Perrin, Wendy, 1965–
    [Secrets every smart traveler should know]
    Wendy Perrin's secrets every smart traveler should know / by Wendy Perrin.
      p. cm.
    Includes index.
    ISBN 0-679-03351-3 (pbk.)
    1. Travel.   I. Title.
G151.P48 1997
910'.2'02—dc21   96-48213
                             CIP

NOTE TO READERS

The anecdotes used in this book were all published in the Ombudsman column in *Condé Nast Traveler* between 1990 and 1996. They are used to illustrate the process of resolving travel complaints rather than the current condition of a particular travel company. Airlines, hotels, shops, tour operators, and other companies change over time. When you read this book, a company that in the past displayed poor customer service may be under new management and treating its customers well. A company that once received our praise may have deteriorated. The anecdotes should therefore not be viewed as an endorsement or a condemnation of any particular company. Where anecdotes describe a situation that was not fully resolved at the time the complaint was published in the magazine, we have explained updated company policies and other information to make them current as of press time.

Table of Contents

TABLE OF CONTENTS

Foreword

For a long time no publication consistently and courageously went to bat for travelers who had been mistreated by an airline, cruise line, or other travel company ... until eight years ago, when *Condé Nast Traveler* founding editor Harold Evans, along with editors Graham Boynton and Clive Irving, dreamed up a new column for the magazine: We would have an ombudsman—a problem-solver who would investigate our readers' complaints and seek justice where appropriate. The ombudsman would contact the companies involved, request an explanation or compensation for the traveler, and publish the results of our investigation so others would learn from it. The column would embody the magazine's mandate: Truth In Travel.

Today, still, no other publication does what the Ombudsman column does. Yet the need for a travelers' advocate is even greater than it was eight years ago. While the travel industry is still largely unregulated and pitfalls abound, more people are traveling in more ways than before, and, in the economically pinched '90s, getting what they paid for is often their foremost concern.

The Ombudsman column grew so popular that Harry Evans decided we ought to publish a book compiled from our ombudsman files. It was during my 3 1/2-year stint as the ombudsman that former managing editor Rick Levine set the wheels spinning and drafted a proposal. Editors Dee Aldrich and Cliff Hopkinson brought the project to fruition.

Several others are owed huge thanks for their contributions to this book: Carol Plum, my successor as ombudsman; Heidi Turner, who has investigated our readers' complaints for more than six years; Condé Nast Traveler contributing editor Michael Shnayerson, who edited a first draft, and Fodor's editorial director Karen Cure, who provided valuable comments on a second; legal counsel Rich Constantine; our readers who have graciously allowed their letters to the Ombudsman to be reprinted here; as well as Nichole Bernier, Peter Frank, Sherrie Liu, John Rand, and David Jefferys, all of whom lent their expertise, not to mention my mother (who taught me how to travel) and my father (who paid for it).

Most deserving of thanks, though, is Tom Wallace, successor to Harry Evans as Condé Nast Traveler's editor-in-chief, who has guided the Ombudsman column's development since my first day on the job. His balanced judgment and keen sense of ethics have ensured the column's unflagging commitment to Truth In Travel.

Wendy Perrin

Wendy Perrin
Consumer News Editor, *Condé Nast Traveler*

Confessions of an Ombudsman

Maybe it was while I was interrogating the airline that handcuffed an innocent passenger, dragging him out of first class and through the airport for needless questioning. Or perhaps it was when I was investigating why thousands of screeching birds had decided to nest at a luxury resort where guests sought peace and quiet. Or while I was tracking down a woman's luggage containing her grandfather's ashes. (The ashes were on a bus—bumping around the great Southwest.) In any case, at some point during my 3½-year term as Ombudsman for *Condé Nast Traveler* magazine, it hit me: This is a really strange job.

Webster's defines an ombudsman as someone who "investigates reported complaints, reports findings, and helps to achieve equitable settlements." But what the *Condé Nast Traveler* Ombudsman does is solve the nation's travel problems. Say an airline lost your ski gear and won't reimburse you. Or the "ocean view" room you paid an arm and a leg for looked onto a septic tank. Or the silk carpet you had shipped from Turkey never arrived. Our team of troubleshooters investigates on your behalf. We do our best to get the airline, hotel, or carpet store either to make good on its promises or to pay up. In fact, over the years, we have negotiated over $2 million in refunds and compensation for wronged travelers.

Now, straightening out everyone's travel snags is no easy task. Some people think that because we're a big, glossy magazine we can bring truth and justice to the travel industry with a snap of our fingers. Let me assure you, it's not as simple as donning a big red cape and a blue suit with a giant O on it. It means wrestling—sometimes for months, or even years—with the more intransigent travel companies. It requires being part consumer advocate, part judge, part FBI agent, part Dear Abby.

Very little surprises me anymore. Very little would surprise you, either, if you had investigated more than 10,000 travel disasters. I've heard the one about the expensive luxury villa that turned out to be a construction site. And the one about the two-day car rental that cost $7,000. And the cabin that was flooded when the ship's swimming pool emptied into it. And the airline that lost the priceless African gray parrots. Not to mention the nonswimmer who fell into the ocean through a hole in the gangplank, the malaria-stricken girl who couldn't get home from Ivory Coast, the man who died over the Atlantic because the flight attendants couldn't perform CPR, the crew member decapitated by a swinging conveyor belt . . .

Being Ombudsman can make you think twice about leaving home. Don't get me wrong: I love to travel. But I find myself worrying about every little thing that can go awry. Plane trips are the worst. I still call four or five times to confirm a flight, arrive at the airport hours ahead of time, refuse to check luggage, and kill time counting the number of regulations being broken.

The strange thing is that ever since I found out everything that can go wrong on a trip, everything *has* gone wrong. The day I was supposed to fly to Eastern Europe, the Persian Gulf War broke out and my flight was canceled. The day I was supposed to fly to New York from Los Angeles, there were riots in L.A. and my flight was canceled. I've been stuck on a six-hour bus ride late at night in the Rockies during a snowstorm with a drunken driver. My rental car has broken down in the jungle. I've been stricken by mysterious bacteria in any number of countries. The worst experience of all was on a transcontinental flight when I found myself seated, to my horror, next to the slimeball defense attorney who had won the criminal case on which I had served as a juror. He proceeded to tell me that he had known from the start that his client was guilty. I spent the rest of the flight feeling nauseated (and not from airsickness).

I'm haunted by the nightmares I've investigated even when I'm not traveling. When I went to the airport to send a friend's cat to her in Los

Angeles, all I could think of was the time the baggage handler dropped a kennel. The door popped open, the cats inside escaped, and one was run over and killed by a baggage truck and the other was lost for six days.

But being the Ombudsman does have its advantages. It's rewarding to know you're helping out the little guy. And I'm lots of fun at cocktail parties. Not only do I have a stockpile of great conversation openers ("Did you hear the one about the pilot who flew to the wrong country?"), but the same law of the universe that makes party guests gravitate toward doctors—everyone wants free medical advice—makes me popular as well. Everyone wants to recount his latest travel mishap and hear what I have to say.

As Ombudsman you hear an awful lot of the same old same old. In fact, one Christmas I set it all to music: "Twelve canceled cruises, eleven missed connections, ten bankrupt agents, nine rotten tour guides, eight stolen passports, seven rare diseases, six noisy cabins, five canceled flights, four missing bags, three skipped ports, two damaged cars, and a silk rug that never arrived."

Still, the outlandish complaints never cease. There was the couple wrongly accused of—and arrested for—having sex in the hotel swimming pool. There was the guy who wanted a refund for his plane ticket to the town where his crazy cousin lives because the cousin had threatened to shoot his rear full of lead if he came anywhere near. The oddball award goes to the Hawaii cruisegoer who brought lava onto the ship. Taking lava from Hawaii is supposed to bring bad luck, so the vessel had to be exorcised.

But the vast majority of the complaints we receive are not so bizarre. They come from intelligent people who have been unable to get an obstinate company to listen to reason and deliver what it promised. When we get results for these travelers, they assume we have some magic formula that they don't. But there is no magic formula. We simply know what the rules are, what your rights are, whom to contact for what sort of problem, and how to beat the system when that's possible.

CONFESSIONS OF AN OMBUDSMAN

Since 1989, when *Condé Nast Traveler* started the Ombudsman column, so many travelers have asked us to share our secrets that we've finally put our accumulated wisdom down on paper, illustrated with anecdotes published in the column over the years. Our guide to traveling trouble-free tells you how to avoid the gamut of problems that can occur and, if disaster strikes anyway, how to salvage your vacation and get your money back.

Bon voyage!

CHAPTER 1

The Fine Art
of Complaining

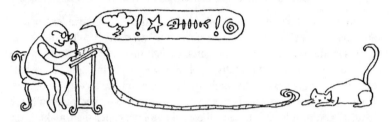

S ome travelers who come to us for help can't get anywhere with an airline, car rental agency, or other travel company because it's being stingy and obdurate. But other travelers run into roadblocks because they've taken the wrong approach. Perhaps they complained to the wrong person. Or they didn't write a letter. Or they wrote it the wrong way. I'll get to the do's and don'ts of dealing with particular types of travel companies in the following chapters, but let me start with some general tips that apply any time you want to insure yourself against travel snags or get a complaint taken seriously.

The Ten Commandments
of Trouble-Free Travel

1. DO YOUR HOMEWORK

A little preparation before leaving home can save a vacation. If you're unfamiliar with a company you want to use, check out its reputation before sending money. If it's a travel agency, find out whether it's registered to sell travel and whether there are complaints filed against it. If it's a tour company, make sure it has posted a bond that protects you in case it goes bust, leaving you with neither your trip nor your money. (The "Where to Turn for Help" section at the end of each chapter lists who you should contact to check out each type of company.)

2. GET IT IN WRITING (AND READ THE FINE PRINT)

Before paying for travel arrangements, get written documentation of what you are supposed to receive. If all your dealings are verbal, write down exactly what was agreed to, the date, the time, and name of the person you spoke to. Take copies of your documents or notes with you on your trip, in case there's a disagreement as to what you were promised.

When you get the written material, read the fine print. Note all exclusions and disclaimers, rather than just accepting whatever you're told about what's included and whether the purchase is refundable. And do your own research to make sure you really want what you're buying. Say you're purchasing a travel package that includes several nights in "luxury" lodgings. Look up the hotels in a guidebook you trust to see whether they really are luxe. If you're told that buying the package is cheaper than making the arrangements on your own, determine the cost of the individual components of your package—airfare, accommodations, car rental—to see if this is really true. Remember that certain headaches that may occur on a trip are more easily dodged if you haven't prepaid. It's easier to switch hotels, for instance, if a company doesn't already have your money.

3. PAY WITH A CREDIT CARD

If you charge a trip and don't receive what you were promised, you can dispute the charge with your credit card issuer and get it wiped off your bill. Credit cards protect you only if you don't get what you paid for—not if you get it but are dissatisfied with it. Even though they don't always come to the rescue when you'd like them to, it's far better to use one than not. If a travel company doesn't accept credit cards, think twice about giving it your business.

4. DON'T PROCRASTINATE

As soon as a problem arises, report it. If you're at a hotel, talk to the general manager. If you're on a cruise, seek out the purser. Find out when the problem can be fixed, and, if it isn't fixed by then, report it once more. A record of your dissatisfaction will help later if you have to file a formal complaint.

What if the problem never gets fixed? What if you're sick of the excuses and delays and don't want to waste any more vacation time? Should you bail out and request a refund later? It depends on how strong your case is (whether the contractual conditions of your purchase were met, whether you've been able to collect supporting documentation), and how financially stable and customer-service-oriented the company is.

Say a resort's brochure promised a swimming pool and tennis courts. You arrive to find that ongoing renovations have made them unusable and that they will remain so for the rest of the week. But when you say you want to go elsewhere, the hotel refuses to refund your deposit. If you can document what you were promised (with copies of the brochure or a descriptive invoice) and what you actually received (with photos of the unusable facilities), and the resort belongs to a reputable U.S. chain, you may do well to leave, find a better hotel, and demand a refund later. If the resort is a small foreign inn, you risk never getting your money back.

The point is that if you decide to bail out of a rotten situation, don't flee without the materials that will help you build a strong case when you request a refund. And if you are told a refund will be sent, get this promise in writing.

5. KNOW YOUR RIGHTS

Sometimes a travel company violates one of its own policies. Sometimes it actually breaks the law. Regulations that protect travelers are limited, but they do exist, and it's important to know when your rights are being transgressed and what compensation you're legally owed. It's also important to know how companies typically attend to travelers in a situation like yours, so you know whether you're getting standard treatment or the brush-off. (Your legal rights, and companies' standard responses to a variety of complaints, are all spelled out in subsequent chapters.)

6. DETERMINE YOUR LOSSES

Compare the amount you paid with the cost of what was delivered. What features of your trip did you not receive? Which weren't as advertised? How much extra did you have to pay to extricate yourself from an awful situation? Determine what damage was done and assign it a cash value.

If you can prove that you were wrongly overcharged, you'll probably get a refund. If you can't document an out-of-pocket loss, you probably won't. But you may be offered a credit toward future travel with the company if it wants your repeat business—and many do, especially hotels and cruise lines.

Keep in mind that a lot of travel suppliers sell a fantasy. If your complaint is based on unrealized expectations rather than a failure to deliver something specifically promised, don't expect much more than an apology letter.

7. WRITE A LETTER

If you can resolve the situation with a phone call or two, terrific. But trying to settle a dispute with a large bureaucracy by phone can be time-consuming, frustrating, and ultimately futile—and leave you without hard evidence of your efforts to resolve the problem. Also, after hearing a traveler's story, some customer-service representatives hazard snap judgments before they've had a chance to research the complaint and study the documents. Not knowing the whole picture, they can inadvertently mislead you, either by instilling false hopes as to the compensation you can expect or by asserting incorrectly that little can be done. Better to write a letter.

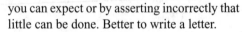

Your formal complaint should be typed and no longer than a page or two. Don't give a long-winded narrative or a laundry list of minor flub-ups. Focus on the company's one or two worst mistakes, and give only the pertinent facts. Provide dates, times, employee names, flight numbers, room numbers, account numbers, etc. Attach copies of all the documents supporting your complaint (tickets, receipts, claim stubs, contracts, correspondence, photographs, police reports, everything). Include your daytime phone number. If there were witnesses to the problem or others who suffered with you, list their names, addresses, and phone numbers. Send your letter by certified or registered mail.

And make sure you write to the right place. If you bought a travel package, write to the party who sold it to you. If you bought directly from an airline, hotel, cruise line, or car rental company, write to the customer relations department at the company's U.S. headquarters. (If you had trouble with a franchise of a hotel or car-rental chain, your complaint may be forwarded to the franchise location.) Don't think you'll beat the system by sending a letter to the company's president. It will most likely be rerouted to customer relations, increasing the chance of its getting lost and delaying the resolution process. Only if the company you had trouble with is small and doesn't have a customer service department should you write to its head.

8. DON'T BE HOSTILE OR GREEDY

Try to sound positive and likeable—so that the person who reads your letter will want to help. Don't be hot-headed or sarcastic. Boasting about how important you are or threatening to instruct everyone at your office never to fly that airline or use that car-rental company again won't make you any friends. On the other hand, mentioning how often you've flown that airline or rented cars from that agency in the past, and how satisfied you used to be, might help a lot.

Don't threaten legal action. If you do, customer relations may forward your letter to legal affairs, which could slow down the whole process and reduce your chance of remuneration; compensation is often viewed as an admission of guilt in court, so a company will be reluctant to provide it if there's a chance that your problem will end up there. If you plan to involve a lawyer, mention it at a later stage.

If you speak to the customer-service agent handling your complaint, don't make threats or lose your temper (forget the squeaky-wheel theory). And don't chronicle the entire frustrating history of your dealings with the company. The agent is not the one responsible for your problem. But he or she does have the power to resolve it and sometimes even to rule on how much compensation to give. I've known plenty who would have been more generous had the customer not behaved like a pit bull.

When requesting remuneration, specify an amount and ask for something the company can deliver (it can give a future discount but can't restore lost vacation time). Don't ask for the moon or you'll lose credibility. If your cruise ship skipped a port, for instance, don't demand a refund of the entire cost of the cruise. A company that thinks you're angling for a freebie won't be as generous as it might be otherwise. If you request an amount that's fair—and explain why you think it's fair—you'll be more likely to get it.

9. DON'T GIVE UP

If the response you receive is a form letter that seems to have been written by a robot and has little connection to your case, send a second letter that explains, point by point, why the company's response did not address your situation.

It's a good sign if you've been offered compensation: It's an admission that your complaint has merit. If you consider the offer inadequate, make a counteroffer. Be willing to negotiate. Some companies simply won't give refunds. If you're agreeable to using the company again, ask for a credit towards future services in an amount somewhat higher than the cash amount you would have settled for.

Set a reasonable deadline, perhaps three or four weeks, for the company to take action on your second letter. If you get no response and your follow-up phone calls prove fruitless, seek help from a third party.

10. BRING IN THE HEAVY ARTILLERY

Send a copy of your complaint, including all background correspondence and supporting documentation, to the appropriate federal or state agency, local consumer protection office or Better Business Bureau, or industry association (provided in the "Where to Turn for Help" section at

the end of each chapter). Chances of outside assistance for a complaint about an airline or travel agency are relatively good. For a hotel, cruise, or car-rental complaint, they're pitiful, as you'll see in subsequent chapters.

Mail or fax a copy of your complaint to *Condé Nast Traveler*'s Ombudsman column (⊠ 360 Madison Ave., New York, NY 10017, FAX 212/880–2190). A local newspaper or radio or television station may have an "Action Line" or "Hot Line" service that can

help, too. If you suspect fraud, notify your district attorney or state attorney general's office as well. If all else fails, consider small claims court. The maximum amounts that can be claimed or awarded vary by state, but court procedures are generally simple, quick, and inexpensive.

CHAPTER 2

Airlines

So this guy walks up to the check-in counter with three bags: a black one to accompany him to San Francisco, a green one he wants to send to Chicago, and a blue one that needs to go to Dallas. "I'm sorry, sir. We can't do that," says the check-in agent. "Whaddya mean?" grumbles the passenger. "Ya did it last week!"

The Ombudsman department hears more sorrowful stories concerning air travel than anything else. As a consequence I've quintupled my supply of airline jokes. If I didn't find some way to laugh about it all, it would be far too depressing.

Much about airline travel is desperately unfair. I'm not talking about minor annoyances like sardine-can seating or transcontinental flights with nothing to eat but peanuts or having to fly from New York to Seattle via Atlanta. (Whether you're going to heaven or hell, you have to change in Atlanta.) These aspects of air travel are inconvenient, but not necessarily unfair, because usually you know what you're getting into ahead of time.

I'm talking about the rules and policies that apply when something goes unexpectedly wrong—say, an airline bumps you from a flight it has oversold, or your luggage is shredded, or you get to your final destination 36 hours late. The few laws that protect travelers who have ceded control over their lives to an airline are outdated and inadequate. When it comes to air travel, it just seems as though the customer is always wrong.

Upon arriving in St. Thomas for my flight to Boston via San Juan, I was bumped because American Airlines had overbooked the plane.

American arranged for Virgin Air to fly me and eight other bumped passengers the 72 miles to San Juan in time for our connecting flights. Everyone on the Virgin Air flight knew where we were going except the pilot, who landed us on St. Barts, 213 miles from San Juan. When we frantically pointed out his mistake, he apologized and took off again.

We finally got to San Juan, and I raced to catch my 6:15 flight. I reached the gate at 6:10, as the sliding glass doors closed. I knocked and waved my boarding pass, but the agent on the other side ignored me. I had to spend the night in San Juan. American apologized for the overbooking with a $150 voucher, but as I see it, I was bumped twice and deserve more.

—*Bernard Harris, Boston, Massachusetts*

We thought so too, so we wrote to American, and it eventually sent an additional $200 voucher. It said that the extra time it would have taken to reconnect the jet bridge, help Harris find his seat, and stow his luggage could have snowballed into a delay. It also did not know of Virgin Air's mistake: Once it arranges alternate transportation for bumped passengers, American said, it is no longer responsible for them. Virgin Air, by the way, had put passengers in a plane originally headed for St. Barts, forgetting to tell the pilot that the destination had been changed.

The way your complaint is handled and the compensation you can expect to receive when something goes wrong on a plane trip differ from airline to airline and, in many cases, from employee to employee. Although airlines are generally sticklers for policy, there is often quite a bit of room for negotiation. Customer service representatives and gate agents are more empowered than you may realize. Not only can they change seat assignments and give free upgrades, they can also waive ticket-changing fees, endorse your ticket to another airline, and settle claims involving relatively small amounts of money. How you go about complaining to them is a big factor in the negotiation process, so keep on their good side; don't treat them like anonymous cogs in a huge machine. Voice displeasure, if warranted, but don't do it at the top of your lungs. Be politely persistent, and document what went wrong with notes from your phone conversations with the airline—including names and dates—and all boarding passes, ticket receipts, baggage-claim stubs, and so on. If you can offer a good reason why the airline should waive its rules in your case, you can go far.

Of course, an ounce of prevention is worth a pound of cure. And there are many measures air travelers can take to minimize screw-ups and make unbearable situations bearable again.

Let's start at the beginning.

Nabbing the Best Fare

Most passengers sitting in the same cabin on the same flight have paid a spectrum of different fares, with last-minute travelers shelling out hundreds of dollars more than those who booked in advance. No wonder people view air fares as a form of extortion.

Just knowing, when you walk onto a plane, that others onboard paid a fraction of what you paid can set your teeth grinding for the rest of the flight. How to avoid feeling like a sucker?

PREDICTING AIR FARE SALES

The first step is to wait for the big sales and then pounce. Domestic air fares tend to drop substantially during three brief periods: (1) late May or early June, (2) late August, and (3) the period between Thanksgiving and Christmas.

These are times when business travel is slow and airlines try to fill jets by luring vacationers. Overall, the cheapest season is spring, when airlines are scrambling to capture their share of the summer vacation market. Prices remain relatively low through summer and climb again in September. They creep higher for the rest of the winter except for the Thanksgiving-Christmas window. As long as travel habits are seasonal and airlines have more seats than they can fill, you can count on these three sale periods.

A good tool for tracking discounts is "Best Fares," a monthly magazine that lists special offers (☎ 800/880–1234; $58 annually).

GETTING A REFUND IF THE FARE DROPS
BEFORE YOU FLY

After you buy your ticket, be on the lookout in case there's another sale and the flight you booked is discounted further. Many airlines refund the difference between the new, lower fare and what you paid. But you have to ask.

We bought tickets on America West for a trip to Mexico. Soon after our purchase, the airline ran full-page ads in several newspapers offering special low fares. Our trip plans met all the requirements listed in the fine print at the bottom. We called America West to obtain the lower fare, volunteering to pay the $35 change fee involved. Our request was turned down. Since we had done this before with no problem, we were surprised. We got the name of a supervisor to appeal to but never received a response.

—*Jim and Suzanne Almas, Jackson, Mississippi*

When Ombudsman asked America West about this, the airline couldn't locate the Almases' letter. But it did promise to refund the difference in fares. It also clarified its policy: If fares are lowered and passengers who are already ticketed meet the new requirements, the airline will refund the difference minus a $35 ticket-changing fee. We asked if the Almases should have proceeded differently and were told no. Apparently, their request was directed to the wrong department and never made it to the right desk.

The policy is pretty much the same with all major U.S. airlines. To get a refund of the price difference, your trip must meet the restrictions of the new fare (if there is a two-week advance-purchase requirement, for instance, you must change your ticket at least two weeks before your flight date). There must also still be seats available at the new fare; if those low-fare seats are sold out by the time you call, you're out of luck. And, you must pay the airline's ticket-changing fee.

So after you buy an airline ticket, review newspaper ads frequently—or check with your agent if you used a travel agency.

PLAYING GAMES

For years travelers needing to make a weekday overnight trip but not wanting to pay the often-exorbitant price of round-trips that don't include a Saturday-night stay have had a trick up their sleeves. Instead of buying one expensive round-trip, they buy two cheap back-to-back round-trips. They use the outbound portion of one ticket to fly to their destination and the outbound portion of the other ticket to fly back. They can later use the second halves of the tickets, or just throw them out.

For example, say you need to fly to San Francisco overnight. The fare is $1,200; but if you were to spend a Saturday night, it would be $450. You buy a New York–San Francisco round-trip for $450, leaving March 3, returning March 12. You buy a $450 San Francisco–New York round-trip, leaving March 4, returning March 11. You use the first half of the first ticket to fly to San Francisco on March 3 and the first half of the second ticket to return the next day. You can either discard the leftover tickets or use them to go to San Francisco on March 11, returning March 12. If you make the first trip, you have saved yourself $300; if both trips, $1,500.

Although using back-to-back fares has saved many business travelers money, it does violate airline rules. If the airline finds out, it will confiscate your tickets and force you to buy new ones if you want to fly. But if you make sure not to present both portions of a ticket at the same time—show only the outbound or inbound portion you're using—and if you book the two tickets on different airlines, chances are that neither carrier will find out. And with more and more low-fare airlines popping up with no advance-purchase or Saturday-night-stay requirements, you may never need this trick at all.

Another maneuver used primarily by business travelers: If flights to a city you're trying to get to are expensive, choose a cheaper flight that stops in that city on the way to somewhere else and get off when it stops. Say you're trying to get from Cleveland to Denver. Say a Cleveland–Denver flight costs about $100 more than a Cleveland–Los Angeles flight that stops in Denver. You buy the ticket to Los Angeles and get off in Denver.

The drawback is that you can't check luggage to the intermediate city where you plan to get off. You are also violating airline rules, and if found out, you may be billed for the difference between what you paid and what you should have paid for the shorter flight.

USING CONSOLIDATORS

If you need to fly overseas, you can often save hundreds of dollars off the cheapest advertised economy fare by using a consolidator. Consolidators buy tickets that the airlines can't get rid of on their own and sell them at a discount. They're the ones who put those small ads in tiny print in the back of the newspaper listing low fares to far-flung places.

You can save the most on flights to Asia and Latin America. Consolidators won't save you much if you're going to Europe in winter because fares are already so low then. But in summer you can find substantial discounts.

Buying from a consolidator can be risky if you don't take certain precautions. Some disreputable consolidators sell stolen tickets and tickets bought with miles purchased from frequent fliers. (This violates airline policy, and your ticket will be confiscated if the airline finds out.) Some take your money and run.

After spotting a newspaper ad for discounted airfares, I sent Twenty Eight Street Travel, Inc., in Manhattan, a $2,300 check for two New York-Bangkok round-trips on Northwest Airlines. After we checked in at JFK, a Northwest supervisor examined the tickets and said they were stolen. Northwest said they would not honor them because Twenty Eight Street Travel never remitted my money to the airline. We were forced to purchase replacement tickets for $3,202.

After returning from Bangkok, we learned that the police were investigating Twenty Eight Street Travel, which had since closed. We seem to have no recourse.

—*Leslie Brown, Greenwich, Connecticut*

Ombudsman advised Brown to inform both the New York City Better Business Bureau and the Consumer Fraud Bureau of the New York State Department of Law. But unfortunately, consumers who get stuck with stolen tickets usually have little recourse. In fact, Brown should consider himself lucky that Northwest waived restrictions on the new ticket, giving him the lowest available fare to Bangkok.

Before using a consolidator, check out its reputation with the Better Business Bureau where it is located and also the local consumer protection agency, which is often the state attorney general's consumer protection division. Also, pay with a credit card even though many consolidators add a small fee for credit-card purchases—so you can dispute the charge with your card issuer if you don't get what you paid for. Be particularly wary of cash-only transactions and of tickets with printed prices that are higher than the amount you paid.

It's a very good idea to use a travel agent when buying consolidator tickets. Savvy agents know and deal regularly with reliable consolidators (who work primarily through agents, anyway). Also, if your transaction is with a travel agent, your payment is protected if the consolidator goes out of business or doesn't deliver what was promised. In theory, at least.

A travel agent in Manhattan booked me on an Air Afrique flight from Angola to Congo through a consolidator called CJA Travel Consultants. In Angola, I discovered that Air Afrique does not fly that route. Not only did I have to lay out $817 in cash, but I also had to fly almost 3,000 miles in the wrong direction—from Angola to Burundi to Rwanda to Ethiopia to Kenya—to get to Congo. When both the travel agent and CJA refused to reimburse me, I took them to small claims court, and they were each ordered to pay me $315 within 30 days. But neither has paid and I am told it will be difficult to get the New York City Marshal to collect. Please help.

—*Gail Wasserman, New York, New York*

Wasserman eventually got paid, but Ombudsman has rarely dealt with a company as difficult as CJA. Its first check to Wasserman, sent nearly two months after the due date, arrived torn in half.

Not only can some consolidators be rude, but there are other drawbacks. Customers often cannot get refunds, change their itinerary, switch airlines if a flight is canceled or if they miss a connection, reserve specific seats, order special meals, or collect frequent-flier mileage for the trip.

In addition, some consolidators are financially unstable. So pay with a credit card. And try to use a consolidator located nearby. If something goes wrong, it's easier to pursue him or, if necessary, take him to small claims court.

For a list of hundreds of consolidators in the United States, Canada, the United Kingdom, and Germany, check out Kelly Monaghan's *Consolidators: Air Travel's Bargain Basement* (The Intrepid Traveler, ✉ Box 438, New York, NY 10034, ☎ 212/569–1081 or 800/356–9315; $6.95).

CHOOSING CHARTER FLIGHTS

Usually a cheaper alternative to scheduled flights on major airlines, these are often sold through tour operators as part of a travel package that includes airfare, hotel accommodations, and guided tours. But some charter companies sell seats directly to the public as well as through travel agents. The drawbacks may outweigh the savings:

- **Refunds and exchanges are difficult.**

- **You're virtually guaranteed a crowded trip.** Most flights fly close to full.

- **Almost everything takes longer.** Check-in, boarding, and baggage claim are often much slower than on scheduled flights.

- **Flight times may be inconvenient.** You may find yourself arriving or departing at odd hours.

- **Delays can last a while.** Charter lines usually operate flights only once or a few days per week. Any significant delay can throw a charter company's schedule out of whack for days. And if a flight is canceled, there's no automatic switching to a scheduled flight; you have to wait for the charter line to make new arrangements.

Tour companies are legally required to protect their customers' payments for charter flights by depositing them into an escrow account. If you buy a charter ticket through a tour operator, be sure to make your check payable to the escrow agent, as listed in the brochure, not the tour operator. And jot down the departure date and destination on the face of the check.

BOOKING BEREAVEMENT FARES

If you must fly on short notice to a family funeral or to the bedside of a critically ill relative, see whether you can get a "bereavement" or "compassion" fare. Sometimes an airline deducts anywhere from 15% to 50% off the full fare you would otherwise pay. Sometimes it simply waives the advance-purchase requirement.

Usually the relative has to be a member of the immediate family—a spouse, parent, child, sibling, grandparent—although a few airlines include more distant relatives. There may be a limit to when you can fly (within 24 hours of the death, for example), and discounts may apply to domestic flights only.

On the first morning of my vacation in England, I was awakened at 5:30 by a phone call from my mother. My brother had just died unexpectedly in the Bahamas. My parents were alone in Omaha, and my father had gone into shock. I had to get home.

At Gatwick Airport, I learned that both a Northwest and a TWA flight to the United States were fully booked. American Airlines told me I could get to Dallas/Fort Worth if I would take a stand-by seat in coach or a confirmed seat in business class. I felt I had no choice but to pay the $2,480.23 business-class fare.

Back home, I obtained documentation of my brother's death and sent it to American, requesting a bereavement fare. American responded that it does not offer compassion discounts on international routes. I am horrified by the implication that I would have been under greater—and somehow more worthy—stress had I been in the United States when my brother died.

—*Lynda B. Watson, Kirkland, Washington*

American ultimately sent Watson a voucher for $1,077, which represents the price difference between the business-class fare and full fare in coach.

Most U.S. airlines do not officially offer international bereavement fares because demand is primarily domestic and because international fare structures are much more complex and strictly regulated than domestic ones (international fares must usually be approved by foreign governments). However, American says it may try to find a way to offer some sort of discount. Rather than offering a specific reduction off a full-fare ticket, for instance, it might choose a lower, restricted fare and waive the restriction. Had a seat in economy been available for Watson, she would have received a voucher representing the price difference between the full fare in coach and the highest excursion fare.

An airline reservationist can grant you an emergency fare over the phone. But when you show up at the airport, you must provide proof of death or critical illness (usually a death certificate, the name and number of the funeral home, or a doctor's note and the hospital phone number). If it is a case of imminent death, most airlines charge you full fare; if the family member passes away, you can submit the death certificate for a refund.

What if you're on vacation when you hear the bad news? You can come back early, using your return ticket to fly standby. Some airlines waive any ticket-changing fee or change in fare at the airport. Some won't, but will instruct you to submit a copy of the death certificate along with a request for reimbursement once you get home.

FLYING AS A COURIER

If you're not on a strict schedule, you can fly internationally for a fraction of the normal price if you go as a courier—which essentially means you share the cost of a ticket with a shipping company that uses your cargo space. The cost of a typical courier flight is often about half the cheapest economy fare; a last-minute trip could even be free.

The catch: You usually can't check luggage or travel with a companion on the same flight. You can only fly from a major U.S. gateway—namely Chicago, Los Angeles, Miami, New York, or San Francisco—to a few dozen of the world's big business centers. You may not receive frequent-flier credit. And there is a remote chance that your services won't be needed after you've planned your trip.

Here are a few courier-flight bookers that we've heard good things about—no guarantees, mind you:

Discount Travel International (☎ 212/362–3636 in New York City).
Halbart Express (☎ 718/656–8189 in New York, 310/417–9790 in Los Angeles, 305/593-0260 in Miami).
International Bonded Courier, Inc. (☎ 305/591–8080 in Miami, 415/692–8106 in San Francisco).
Jupiter Air, Ltd. (☎ 718/656–6050 in New York, 310/670–5123 in Los Angeles, 415/697–1773 in San Francisco).
Now Voyager (☎ 212/431–1616 in New York City).

For more information and an extensive list of courier companies, try **Air Courier Bargains,** by Kelly Monaghan (The Intrepid Traveler, ✉ Box 438, New York, NY 10034, ☎ 212/569–1081 or 800/356–9315; $14.95).

FLYING WITHIN FOREIGN COUNTRIES

Many foreign airlines sell air passes that make extensive travel within a single country or region a bargain. The passes typically entitle you to several flight segments (usually three), and you can add additional segments at extra cost. Air passes abound in Europe—look for those that allow travel on more than one airline—and are also available for countries in Southeast Asia and South America, and throughout Australia and the South Pacific.

FLYING WITHIN EUROPE

European intercity airfares can be truly pricey. You often get the best deals from London's numerous discount travel agencies, sometimes called "bucket shops," which specialize in different parts of the world. The agencies listed here will trade information by phone or fax and can either ship advance-purchase tickets or hold them until you arrive. (But don't try their patience: Even a few transatlantic faxes reduce their small profit margins.)

Benz Travel (London, ☎ 44–171/439–4181, FAX 44–171/287–9721; for Germany).
Bluebird Express (West Sussex, ☎ 44–1444/235–678, FAX 44–1444/235–789; for France and Italy).
Hamilton Travel (London, ☎ 44–171/344–3333, FAX 44–171/344–3347; for Scandinavia).
Major Travel (London, ☎ 44–171/485–7017, FAX 44–171/267–6780; for all of Europe).
Mondial Travel (London, ☎ 44–181/777–7000, FAX 44–181/776–2000; for Austria, Czech Republic, Hungary).
STA Travel (London, ☎ 44–171/361–6161, FAX 44–171/937–9570; for all of Europe).
Trailfinders (London, ☎ 44–171/937–5400, FAX 44–171/937–9294; for all of Europe).
Unijet (West Sussex, ☎ 44–444/458–611, FAX 44–444/417–100; for all of Europe).

If you want to use one of these discounters:

- **Comparison shop.** Check the airlines' rates as well; they may be running special promotions that can't be beat.

- **Don't buy unless the discounter is bonded.** Make sure the discounter is bonded with the International Air Transport Association or the Association of British Travel Agents—a safeguard should the agency go out of business before sending your ticket.

- **Confirm the airport.** Be certain of which airline you're flying, and from which London airport (Heathrow, Gatwick, London City, or Stansted).

- **Pay with a credit card.** Ask if you can pay a deposit first, with the balance due when you receive the ticket. Most reputable firms will accept this arrangement.

- **Confirm with the airline.** Verify that you are booked for the flight and dates requested. When you get your ticket, check that there is a coupon for every leg of your trip, that your name and flight numbers are correct, and that the status box next to each flight is marked "OK," which indicates that you have a confirmed seat.

Choosing a Flight that Won't Be Delayed

Yes, you can actually select flights so as to improve your chances of arriving on time.

- **Fly early in the day.** Later departures are more likely to be delayed, because they are susceptible to ripple effects throughout the day. Also, if an early flight is delayed or canceled, you have more rerouting options. If you book the last flight of the day and it is canceled, you may get stuck overnight.

- **Choose a nonstop flight.** If you must change planes, choose the route with the least congested connecting airport or the city with the least chance of inclement weather. Keep in mind that a so-called "direct" flight is not a nonstop. Even if a flight has only one flight number, it can involve a change of planes.

- **Choose flights with higher on-time performance ratings.** Before booking a flight, find out what percentage of the time it is delayed by asking for that flight's on-time performance rating. Major U.S. airlines are required to publish in the computer reservations system a one-digit code for each flight that indicates how often it arrives on time. ("On time" means within 15 minutes of schedule.) If the code is 7, for instance, that means the flight arrives punctually between 70% and 79.9% of the time. When choosing between flights with similar schedules and fares, opt for the one with the higher on-time rating.

Ticket Trouble

On international flights, make sure the name on your ticket is exactly the same as the one on your passport. On domestic flights, make sure it's the same as the name on the photo I.D. you'll be carrying with you.

TICKETS ON "CODE-SHARING" AIRLINES

On international flights, it is becoming more and more common that the airline written on your ticket is not the one you end up flying. Say you book a Delta Airlines flight from Los Angeles to London. At LAX you would board a Virgin Atlantic plane, as Delta does not fly to London. Or, say you've got a Continental Airlines ticket from Houston to Rome. Chances are you will need to stop in New York and switch to an Alitalia plane for the New York–Rome leg.

Welcome to the crazy world of "code-sharing," which, in a nutshell, means that certain airlines that have formed international partnerships (United and Lufthansa, Northwest and KLM) sell seats on each other's flights. The partner airlines share flight numbers, or codes—hence, "code-sharing." For example, a computer reservation system may show a Canadian Airlines flight number for a New York–Vancouver flight, even though the trip will actually be flown by American Airlines. Airline reservationists and travel agents are required to inform travelers if a different airline will operate their international flight, but that doesn't mean they always do. To avoid booking your favorite airline and ending up on one you hate, it's safest to ask your travel agent or  reservationist whether the flight is indeed on the carrier you think it's on. And don't forget to ask whether the flight is nonstop or "direct" (which involves a layover).

STOLEN TICKETS

A relatively small number of tickets—usually issued by disreputable travel agents or consolidators—are actually *stolen* from airlines. If you get to the airport and the check-in agent identifies your ticket as stolen, it will probably be confiscated and you will be forced to buy a new one if you want to take the flight. You may even have to pay full fare because you're buying your new ticket at the last minute. If the airline doesn't discover that your ticket is stolen until you've already used the first segment, you may be hit with an exorbitant one-way return fare.

Airlines are within their rights to do this, but the Department of Transportation thinks it's pretty rotten: If it's clear that the passenger didn't know and couldn't have known that he was buying an illegal ticket, the airline should accommodate him anyway, especially if he's already been allowed to fly part of his trip.

So if you find out at the airport that your ticket was stolen and you have to buy a new one, write customer relations when you get home. Ask for a refund or voucher for a future flight, and provide whatever evidence you may have that you bought the tickets in good faith. Write to the Department of Transportation as well (☞ Where to Turn for Help, *below*). If you bought the ticket with a credit card, dispute the charge with your card company.

LOST TICKETS

Jot down your ticket number and bring it with you on your trip. This makes it easier to get a refund if your ticket is lost or stolen, and may enable the airline to replace your ticket if you must actually buy a new one. Although you'll eventually get a refund, it may take a good two to six months—if not a year—and the airline may charge a lost-ticket fee.

More and more airlines are selling electronic tickets, paving the way for the new age of ticketless travel, where you simply book a flight over the phone or through your computer, are given a confirmation number, show your ID at the airport, and walk onto the plane. You are sent a receipt in the mail. This will reduce the number of misplaced tickets: If you have no ticket, you can't lose it.

Why You Should Reconfirm Your Seat

A family from my constituency was bumped from a Venezuelan International Airways flight from Caracas to Houston. They expected to be compensated or placed on another flight, but VIASA said their tickets were worthless because they had not called to confirm 72 hours before the flight. VIASA offered no help, so the family found and paid for a flight home on another airline, at great additional cost. Nine months later,

VIASA has finally compensated them with $350 each. This covers the cost of the unused tickets but not the additional cost of getting home.

—*Fife Symington, Governor, Phoenix, Arizona*

This was not an easy case. VIASA's customer relations department refused to help, so we forwarded the complaint to a public relations official for the International Air Transport Association in Montreal. He passed it to a senior officer at VIASA, and shortly after, the airline offered each family member a free round-trip ticket to Caracas. But it was not legally obligated to do so. On international flights, many airlines require that passengers reconfirm their seats 72 hours in advance. If you don't, your reservations may be canceled.

The smaller and less organized the airline you're flying—and the less technologically advanced the country you're visiting—the more important it is to call and reconfirm flights as close to the 72-hour mark as possible. Airlines with modern reservations systems don't always require it, but they do when they operate in less-developed countries that still use primitive reservations systems.

Reconfirming also lets you check that any special requests have been noted and makes you aware of possible schedule changes.

We called Avianca Airlines to confirm our reservation five days before our return trip from Colombia to Michigan via Miami. The day before the flight, we learned that our son at home was ill, so we needed to get back immediately. At the airport the next morning, we were shocked to learn that our flight had left 3½ hours earlier than scheduled. An Avianca supervisor said that the airline had telexed us at the Hotel Inter-Continental the night before to warn us of the time change, that it was the hotel's fault if we didn't get the message, and that he would put us on a flight to Miami the next day. We refused—we needed to get home right away—and asked for the next flight to the United States. He put us on a New York flight but insisted on charging the full coach fare. We had to buy new tickets home from New York as well.

—*Richard M. Laine, Ann Arbor, Michigan*

What a rip-off. After several letters to the airline, we finally persuaded it to send Laine a check for $1,756, which covered the cost of the extra tickets he had to buy. We have received quite a few letters from *airline passengers who were not notified of a change in flight time. If you miss a flight because of a scheduling change, the airline will not assume liability, even if it never notified you. So if you're flying a small foreign airline, call the day before to double-check the departure time.*

Why You Should Check in on Time

Many readers ask us whether it's really necessary to meet the check-in deadline. I'd rather spend the extra hour in bed too, but it's safer to play by the rules: If you're late, the airline is within its rights to give away your seat.

I left London for Gatwick Airport at 8 AM to catch an 11 AM flight to Los Angeles. Highway construction caused traffic problems, and it took two hours to get there. When I arrived at the British Airways counter at 10:05, the agent said that it was too late to board the flight: It was five minutes past check-in time. I begged him to let me on the plane, since 14 people were coming to my house for Thanksgiving dinner the next day, but he refused.

At about 10:30, the airline boarded some standby passengers but not me, despite my confirmed reservation. I was booked on a flight the next day instead. When I wrote customer relations asking for an explanation, the airline insisted that the passenger is contractually obliged to arrive an hour early, as stated on the ticket.

—*Wendy Haynes, Simi Valley, California*

The airline eventually sent Haynes a $200 goodwill voucher. British Airways' customer relations department told us that the check-in agents were originally instructed not to let any passengers on the plane after 10 AM because of a "weight problem." Shortly before departure they received new instructions to add five more passengers. Haynes was not among them because the airline chose to accommodate those who had been standing by, ready to board, at 10 AM.

British Airways requires check-in for coach passengers two hours before departure, "to allow for proper security checks, efficient baggage handling, and a timely departure." The airline will do its best to accom-

modate you up to the one-hour mark but, after that, there are no guarantees.

———

The check-in deadline depends on the airline and airport. But for international flights, it's usually two hours before departure, occasionally even three. Sometimes that's for getting to the check-in counter, sometimes for getting all the way to the boarding area.

Domestically, the deadline is often an hour before flight time, or 30 minutes for passengers with advance seat assignments. If you miss the half-hour deadline but have a boarding pass, you may lose your specific seat but probably not your reservation. If you miss the 10-minute deadline, your reservation may be canceled.

The first passengers to be bumped are usually the ones who checked in last—even if they met the deadline. "Checking in" does not mean simply checking your luggage at the curb or holding an advance boarding pass, it means getting your name punched into the computer. So if you arrive at an airport late, get your name punched in fast. In fact, if you arrive within a few minutes of the deadline, don't automatically rush past the baggage check-in counter and all the way to the gate, even if you have your boarding pass and don't intend to check luggage. If the line is minimal at the baggage check-in counter and it's a 10-minute walk to the gate, where there may be another line, get your name punched into the computer system at the check-in counter.

Luggage Snafus: Reducing the Risks

A hundred things can go wrong with luggage. It can sit out on the runway in the rain and get drenched. It can be pilfered by baggage handlers. Its tag can get torn off by the conveyor belt. It can end up in Bombay.

I've heard so many deplorable tales about lost and damaged bags that I vowed several years ago never to check luggage again.

HOW TO AVOID CHECKING LUGGAGE

Carrying everything onboard yields not only peace of mind but also no wait at the check-in counter or baggage carousel. Of course, the race to nab enough space in the overhead compartment can be stressful. And you can feel a pang or two of guilt as your seatmates search for a place to put their coats.

Carrying everything onboard means packing carefully (☞ Packing Tips *in the appendix*). And it may mean taking more than the number of carryons permitted per passenger by your airline, which can be tricky, since airlines are becoming stricter about carry-on luggage. The limit is usually two bags on domestic flights and sometimes only one internationally. Check your airline's policy and ask about your particular flight, as different planes have different limits. Often there are limits on the size and weight of carryons as well.

Carrying more than the airline's prescribed limit may require some sleight of hand as you maneuver past eagle-eyed gate attendants and onto the plane. Trompe-l'oeil tactics that have worked for me include: hiding my laptop case by folding my garment bag over it; hanging my laptop case or strap briefcase inside the garment bag; zipping smaller bags inside larger, malleable bags; wearing a shoulder bag underneath a voluminous coat; and carrying only black luggage so that the various pieces kind of blend in with each other and with the dark coat, so that it's hard to tell where one thing ends and another begins.

It's easier to carry onboard more than the per-passenger limit if you:

- **Travel at off-peak hours.**

- **Choose larger aircraft rather than smaller.** On some small planes, you won't be allowed to carry on oversize bags or bags with wheels, and some have no hanging space for garment bags in coach class.

- **Avoid the bulkhead row.** It has no under-seat storage.

- **Board early.** You'll get to the overhead bin before anyone else.

- **Sit next to a vacant seat.** You can use the space under the seat in front of it (☞ How to Sit Next to an Empty Seat, *below*).

If there's just no room for all your stuff, you may have to surrender one of your carryons to the flight attendant so she or he can check it. Give up your sturdiest piece—removing all valuables and anything breakable, of course—and get a receipt for it. If you don't take your valuables, or don't get a receipt, and your bag gets lost, the airline will probably deny liability.

If all this fuss makes checking luggage look like a day in the park and you're willing to live with the risks involved (☞ When Luggage Disaster Strikes, *below*), then go ahead and check your bags. But please take precautions.

HOW TO PREVENT CHECKED LUGGAGE FROM GOING ASTRAY

- **Choose flights with lower baggage-loss potential.** A bag is more likely to go astray if you are changing planes than if you aren't, and even more likely if you are changing airlines as well.

- **Check in on time.** If you show up at the last minute, you may make the plane but your suitcase may not. If you arrive at the airport so early that the airline has another flight to your destination before yours, either switch to the earlier flight or wait until the first one leaves to check your luggage. Otherwise it could get put on the earlier flight and sit for hours at your destination airport, unattended and vulnerable.

- **Tag your luggage.** Put your name, address, and phone number—both at home and at your destination—on both the outside and inside of your luggage.

- **Make sure you're given a claim stub for every bag you check.** Glance at the tags to make sure the correct flight number and three-letter airport code is on each.

- **Rip off the luggage tags from previous trips.** Don't make life confusing for busy baggage handlers.

WHAT IF YOU'VE GOT EXCESS LUGGAGE?

You're allowed two checked bags on most U.S. and international flights. If you bring more, or if you exceed your airline's limit on the size, weight, or dimensions of those bags, you'll probably have to pay extra. U.S. travelers are sometimes hit with a luggage surcharge when flying between foreign cities.

When my party of three checked in for our flight from Verona to Paris, the Air France agent insisted that our baggage was 44 kilograms

(97 pounds) overweight, even though it weighed no more than on any other segment of our trip (we had flown from New York to Nice via Paris). Several others on our flight also thought they were being unfairly charged for excess baggage. When we arrived in Paris, we demanded that our luggage be reweighed and learned that we had indeed been overcharged. I wrote Air France requesting reimbursement of the charge and also of the $116.50 I had to spend on a new suitcase in Paris to replace the one that the airline destroyed on the same flight. It never even responded. Please help me retrieve the money that Air France has owed me for the last two years.

—*Raymond R. Macaluso, Leucadia, California*

We finally persuaded the airline to issue a refund, but it wasn't easy. At first it agreed to reimburse Macaluso for the cost of a new suitcase but not for the excess-baggage charge, arguing that different baggage allowances apply to transatlantic routes and to routes within Europe. The airline permits each passenger up to 64 kilograms (141 pounds) of luggage on transatlantic and through flights but only 23 kilograms (51 pounds) on intra-European flights. Air France changed its tune, however, when Macaluso sent proof that his party consisted of three passengers whose bags were checked together. The airline now says the allowance was actually 69 kilograms (three times 23). The bags weighed a total of 97 kilograms, so Macaluso should have been charged for only 28 kilograms of excess baggage. Air France eventually, 2½ years later, sent him $220.70. Better late than never.

The moral of the story, for non-mathematicians and those anticipating overseas shopping sprees: The same two bags that cost you nothing to check at the start of your trip could cost you a small fortune later, since baggage allowances vary in terms of weight and number.

HOW TO MINIMIZE POTENTIAL LOSSES

If you do not have homeowner's or travel insurance that covers luggage, consider purchasing something called "excess valuation" from the airline when you check in. It increases the airline's liability limit for mishandled luggage. Some airlines don't offer it, but most do, although not always on international flights. The cost is $1 to $2 for every $100 of coverage. Valuable or breakable items such as cameras, jewelry, antiques and musical instruments may not be covered, and there may be a $5,000 maximum.

Flight Delays and Cancellations

Just in case a delayed or canceled flight isn't frustrating enough, airlines provide an added pill to swallow: No matter how long or uncomfortable the delay, they are not obligated to make any peace offering. They don't have to put you up in a hotel overnight, or give you a meal, a drink, or even money for a phone call. And they're not liable for any damages or expenses incurred. That said, if a delay or cancellation causes undue hardship, some airlines try to make up for it.

My party of three was supposed to fly from Portland to Cayman Brac via Dallas/Fort Worth, Miami, and Grand Cayman. When the Portland–Dallas flight was diverted to Denver because of mechanical problems, American Airlines in Denver altered our itinerary; we would be arriving in Cayman Brac two days later than planned. The Denver agent sympathized with our plight and instructed us to keep receipts of hotel, food, and transportation expenses caused by the delay. She typed a message in the airline's computer system authorizing reimbursement.

We lost prepaid hotel reservations, scuba diving packages, and two days of vacation, but American now says it is not liable for our losses. We find its offer of $300 in travel vouchers unacceptable and have rejected it.

—*Michael Walker, Tualatin, Oregon*

Although American certainly didn't have to, it ended up sending $455 in cash and $276 in travel vouchers. Because the Denver agent's computer message did not specify the number of days for which Walker should be reimbursed, the airline decided to absorb the cost of the first day's delay and to compensate for the second with vouchers. Most U.S. airlines do not compensate for even one day's delay, so we applaud American's generosity.

Airlines are more likely to offer amenities to stranded passengers—overnight accommodations, meal vouchers, a phone call home—if a delay is for mechanical reasons or because the crew hasn't arrived from a delayed incoming flight, than if it is weather-related. (A mechanical or operational problem is within the airline's control; the weather isn't.)

If you suspect a delay may turn out to be substantial, find a phone, call your airline, and book a seat on the next flight. If there's another airline flying your route, call and reserve a seat on that plane as well. If the delay is protracted or your flight is canceled, ask the gate agent to reticket you on the next flight or endorse your ticket to the other airline.

In the case of cancellation, the airline is required to put you on the next flight on which seats are available or endorse your ticket to another carrier, although passengers with discounted or frequent-flier tickets may not be offered this latter option.

The delayed airline is not necessarily responsible for getting you to your final destination. Say your United Airlines flight from Denver to New York runs late, causing you to miss your Iberia flight to Madrid. United is not obligated to fly you across the ocean. If you need to take two or more flights to get where you're going, book them all through one airline.

If a cancellation causes extreme hardship and you think the airline should be held liable, you can take the case to court.

When You're Bumped

Airlines routinely oversell their flights, counting on a certain number of no-shows. If too many people with reservations turn up, the airline is supposed to ask those who aren't in a hurry to give up their seats and take a later flight, in exchange for compensation such as a free ticket.

IF YOU VOLUNTEER TO BE BUMPED

Before volunteering, ask a few questions:

- **Can the airline provide a confirmed seat on the next flight?** If you're put on standby, you could be stranded.

- **What amenities will the airline provide while you wait?** Meals? Phone calls? A hotel room if you're stuck overnight? Transportation to the hotel?

- **If the compensation is a free ticket, what are the restrictions?** Is there an expiration date? (Sometimes you must use it within a year.) Are there blackout dates? How long before departure are you allowed to make reservations? (Sometimes you must wait until 48 hours before a flight to try booking a seat on it.)

IF YOU'RE BUMPED AGAINST YOUR WILL

There's a small chance you could be bumped involuntarily. If so, you may be entitled to "denied boarding compensation." The amount depends on the price of your ticket, the length of the delay, and whether you've played by the rules. The airline must also give you a written statement explaining your rights.

Here's what you're owed by law: If the airline arranges substitute transportation scheduled to get you to your final destination (including later connections) within an hour of your original scheduled arrival time, you're owed nothing. If the substitute transportation is scheduled to get you to your final destination between one and two hours late (between one and two hours late (between one and four hours on international flights), you are owed the one-way fare to your destination, up to $200. If the substitute transportation is scheduled to get you to your final destination more than two hours late (more than four hours internationally) or if the airline does not make alternate arrangements, the compensation doubles to twice the one-way fare, with a $400 maximum. If the airline offers a free future flight, you have the right to insist on a check.

This is the minimum an airline must do for you. If being bumped is a real inconvenience and causes you to lose more than the $200 or $400 the airline offers, by all means write to customer relations and demand more.

My girlfriend and I arrived at JFK two hours before our Alitalia flight to Rome, where we were to catch a connecting flight to Sicily. After waiting to check in for more than an hour, we were told that the flight was overbooked, our seats had been given away, and Alitalia was trying to put the bumped passengers on a Swissair flight to Zurich and a connecting flight to Rome. This alternate plan would mean missing our connection to Sicily and forfeiting our prepaid arrangements.

So we spoke to a second check-in agent, who said that no seats were available in any class on our Alitalia flight. A third agent said he could get us seats in first class, but that we would have to pay an extra $4,592. We reluctantly paid it. Onboard, we were surprised to see empty seats in first class . . . and the second check-in agent sitting in coach. Alitalia had bumped a paying passenger so an employee could fly instead! I think that the airline should have given us the first-class seats.

—*Edward Davis, New York, New York*

All Alitalia owed Davis and his girlfriend, the airline insisted at first, was "denied boarding compensation" of $200 each—which it consented to double as a show of goodwill. Then we asked the airline why an employee was given priority over a paying passenger. She wasn't, an Alitalia spokeswoman told us: The employee sat on a jump seat that the airline cannot assign to passengers.

Alitalia rarely upgrades travelers to first class in an overbooking situation, the spokeswoman added, because the fare difference between coach and first class is huge. It might upgrade them to business class, because the fare difference is comparable to the denied boarding compensation, but there was no business-class section on Davis's flight. Fortunately, Alitalia eventually gave him two round-trip business-class tickets to Italy.

If you're unhappy with your denied boarding compensation and intend to try negotiating a higher settlement, don't take your free trip or cash your check (you usually have 30 days from the date on the check to decide whether to accept it). Once you do, you waive your right to demand more compensation later.

If your efforts with customer relations are fruitless, either write the Ombudsman column or consider taking the airline to court to obtain a decent settlement. Other travelers have, with some success.

WHEN YOU'RE NOT OWED COMPENSATION

Not everyone is eligible for "denied boarding compensation." You must have a confirmed reservation (indicated by an "OK" in the status box on your ticket). And you must have met the check-in deadline.

You may not be offered "denied boarding compensation" if you are using a frequent-flier ticket, if the flight is a charter, if it is a scheduled flight with 60 or fewer passengers, or if the airline substituted a smaller plane for the one it originally planned to use. Nor do the rules necessarily apply to international flights into the United States or to flights between foreign cities. International carriers, especially those in less developed countries, can be unpredictable. Some might bump you, even though you have checked in on time, simply because you are using a heavily discounted or frequent-flier ticket.

IF YOU'RE BUMPED IN EUROPE

The European Union has its own set of rules. If you're bumped from a flight originating in any E.U. country—Austria, Belgium, Denmark, France, Finland, Germany, Greece, Ireland, Italy, Luxembourg, the Netherlands, Portugal, Spain, Sweden, and the United Kingdom—you may be eligible for immediate cash compensation (paid in European Currency Units, or ECUs). The amount depends on the distance of the flight and the length of the delay.

When the distance is less than 3,500 kilometers (2,170 miles), you are owed 75 ECUs ($96 at press time) when the delay is two hours or less, 300 ECUs ($384) for delays of more than two hours. When the distance is greater than 3,500 kilometers, you're owed 150 ECUs ($192) if the delay is four hours or less, 300 ECUs ($384) if it's more than four hours.

Bumpees must also get a free phone call or fax message and, depending on the length of the delay, free meals and hotel accommodations.

But there's a wrinkle: The compensation cannot exceed the value of your ticket. And you're not entitled to remuneration if the flight is a charter or if you are using a frequent-flier ticket. We've even seen airlines deny compensation to passengers who were using discounted tickets.

When You're Stuck at the Airport

Whoever said getting there is half the fun probably didn't spend much time in airports. Most passengers subjected to a lengthy layover or delay sit around for hours with nothing better to do than browse at newsstands and booze it up at the bar. Travelers lucky enough to be stranded at a particularly user-friendly airport might get to watch CNN at the gate or stroll through stores like the Sharper Image and the Body Shop. If they're at a major connecting hub, they can even rent rooms with beds, showers, and phones on a four- or six-hour basis.

But some airports offer far more interesting possibilities—everything from city tours to movie rentals, from casino gambling to striptease acts, from virtual-reality golf to water skiing. Here are the best ways to kill a few hours at some of the world's busiest airports:

IN THE UNITED STATES

- **Baltimore-Washington International.** In the Observation Gallery, computerized interactive exhibits describe the history of air travel and provide current weather and air traffic data from across the country (it's the same system the FAA uses to monitor aircraft). There's even an entire Boeing 737 with a flight simulator in the cockpit. Sitting in the pilot's seat and studying computer-generated images, you can maneuver the plane and "land" it at BWI.

- **Boston (Logan).** Take the complimentary minibus to the Harborside Hyatt, check your carry-on bags at the bell desk, hop on the hotel's water shuttle for a 7-minute ride across Boston Harbor to downtown (it leaves every 15 minutes), and explore Boston's historic center or the aquarium.

- **Chicago (O'Hare).** Even if it's snowing and ten below, you can pretend you're playing Pebble Beach. Virtual-reality golf is available at the O'Hare Hilton, smack in the middle of the airport, along with a putting green and lessons. A sports bar with 13 televisions broadcasts sporting events from around the world. Also available are massages, manicures, tanning beds, a dentist, and 60 first-run movies for use in guest rooms, which can be rented on a four-hour basis.

- **Dallas/Fort Worth.** Head for the Hyatt Regency DFW, where you can catch a shuttle to the Hyatt Bear Creek Golf and Racquet Club for tennis, golf, or just a leisurely lunch amid the greenery.

- **Denver.** There's plenty to gape at here—from the 125-foot-high ceilings to the $7.5 million art project to the stunning Rocky Mountain vista (best viewed from the terminal's southern end) that stretches from south of Pike's Peak to the Wyoming border. In case an uncomfortable flight has got your back in a tangle, there's a chiropractor in Concourse B.

- **Honolulu.** Visit the Pacific Aerospace Museum, complete with singing-and-dancing robot, or loll in the Sino-Japanese-Hawaiian garden. If you have several hours, for only $1 you can catch a public bus immediately outside the terminal to Pearl Harbor (10 minutes away), to Waikiki (an hour away), or even around the entire island, through pineapple plantations and along the north shore (a four-hour round-trip).

- **Los Angeles.** Check out the city through a telescope on the observation deck of the Theme Building. Or cab it to Marina del Rey—a 15-minute ride—for a stroll along the harbor and some café-hopping.

- **Miami.** For $5 you can use the rooftop pool, health club, racquetball court, running track, Jacuzzi, and sauna at the Miami International Airport Hotel in Concourse E. If there's no time for a work-out, treat yourself to a quick poolside lunch or a piña colada with a panoramic view.

Water-sports fans with several hours to spare can take the shuttle bus to the Miami Airport Hilton and Towers for water skiing on its 100-acre freshwater lagoon. Jet skis and wave runners can be rented as well.

- **Orlando.** Ride the elevated rail that glides over 450 acres of lush tropical gardens, then view them from a different angle at the Hemisphere Restaurant on the ninth floor of the mid-airport Hyatt Regency.

- **Pittsburgh.** Those suffering from aches and pains can visit Stressbreakers, in Concourse C, for a massage; if that isn't sufficient, stop by the medical center sponsored by the University of Pittsburgh for a free consultation.

- **San Francisco.** Bay Front Park stretches for 7 miles along the coastline; go for a stroll, bike ride, or run on trails winding through nature preserves with hundreds of varieties of wildflowers. To get there, grab the shuttle bus to the Westin San Francisco.

- **Washington (Dulles).** A taxi can have serious shoppers at the Galleria Mall in MacLean, Virginia, in 15 minutes. For a massage or swim, head for the airport Hilton.

AT AIRPORTS ABROAD

- **Amsterdam (Schiphol).** Take a two-hour city or countryside tour operated—in luxury mini-buses—by Holland Tours Schiphol. If you prefer to linger at the airport, work on your tan at the Sun Center, your body at the Fitness Center, or your swing at the Golf Center, where a golf simulator lets you play any of 24 international courses and pros are available for lessons. High rollers can visit the casino (not to worry: this casino has clocks on the wall and broadcasts boarding announcements).

- **Berlin (Tempelhof).** Catch some cabaret at La Vie En Rose, the only revue theater at an airport. The show might spotlight an illusionist, a striptease artist, and an exotic dancer (at press time, you could see El Phytonia, who performs with her rare white tiger pythons). Check out the Magic Bar next door, which resembles a Disneyland castle and features a magician barkeeper.

- **Frankfurt (Frankfurt-Main).** Stop by the disco, bowling alley, games arcade, sex shops, and pornographic cinemas in Terminal 1, or watch local bands on the stage outside the McDonald's in Terminal 2. There is also a collection of vintage aircraft, and airport tours that include a trip through the impressive baggage conveyor system. If time is short, stick to the monorail that shoots between terminals (a round-trip ride takes 5 or 6 minutes) or the observation deck at the visitors' terrace, where you can get a bird's-eye view of takeoffs and landings.

- **Hong Kong (Kai Tak).** A 15-minute cab ride will have you in the Tsim Sha Tshui shopping district. Stop by the Peninsula Hotel for high tea accompanied by harp music in the elegant lobby or for a meal and a stunning view of Hong Kong at the Philippe Starck–designed rooftop brasserie.

- **London (Heathrow).** You can shop at Harrods, Burberry, Liberty and other distinguished British stores—they charge the same prices as in town. Or hop a cab to Windsor Castle (a 15-minute ride) and tour one of the royal residences.

- **Munich (Franz Josef Strauss).** Head for the Hotel Kempinski (it's connected to the airport by a walkway) for fresh draft beer and pretzels straight from the oven. Its outdoor Bavarian beer garden borders a 16,000-square-meter geometric garden. You can use the hotel's pool, take an aerobics class at its health club, even get a massage.

- **Paris (Charles de Gaulle).** If you can afford it, consider dinner at Maxim's, in Terminal 1, followed by a duty-free shopping spree at Cartier, Chanel, Dior, Hermès, Guerlain, Pierre Cardin, and Yves Saint-Laurent.

- **Singapore (Changi).** Travelers with several hours to spare can take a free city tour (offered three times a day) or head for the free movie theater. Those with less time can visit the rooftop pool and Jacuzzi, then sauna and shower at the fitness center. Stop by the Science Discovery Corner, which has exhibits of interest to both kids and adults, on your way to the karaoke lounge. You'll probably leave Changi wishing you had more time to spend here.

- **Sydney (Kingsford-Smith).** Hop on the complimentary shuttle bus to the airport Hilton—three minutes away—for a jog, a swim, or 18 holes at the Kogarah Golf Club next door. The shuttle also takes sightseers and shoppers to downtown Sydney.

- **Tokyo (Narita).** Let the kids play computer games in the playroom while you rent music, a movie, or a news program in the audio-video room. "Sit in a bodysonic chair," says the airport brochure, "and enjoy dynamic sound throughout your body."

- **Zurich (Kloten).** A train runs through the airport's lower level and can zip you to the heart of Zurich in 10 minutes. A free shuttle bus from the airport can whisk you to the Hilton, 2 kilometers (1.2 miles) away, for a massage at the health club. Or explore the airport's enormous food market, where locals shop on weekends. You'll find just about every Swiss food specialty—Sprüngli chocolates, fresh produce, breads, pastries, liqueurs, and cheeses that can be shrink-wrapped so that you can take them through U.S. Customs.

Getting the Seat You Want

When it comes to airplane seats, different passengers have different priorities. If yours is extra leg room, you may want a seat in the bulkhead or in an emergency-exit row. If it's a smooth ride, you'll want to be over the wings rather than in the back. For minimal distractions, you'll want to avoid seats near galleys and lavatories, which attract traffic and chatter. If you need to disembark quickly so you can make a fast connection, you'll want a seat up front. If you hope to lie down across several seats, you'll want to be in the center section toward the back, but if you need the seat to recline, you'll have to avoid the last row. . . .

The wrong seat can ruin a trip. I still remember Norman Peters of Washington, D.C., who wrote to the Ombudsman column about being seated on a transatlantic flight next to a man who weighed 400 pounds. The man raised both armrests and took up half of each of the seats adjacent to his own, pinning Peters on half of his own seat. It was quite an uncomfortable ride.

The most common seating gripe we hear is from travelers stuck in the smoking section.

HOW TO GUARANTEE YOURSELF A NON-SMOKING SEAT

The answer is pretty simple: Fly a U.S. airline.

On international flights, U.S. carriers are legally required to provide you with a non-smoking seat as long as you request it by the airline's seat-assignment deadline (which differs from flight to flight), arrive by check-in time, and are not flying stand-by. If no seats remain in the non-smoking section, the airline must expand it.

The situation is dicier if you're flying a foreign airline. They generally set aside a limited number of non-smoking seats, which are available only on a first-come, first-served basis. And the crew does not always prevent passengers from smoking in or very near areas of the plane where cigarettes are outlawed.

I become ill when exposed to even the slightest trace of cigarette smoke, so I seldom fly internationally. When I had to fly to New Zealand, I called Air New Zealand and explained my predicament. I was told that its 747s have a small upper deck where smoking is not allowed. The round-trip from Los Angeles to Auckland was $3,225—the upper deck is entirely business class—but I was willing to pay it for a smoke-free trip.

Unfortunately, the flight attendants smoked in a galley a few feet behind me, pilots smoked in crew rest seats a few feet in front of me, and I was ill for most of the flight and for days afterward. For more than a year, I've been asking the airline to compensate me, but it refuses.

—*Michael Miller, Hana, Hawaii*

When we asked Air New Zealand, we asked very nicely, and it changed its mind and issued Miller a $2,250 refund representing the extra amount he had to pay to fly in business class. We've seen other airlines' reactions to similar complaints from travelers subjected to smoke against their wishes, and we consider Air New Zealand's response to be extraordinarily generous.

Since Miller took his trip, several airlines have declared all flights non-smoking or have made particular routes smoke-free. In fact, Air New Zealand's flights between the United States and New Zealand are now entirely non-smoking.

The only time smoking is allowed on U.S. flights, by the way, is if the flight is a charter or lasts more than six hours (which means to or from Alaska or Hawaii).

HOW TO SIT NEXT TO AN EMPTY SEAT

How can those of us relegated to coach avoid the occasional seatmate from hell? You know: chatterboxes, noisy gum chewers, crying babies, ladies applying nail polish, snorers whose heads collapse on your shoulder, proselytizers who ask if you believe in God and then whip out their Bible, passengers between you and the aisle who fall asleep just when you need to use the lavatory, kids behind you who won't stop kicking, kids in front who hang over the seat, making faces and drooling onto your laptop . . . Here are some tried-and-true techniques:

- **If several airlines offer equally convenient flights, book the least crowded.** Reservations agents can tell you how crowded a flight is.

- **Try for emergency-exit rows.** There's more leg room, many have had a seat removed—which means one seatmate rather than two—and it's kid-free: Only adults capable of assisting with an emergency evacuation are allowed. Seats in the emergency-exit row can only be assigned at the airport, so check in early.

- **To avoid sitting next to infants, steer clear of bulkhead rows.** This is where airlines often put families.

- **On narrow-bodies, if you're traveling with a companion, ask for the window and aisle seats in a three-seat row.** On flights that aren't full, the middle seat often remains empty; on sold-out flights, the person in the middle is usually happy to switch with one of you.

- **On wide-bodies, try for an aisle seat in the center section, toward the rear.** Middle seats here are typically assigned last. On flights that aren't full, you can increase the odds of having the row to yourself by requesting an aisle seat and sitting not in it but in the next seat over. The passenger assigned to the aisle seat at the other end of your row will then have an inducement to move to another row, hoping for more vacant seats beside him.

- **Ask the gate agent to switch you to a seat next to an empty one.** It may be easier once everyone has boarded and the agent knows for sure where everyone is sitting. Gate agents can actually block off an empty middle seat if you're nice enough to them (or you're a very frequent flier).

- **After everyone has boarded, move to the nearest pair of empty seats.** When you board, scout out seats next to vacant seats and bolt the moment the plane door starts to shut.

If all else fails, fend off loquacious or unpleasant seatmates by donning headphones (they don't have to be plugged in), burying your nose in a book, or using a conversation stopper like "This is my seventh glass of water today on the Calorie Counter Diet" or "My psychiatrist says it's good for me to talk about my divorce" or "I teach economics."

HOW TO GET A FREE UPGRADE

- **If you are a very frequent flier, mention it when checking in.** Very frequent fliers (the elite members of frequent-flier programs who rack up more than 50,000 miles per year) have the best chance. They can even call the airline several days ahead to be put on an upgrade waitlist. And they often receive free upgrade coupons.

- **If you have paid full fare, be sure to ask.** Some airlines automatically upgrade full-fare coach passengers to business class, if seats are available. This is why upgrades on discounted tickets are unlikely unless coach is over-booked.

- **Choose flights carefully.** If you know when you book your flight that you intend to try for an upgrade, and you have a choice between different flights with equally convenient schedules, go for the one with the largest number of empty seats in business or first class.

- **Make friends with a savvy travel agent.** Some have good relationships with airline sales managers and can pull strings. Some have a supply of upgrade coupons or know which airline is likely to grant upgrades on a certain route.

- **Ask to sit together if you're flying with someone who has a first or business class ticket.** Your best bet is to try to arrange this through the ticket agent in the club lounge, if either of you has access.

- **Dress well.** An upgrade is far more likely if you're wearing a suit than if you're in sweatpants.

- **Don't keep it a secret if you're on your honeymoon.**

- **Ask for an upgrade—and hover.** If you've requested an upgrade from the gate agent but can't get an immediate answer, stay nearby until close to boarding time. If a seat opens up, a busy agent who has not had time to compile an upgrade waitlist may simply choose the nearest person who jumps.

You can also buy upgrade coupons for a modest fee and use them on a stand-by basis. You may have a hard time using them at peak hours and on popular routes.

Staying Healthy and Comfortable in the Sky

I catch a cold on about half the transoceanic flights I take, so I'm particularly sympathetic when people complain to me about sore throats, itchy eyes, headaches, nausea, swollen ankles, backaches, and the flu, all traceable to air travel. It's gotten worse in recent years: Because recirculating air requires less fuel, airlines have reduced the influx of fresh air on planes (not to mention the size of the seats and the amount of leg room).

Still, there are a few steps you can take to protect yourself against airborne germs and other in-flight hazards:

- **Combat dehydration.** The air on planes is literally drier than the Sahara. The low humidity dehydrates your body, which can cause excessive fatigue and jet lag, make your eyes red and sore, and irritate upper respiratory passages, making them more susceptible to infection.

  So drink plenty of water in-flight—at least eight ounces per hour. (I often take along my own bottled water.) Avoid alcohol, caffeine, and salty drinks like tomato juice—all of which dehydrate—as well as salty peanuts and pretzels. Apply moisturizer and use saline eye drops. Contact-lens wearers are especially prone to discomfort because dehydration reduces tear volume.

- **Keep your ears from popping.** Try to keep your Eustachian tube open by taking a decongestant and chewing gum. Relieve ear pressure through the Valsalva maneuver: Close your mouth, pinch your nose, and breathe out, forcing air up from your lungs into your ears.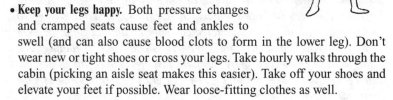

  If you have a cold or think one may be coming on, take a decongestant both before the flight and an hour before landing. Use a nasal spray as well, and take megadoses of vitamin C for a couple of days before and after the flight.

- **Keep your legs happy.** Both pressure changes and cramped seats cause feet and ankles to swell (and can also cause blood clots to form in the lower leg). Don't wear new or tight shoes or cross your legs. Take hourly walks through the cabin (picking an aisle seat makes this easier). Take off your shoes and elevate your feet if possible. Wear loose-fitting clothes as well.

- **Keep yourself fueled.** Bring along nutritious snacks—a sandwich, an apple, a granola bar. Full meals aren't served anymore on many U.S. flights—all you may get is a tiny bag of pretzels—and you never know how long you may be delayed and trapped without sustenance.

Which brings us to . . .

Airline Food

Time was when everyone used to complain about how awful airline food was. They said there wasn't anything on the plate they recognized. One of the "Top 10 Ways to Annoy a Flight Attendant," David Letterman joked, was to ask whether the Salisbury steak could be used as a flotation device.

Well, the airlines listened . . . and eliminated meal service almost entirely. And now everyone complains that there isn't enough airline food. Go figure. So when planning a flight, ask in advance whether a full meal will be served, just a "snack," or merely beverages.

Food is still served on most international flights, and can still be less than appetizing.

On a flight from Frankfurt to Los Angeles on Lufthansa German Airlines, I found a roach in my dinner. It was in a bite of spinach that I had put in my mouth and was about to start chewing. I and the passengers around me complained to the flight attendant, who took the plate away and brought me a new dinner. By then, of course, I had lost my appetite. When I wrote to Lufthansa, it offered a compensatory voucher worth $60. I think I deserve more.

—Jeff Minkin, San Diego, California

Lufthansa disagrees. At first it told Minkin that it was unable to verify his "meal irregularity." Then the airline changed its mind, apologizing and saying it didn't doubt that the incident occurred. Although Lufthansa's caterer has the "highest hygienic standards," a member of Lufthansa's executive board told us, "it can still happen that a bug will find its way into the greens undetected." But he did not think Minkin was owed further compensation. "Whereas I confirm that finding such a life-form in one's meal may be quite disagreeable, I fail to see the damage it could cause," he said. "The matter as such offers no basis for financial remuneration."

As ugly as some airline food may be, it's even uglier when it ends up in your lap.

My wife and I sat in seats 16A and B in the upper-deck business class of a United Airlines transpacific flight. The flight attendant served our meal and then left the food cart in front of us, in the large emergency-exit space between rows 15 and 16. The cart was not locked in place. As we were eating, the man sitting in 15A reclined his seat, which sent the cart toppling onto my wife and me, spilling food and liquid all over us. Dripping from top to bottom, we shouted for help. It took seven or eight minutes for someone to come clean us up and find us new seats. Needless to say, we were very uncomfortable for the rest of the trip. We are shocked by the flight staff's poor training and the threat to passenger safety caused by an unsecured cart in an emergency-exit row.

—*Alfred A. Ash, Pittsburgh, Pennsylvania*

So was Ombudsman. When we questioned United about the episode, it apologized "for the incident and for the unresponsive and insensitive manner in which it was resolved" and compensated the Ashes with two transpacific upgrades. It said that food carts should not be left unsecured or unattended and that a flight attendant should have responded to the Ashes' problems in less than seven minutes. United added that it would review this incident with the crew and provide supplemental training to make sure it didn't happen again.

We've received several complaints about flight attendants who spilled wine, coffee, and other staining liquids on helpless passengers. Should this happen to you, ask the crew for an in-flight accident report as proof of the spillage. Otherwise, when you write customer relations, you won't be able to document that the incident actually occurred.

Flying with Pets

Most animal-related mishaps we hear about happen to pets that fly in the plane's cargo area rather than in the cabin with their owners. (Different airlines have different policies concerning how many animals can travel per plane or per cabin.) Sometimes Rover's kennel gets dropped by baggage handlers; sometimes Fluffy is nowhere to be found upon landing.

I flew American Airlines from Dallas to San Jose, Costa Rica, thinking my two West Highland white terriers were traveling along in the cargo compartment. When we landed, I discovered they were missing. I was up all night trying to get information from the airline and finally learned that the dogs had been sent to London by mistake, then immediately flown back to Dallas.

A friend picked them up at the Dallas airport with a veterinarian on hand. My female dog had scratched herself raw from the trauma of the journey. The vet said the dogs had to stay in Dallas until they were healthy enough to fly to Costa Rica. Finally, a week later, I got my dogs back. The female is still on medication.

Apparently the Animal Welfare Act requires airlines to give animals water every 12 hours and food every 24 hours. The Dallas–London flight takes 10 hours and the flight back 11½. If the dogs were immediately put on a return flight, then it's possible that they went almost 22 hours without being fed or watered.

—*Lee Doss, Playa Carrillo, Costa Rica*

American told us that the dogs were fed and watered upon arriving in London and watered again just before their return flight. The airline apologized for the mishap: The plane for San Jose was sitting next to the plane for London, and the dogs were simply loaded onto the wrong one. American ultimately sent Doss a $1,280 check, representing the liability limit for two pieces of baggage lost on an international flight. It also sent a $500 voucher and added 10,000 miles to Doss's American AAdvantage account.

Airlines view pets as baggage: If your animal is harmed or lost while in its care, an airline will probably apply the liability ceiling that applies to damaged or lost luggage: $1,250 on a domestic flight, $640 internationally.

When you take an animal on a plane, you must make sure that it is old enough (at least 8 weeks old and fully weaned) and healthy enough (most airlines require a health certificate issued by a vet no more than 10 days before departure). You must have the right kennel and make advance arrangements with the airline. You should also select your flight carefully to make the trip as easy as possible for your pet: Try to take nonstop flights and avoid travel in excessively hot or cold weather (☞ Where to Turn for Help, *below*).

Flying with a Disability

I head a philanthropic organization that brought a child to San Francisco for spinal surgery. Knowing that the child would be in pain and would need to travel in an almost horizontal position on the San Francisco–New York leg of her journey home, I bought seats in first class, requesting that they not be in the first or last row, where it is impossible to recline fully. We were assigned second-row seats.

Upon boarding, we were surprised to find our seats occupied. A flight attendant asked the occupants to move, but they refused. I explained the child's predicament, but was ordered either to sit in the last row, where there were seats available, or get off the plane. So we sat, and the child was miserable until, halfway through the flight, two kind-hearted passengers who heard her moaning volunteered to switch seats.

The only reason my organization bought first-class tickets was so that the child could recline properly. I've complained to TWA, but its unsympathetic response is that the airline does not guarantee seat assignments.

—*Adam P. Bernstein, San Francisco, California*

Ombudsman finally got some sympathy from TWA, but it wasn't easy, and the three upgrade certificates it sent hardly seemed just compensation. We began by asking TWA why it had not made an exception for the sake of the child. It acknowledged that the crew "should have insisted on the passengers in row two either moving or deplaning, but time was of the essence and the plane had to be gotten under way." Ombudsman wrote back, asking how the airline could admit that its crew was at fault and yet refuse to offer compensation. This time TWA sent Bernstein the upgrade certificates, "as a gesture of goodwill." When we asked Department of Transportation spokesman Bill Mosley his opinion, he said that TWA did not violate the Air Carrier Access Act, which protects airline passengers with disabilities, but added, "That does not imply that we approve of the way TWA handled the situation."

When travelers with a disability complain of unfair treatment, it is usually not that the Air Carrier Access Act has been violated but that the crew has shown insensitivity.

The act also prohibits airlines from refusing transportation to someone on the basis of a disability or requiring someone with a disability to travel with an attendant.

Two friends booked a round-trip flight on Bahamasair for a weekend fling in Freeport. At Baltimore–Washington International Airport, they were told to wait until the last passengers had boarded the plane. Since both of them are deaf, they assumed that Bahamasair was going to give them the much disliked "special treatment" that airlines commonly give people with disabilities.

To their surprise and amazement, they were not allowed to board the flight on the grounds of their disability. They were told they had to bring along a hearing companion or interpreter for the sole purpose of easier emergency-evacuation procedures. This is absurd. If a passenger does not speak or understand English, would he be considered a hindrance in an emergency evacuation?

I'd like to know whether Bahamasair had the right to revoke my friends' tickets because of their deafness, and whether my friends can expect a refund. One of them is a travel agent. They have traveled freely across the world and are capable of managing on their own, without dragging along a hearing companion. It was the first time in their lives they had felt so helpless and handicapped.

—*Dan Brubaker, Seabrook, Maryland*

It should never have happened. The discrimination that occurred here was a violation of both the Bahamian constitution and U.S. law. Bahamasair apologized, refunded the cost of the unused tickets, and promised to clear up the matter with its handlers at B.W.I. Airport. "We were as surprised as your two friends to learn they were denied boarding," the airline wrote to Ombudsman. "It is not our policy that deaf or blind passengers must be accompanied on Bahamasair flights."

"Problems often stem not from the airlines' rules but from their training programs," Sid Wolinsky, director of litigation for Disability Rights Advocates, told us. "Usually the rules are okay, but the employees are totally ignorant of them."

According to the Air Carrier Access Act, an airline can exclude a traveler with disabilities from a flight only if carrying that person would compromise the flight's safety (and it can refuse to seat people with a disability in emergency-exit rows, because passengers in those rows must be able to perform emergency evacuation functions). But if someone with a disability is excluded for safety reasons, the airline must provide a written explanation of the reasons.

If you think an airline has violated the Air Carrier Access Act or if you have complained to the airline's customer relations department but have received an unsatisfactory reply or no reply at all, write the Department of Transportation (☞ Where to Turn for Help, *below*), which says it will follow up with the airline on your behalf.

Mid-Air Medical Emergencies

When someone takes ill in the sky, what medical help is available?

Two hours before landing at JFK, on a flight from Belgrade, Yugoslavia, a call went out through the plane for a doctor. Since I'm a registered nurse, I and a young Yugoslavian female doctor volunteered and were led to a man who had just had a heart attack. I placed an oxygen mask on his face but could not palpate a carotid pulse. We lowered him to the deck, and I started oral resuscitation while the doctor percussed the man's chest. When the doctor needed relief, a flight attendant tried to take over, but he could not percuss properly. It was obvious that he had had little instruction and less experience in CPR, but he was the only crew member who even attempted to help! I called several times for relief, but the calls went unheeded until another passenger came to my aid. After an hour of CPR, we had to face the fact that the man had died. I'm very concerned about passengers who have a respiratory crisis on a plane whose crew has little or no emergency training.

—*Marianne M. Dudley, RN, Fairbanks, Alaska*

Ombudsman applauds Dudley. She puts her finger on a critical issue. Neither U.S. nor international law requires that flight attendants know CPR. Yugoslav Airlines told us that they do teach their flight attendants CPR but suggested that "logic and better procedure call for taking a subordinate role." Airlines, in effect, depend on there being a doctor on board. As a Federal Aviation Administration spokesman told us, "We do not expect flight attendants to act as trained physicians."

—

But many physicians refuse to aid sick passengers for fear of malpractice suits. While it is not much of a problem in Canada and Europe, it is the biggest obstacle to in-flight emergency care on U.S. airlines, according to Dr. Claus Curdt-Christiansen, chief of aviation medicine for the International Civil Aviation Organization. Physicians flying to Islamic countries are also reluctant to help, even on western airlines. They fear being subjected to Islamic law, says Dr. Curdt-Christiansen, which requires that people viewed as responsible for someone's death pay blood money to the deceased's spouse. He adds that Air Canada's good Samaritan policy, under which the airline gives full legal protection to doctors who render assistance, should set an example for the industry.

When Luggage Disaster Strikes

If your checked luggage arrives damaged, or if it never arrives at all, 99 times out of 100 you won't be reimbursed nearly as much as you should be. Sure, it's unfair. Sure, it's a total rip-off. But those are the rules. You'll get over it eventually. And next time you'll try to carry all your stuff onboard.

WHAT TO DO IF YOUR LUGGAGE IS DAMAGED OR PILFERED

When you grab your bag off the conveyor belt, if it appears to be mangled, damp, open, or unlocked, inspect the contents right away. If anything is missing or damaged, report it before leaving the airport. If your luggage looks fine, you don't need to open it at the airport, but do so as soon as you can, and check to make sure everything is there and intact. If it's not, notify the airline immediately. Jot down the name of the person you spoke to and the date and time you called, and follow up with a letter.

—

My garment bag was shredded and $1,428 worth of clothing damaged beyond repair on a flight from Los Angeles to New York. After I reported the damage at JFK, TWA asked for receipts to support the value claimed. Since I did not retain the receipts, I provided TWA with descriptions of the items, including purchase date, store, and price. I even sent them the ruined garments. I've waited four months, sent letters, made numerous phone calls to TWA's customer relations department, left umpteen unanswered messages, and gotten no satisfactory response.

—*Mary Natalizio, La Crescenta, California*

TWA finally reimbursed Natalizio $915, the depreciated value of the garments, but Ombudsman considers it a poor performance that she was put through such an obstacle course.

Airlines compensate for damaged luggage on a case-by-case basis, and on domestic flights they may place a $1,250 ceiling on their liability. If your suitcase is smashed or torn, airlines usually pay for repairs (although seldom to damaged wheels, handles, and straps). They may also refuse to pay for damages to fragile merchandise that wasn't packed properly (although they generally cover items packed in containers designed for shipping—such as the original factory-sealed carton or a cardboard mailing tube—and packed with protective padding material).

If articles are stolen from your luggage, the airline may ask for receipts and may cover the depreciated value. Policies vary from airline to airline.

WHAT TO DO IF YOUR LUGGAGE DISAPPEARS

When the last bags from your flight float down the conveyor belt and yours isn't among them, don't panic. Your luggage isn't necessarily gone for good. According to the Department of Transportation, the great majority of misplaced bags do turn up and are reacquainted with their owners in a matter of hours.

Still, even if you're told your suitcase will be on the next flight:

- **Insist on a missing-luggage form.** Make the airline fill it out and request a copy. Get the name of the agent who fills out the form and a follow-up phone number. (Don't let him give you the reservations 800 number.)

- **Hold onto your baggage-claim tags.** If you must surrender them, make sure the agent gives you photocopies or notes on the form that he took them.

- **Ask whether your bag can be delivered without charge once found.** Sometimes you're charged the cost of getting your bag to you.

- **Ask how much the airline will reimburse you for emergency purchases you must make while your luggage is missing.** The amount depends partly on whether you're away from home and how long your bags are delayed. But it's also subject to negotiation, so summon up all your persuasive powers.

My wife and I flew USAir to Denver and United to Aspen for our honeymoon. When we arrived, our luggage was missing. After waiting for three days, we received permission from United to replace some of our lost gear. Well, Aspen is an expensive town, and the basic necessities for our week-long ski trip totaled $2,321.24.

Back home, we discovered that American Airlines had found our baggage and had contacted United about it on the day we flew to Aspen! If United had retrieved the luggage then, we wouldn't have had to make the purchases. But United says it will reimburse only half the amount we spent. I think we're entitled to the full amount.

— Ira Feigenbaum, West Hartford, Connecticut

United didn't, but it eventually gave Feigenbaum a $50 voucher and four domestic upgrade certificates in addition to the $1,160.62. United will refund up to 50% of the amount spent on emergency purchases due to delayed baggage. The airline told us it was not solely responsible for the mishandling of the luggage; it billed a percentage of Feigenbaum's reimbursement check to USAir.

The amount you are reimbursed for purchases you must make while awaiting your luggage varies from airline to airline. Some give you $25 for the first 24 hours your luggage is missing and toss in a free overnight kit. Some don't give you a cash advance but reimburse you later if you keep receipts. Ask what items are reimbursable before you go on an emergency shopping spree. Some carriers absorb up to 50% of your expenditures as long as they are reasonable and you keep receipts. Some don't reimburse anything unless your luggage has been missing longer than 24 hours. Some give you a flat per diem (usually in the $25 to $50 range) and, if your luggage turns out to be lost for good, deduct that amount from your final settlement.

In short, it's a crap shoot.

WHAT IF YOUR LUGGAGE NEVER SHOWS UP?

This next part is best swallowed with a martini. An airline's liability limit for lost luggage is only $1,250 per person on domestic flights and a mere $640 per bag internationally.

That's the maximum it has to pay. An airline may pay less if it decides that the depreciated value of your property is worth less, or if it opts to pay an amount based on your luggage weight. According to an international treaty called the Warsaw Convention, if an airline weighs your luggage at check-in and records the amount on your ticket, then its liability is limited to $9.07 per pound ($20 per kilo). Airlines that don't record a passenger's baggage weight assume that each bag weighs 70 pounds (32 kilos), thus the liability ceiling of about $640 per bag.

This amount is, of course, ludicrously low. The Warsaw Convention dates from 1929. The $1,250 liability limit for domestic flights is also unrealistic, and there has been recent talk of increasing it to $1,800. Stay tuned. (And cross your fingers.)

You'll have to send the airline a lost-luggage claim, including a list of the articles your bag contained, their estimated value, and any receipts you still have. Without them, you can expect to haggle with the airline over the value of your property. It probably won't reimburse the full amount of your claim—because it pays based on the depreciated value of your belongings rather than on their original price or replacement cost—and it won't cover the loss of any valuables such as cameras or jewelry.

If your trip involved two different airlines, it is the final one that is responsible for handling your claim, even though the fault may lie with the first. And if your international trip included a domestic segment, it is the $640 liability limit (not $1,250) that applies.

As if all that weren't bad enough, the airline will take six weeks to three months to reimburse you.

A word of warning: Don't exaggerate a claim in an attempt to finagle more money out of an airline than you're owed. If an airline thinks a claim is inflated or fraudulent, it will work against you, especially if you can't cough up receipts and most especially if you've filed lost-luggage reports in the past.

Instead of cash, you may be offered a settlement of free tickets (in an amount higher than the sum in question). Before accepting them, be sure to ask about restrictions—whether there are blackout dates, for instance, and how long before departure you can make your reservation.

WHAT ABOUT CARRY-ON LUGGAGE?

Airlines are not liable for lost or damaged carry-on items, so when moving around or off a plane, keep your wits about you.

After all the passengers had boarded American Airlines Flight 403 from Dallas to Mexico City, the pilot announced a delay because of mechanical problems. The time was 6:55 PM. He said that passengers could get off if they wished and that an announcement on the status of the flight would be made in the gate area at 7:30.

I was one of two passengers who deplaned. I made some phone calls and returned to the gate area at 7:30 only to learn that the plane had taken off at 7:20. I had left a coat containing my wallet, passport, credit cards, driver's license, and $700 in cash in the plane's overhead bin.

An American ticket agent booked me and the other stranded passenger on another flight to Mexico City. When I arrived there the following morning, my coat, wallet, and documents were waiting for me, but the $700 was missing. I believe that had the pilot followed his own directive, this unfortunate incident would not have occurred.

—*Nicholas Granado, Sewell, New Jersey*

Although American will not assume responsibility for personal items left in the cabin, it has sent Granado a $150 voucher as a goodwill gesture. American says that at 7:15, numerous announcements were made throughout the terminal advising that Flight 403 was ready for immediate departure.

Ombudsman urges travelers to remember that an airline cabin is not necessarily any safer than a busy airport and that valuables should not be left unattended in either place.

Frequent-Flier Mileage Mishaps

Ah, yes. Frequent-flier mileage. It sounded like a swell idea at first. Travelers get something for nothing. Airlines get customer loyalty. Everybody wins. Problem is, the airlines got themselves into a jam. Pretty soon they owed passengers hundreds of thousands of free tickets. Life became more difficult for people trying to cash in their miles. On popular routes, seats allocated for frequent fliers grew scarce. Anyone trying to use miles to fly to Hawaii in December or France in July had to book eight months in advance. And you could forget about the times when you actually needed to travel. Thanksgiving, Christmas, and Easter were all "blacked out."

Then the airlines added salt to our wounds. They changed the rules: Now miles may expire after three years. Just when you are about to hit the 25,000-mile mark that entitles you to a free domestic round-trip, all your mileage more than three years old vaporizes. The airlines do not have a problem with this: They still view mileage as a gift they choose to bestow. But passengers are irked: We now view mileage as our God-given right. Infrequent fliers find it much tougher to earn a free trip. Those who travel on business constantly can collect enough miles for far-flung journeys—but then, these are precisely the people who don't want to go anywhere near an airport during their precious time off.

Add to all this the fact that a lot of errors spring up in the airlines' computerized mileage-tracking systems, and you've got a major source of frustration for air travelers and of letters to the Ombudsman column.

COMMON COMPLAINTS

The biggest mileage-related problem we hear about is when the airline fails to credit your frequent-flier account with miles you've flown. How to minimize screw-ups?

- **Be armed with your frequent-flier membership number when you fly.** Ask to have it recorded at check-in, in case you forgot to give it when you made your booking.

- **Hang onto all boarding passes and ticket receipts.** Keep them until your statement arrives showing you've been credited properly. To rectify any mistake, you usually need both pieces of documentation—boarding pass and ticket receipt.

- **Check mileage statements and report discrepancies quickly.** Look them over as soon as they arrive in the mail. If you notice a problem, contact the airline immediately. Most do not credit miles that are six months or a year old.

The new age of electronic ticketing poses a new problem for frequent fliers: If you're not given a ticket, how can you document that you flew?

My 13-year-old daughter recently flew on United Airlines from San Diego to Seattle and back. When she arrived at the airport, she was given ticket stubs that also served as her boarding pass. After she returned home, I sent the stubs to United Airline's Mileage Plus so she could collect the miles traveled. They refused to credit her account without more documentation, such as a copy of a ticket or a ticket number. She was never issued one—this was one of the airline's "ticketless travel" routes. If I had had her account number with me when she checked in, United probably would have taken it then. But now it is asking for papers we never had.

—*Sharon Linzey, San Diego, California*

Linzey's daughter did eventually get her miles, and we got an explanation. With its new electronic ticketing process, United said, "A receipt and itinerary are always printed at the point of issue." The receipt replaces a conventional ticket when the customer requests mileage credit. Apparently, Linzey wasn't given one, which is what created the problem. Copies of electronic boarding passes aren't recognized without the additional proof of purchase.

Make sure you get your receipt, and keep it until you see that the miles have been credited to your account.

Another common mileage complaint we hear: You fly a U.S. airline's international partner in order to accumulate miles, only to discover that because you paid a restricted fare, you aren't eligible for mileage credit. This seems to happen mainly on flights to and around the South Pacific and Asia. Sometimes you receive miles only if you fly in business- or first-class on these partner airlines. Sometimes only flights on particular routes are eligible. So, before buying a ticket on a partner airline, read the fine print in the U.S. airline's frequent-flier member's guide or call its mileage department. Don't trust what an airport ticket agent tells you; they don't always know the ins and outs of mileage accrual.

A third big gripe: Your flight was canceled, you were transferred to another airline, and you did not receive mileage credit. Some U.S. carriers don't give credit to passengers forced onto another airline unless the other airline is one of its international partners. Some give mileage credit if the cancellation was caused by mechanical or operational problems but not if it was weather-related.

Be aware that if your flight is delayed or canceled and your ticket was paid for with frequent-flier miles, you may not be treated as well as paying passengers, particularly on foreign airlines. The carrier may be less likely to switch you to another airline, and if you're stranded overnight, you may not receive the same amenities—hotel and meal vouchers and such. How to avoid second-class treatment? Airlines often make exceptions for "highly valued customers," so if you have very-frequent-flier status, make sure the counter agent knows it. Other passengers may have to settle for traveling standby on the airline's next flight out, a potential nightmare during peak travel times. If you really do get jerked around, write customer relations.

HOW TO MAKE THE MOST OF YOUR MILEAGE

- **Rack up miles through other programs.** These include affinity credit cards that net miles for every purchase, long-distance calling cards, even flower delivery services.

- **Use miles as you accrue them.** This is especially true if you're an infrequent frequent flier. If you hold out for pie in the sky—e.g. those two first-class tickets to Asia you've been dreaming about—your miles may expire, the requirements may go up, the rules may change.

- **Use mileage for flights that are ordinarily expensive.** Don't use miles for a round-trip to Florida that you can get for $198. Use them for a $700 flight to Colorado in ski season. I use my miles when I need to fly somewhere at the last minute and, because I've missed the advance-purchase deadline, would otherwise have been forced to pay full fare.

- **Consider insuring your miles.** A unique program run by the publisher of *InsideFlyer* magazine (☞ *below*) provides a number of services to serious frequent fliers, including a mileage insurance plan. There are two options: AwardGuard, which costs $20 per year, protects unused miles and tickets if an airline goes bankrupt; AwardExtender, which costs $60 annually, honors miles and awards once they expire.

InsideFlyer is an exhaustive source of news on both discounts and frequent-flier programs (☎ 800/487–8893; $33 annually). The *Official Frequent Flyer Guidebook,* published by InsideFlyer, is an annual catalog of programs, comparison charts, and advice ($14.99).

Where to Turn for Help

QUESTIONS AND COMPLAINTS ABOUT AIRLINE REGULATIONS, POLICIES, SERVICE, ADVERTISING

U.S. Department of Transportation (DOT)
✉ Office of Consumer Affairs (I-25)
400 7th St. SW
Washington, DC 20590
☏ 202/366–2220

This agency tracks and investigates consumer complaints; provides fact sheets with advice when an airline ceases operations or a scam is uncovered; and compiles monthly and quarterly statistics on delayed and canceled flights, overbookings, baggage problems, and consumer complaints to the DOT (published as the **"Air Travel Consumer Report,"** available for $1.75 from Consumer Information Center, ✉ Department 133-B, Pueblo, CO 81009).

The office also publishes **"Fly-Rights: A Consumer Guide to Air Travel,"** which everyone should read (available from Department 136C at the Consumer Information Center; $1.75). Available free from the DOT are **"Plane Talk,"** a series of fact sheets that cover tips for airline travel, frequent-flyer programs, transporting live animals, charter flights, flying with disabilities, and how to avoid baggage problems; the **"Informal Summary of Aviation Consumer Rules,"** a summary of airline regulations that is more exhaustive and not as easy to understand as "Fly-Rights"; and **"Air Travelers Tell It to the Judge: A Consumer's Guide to Small Claims Court."**

QUESTIONS AND COMPLAINTS ABOUT AIRLINE SAFETY AND MECHANICAL PROBLEMS

Federal Aviation Administration
✉ 800 Independence Ave. SW
Washington, DC 20591
☏ 800/FAA–SURE (hot line)

The FAA is the publisher of **"Hazardous Material? Tips for Airline Passengers,"** a free brochure detailing materials prohibited in checked and carry-on luggage.

CONSUMER ISSUES, SAFETY CONCERNS

Aviation Consumer Action Project
✉ Box 19029
Washington, DC 20036
☎ 202/638–4000
This non-profit organization works to improve safety and strengthen consumer rights for airline passengers; handles complaints about airline service and safety; and publishes **"Facts and Advice for Airline Passengers"** ($4) and the quarterly *ACAP News* ($21 annually).

INFORMATION ABOUT FARES, DEALS, AND TRENDS

Consumer Reports Travel Letter (subscriptions ☎ 800/234–1970; $39 annually, $5 per back issue) is a superb overall resource for anyone who travels frequently and wants to do it economically.

INFORMATION ABOUT HOW TRAVELERS HAVE SUCCESSFULLY SUED AIRLINES

Travel Law, by Thomas A. Dickerson, is a comprehensive legal reference that discusses a vast range of airline problems, airline liability in a variety of circumstances, and court cases in which liability limits have been overridden (available from Law Journals Seminar Press, ✉ 345 Park Ave. S, New York, NY 10010, ☎ 212/779–9200; $98).

INFORMATION AND COMPLAINTS ABOUT HOW AIRLINES TREAT PEOPLE WITH DISABILITIES

U.S. Department of Transportation
Office of Consumer Affairs (I-25)
✉ 400 7th St. SW
Washington, DC 20590
☎ 202/366–2220
The office publishes **"New Horizons for the Air Traveler with a Disability,"** which describes accommodations, facilities, and services required by law (available from the Consumer Information Center, ✉ Dept. 484Z, Pueblo, CO 81009; $.50). **"Access Travel: Airports"** gives tips for easier travel and lists the design and facilities at 553 airports worldwide (available from ✉ Dept. 578Z at the Consumer Information Center, above).

Society for the Advancement of Travel for the Handicapped
✉ 347 5th Ave., Suite 610
New York, NY 10016
☎ 212/447–7284
A non-profit membership organization, SATH advises and assists travelers with disabilities (membership $45 annually).

INFORMATION AND COMPLAINTS ABOUT
AIRLINE TREATMENT OF ANIMALS

U.S. Department of Agriculture
Animal and Plant Health Inspection Service
Regulatory Enforcement and Animal Care
✉ 4700 River Rd., Unit 84
Riverdale, MD 20737
☎ 301/734–8645
The Department of Agriculture publishes **"Air Travel for Your Dog or Cat,"** **"Traveling by Air with Your Pet,"** and **"Regulatory Enforcement and Animal Care"** (free).

CHAPTER 3

Lodgings

The more money you spend on a hotel vacation, the fewer problems you'll have. This may sound obvious, but it is actually truer of hotel stays than it is of plane trips, car rentals, or cruises. If you splurge on a business-class plane ticket, and the flight is delayed or the airline loses your luggage, you'll be no better off for having paid your premium. Car renters who use an expensive company are just as likely to have problems with collision-damage coverage and drop-off fees as those using the cheapest firm. Whether you've opted for a cruise ship's penthouse suite or the cheapest inside cabin, you'll likely receive the same level of service.

But with hotels, the more you pay, the less chance you'll encounter overbooking problems, hours-long waits to check in, out-of-order facilities, advertised amenities that don't exist, poorly informed concierges, wake-up calls that never happen, theft of your belongings, or any of a host of other possible glitches. This is because the biggest difference between a room that costs $150 a night and one that costs $300 a night is often the level of service. We rarely receive complaints about a Four Seasons or Ritz-Carlton. We most often hear about hotels belonging to lesser U.S. chains, about small independent establishments in Europe, and, most of all, about large beach resorts in the Caribbean and Mexico.

On our first night at the Halcyon Cove Beach Resort and Casino in Antigua, my husband and I opened the door of our room and saw something scurry across the floor. The next morning we saw it again. Then our daughter, who was staying next door, showed us a partially eaten bar of soap and rodent droppings on the lingerie in her bureau.

We complained to the manager, who said it was impossible to move us to new accommodations but promised to place rodent traps in our rooms. We washed our clothes and bought new toothbrushes and toiletries, which we kept in the refrigerator. The next night, we found a rat writhing on our floor, trying to free itself from the glue trap by gnawing off its leg. We immediately told the night manager we would camp out in the lobby if he did not move us. He found two rooms, but we could barely sleep.

I sent the hotel four letters of complaint, but got not one response. Then my travel agent wrote, and the hotel refunded the cost of a night's stay. I think I deserve more.

—*Betty Lou La Rocco, Brick, New Jersey*

So did Ombudsman. Our first move was to forward La Rocco's letter to David Fernandez, director of the Antigua and Barbuda Department of Tourism in the United States, who said he was "appalled," adding that "the Halcyon Cove Hotel has carried out a thorough eradication program under the supervision of the Department of Health. It is unlikely that this phenomenon will recur." Unsatisfied, Ombudsman wrote him again, demanding to know why the Department's health standards were not met in the first place. This time, Yvonne Maginley, director general of tourism, replied that construction work had been going on nearby and that "the refuse from the workmen's meals must have attracted rats." She also persuaded the resort to offer La Rocco a complimentary two-week stay.

The good news: Hotels do a much better job than airlines of making unhappy customers happy again, perhaps because hotels have to work harder at luring travelers back for more. The bad news: No federal agency regulates hotels or aids consumers by investigating and tracking their complaints. If something goes wrong at a hotel, it is usually the individual establishment's decision whether or not to make up for it, and some properties are far more sympathetic than others.

If an unfortunate situation can be remedied, take immediate action. If you were promised an oceanfront room and you've been assigned one overlooking the parking lot, ask to switch. Start with the front desk and, if need be, huff and puff all the way to the general manager. If a better room is not available, think up solutions. Can you move to an oceanfront room in a couple of days and agree to some sort of compensation for the nights spent in the inferior room? Can an acceptable room at another hotel be arranged?

If your needs aren't met, request a fair refund. If the hotel agrees to compensation, don't leave without proof of the agreement—either a deduction on your bill, or a promise in writing, which will help if you need to contact the customer relations office later.

Should complaints to the management get you nowhere, document the problem (with photographs if pertinent), make a diary of your attempts to right it (including the names of everyone involved, dates and times, room numbers, etc.), and, after your stay, write to the property (or to the tour operator, if you bought a hotel-plus-airfare travel package).

If the response you receive is unsatisfactory, and the hotel belongs to a larger chain, write to the company's headquarters. Sometimes franchisees don't comply with company policies until the corporate office starts breathing down their neck. As for independent hotels, try contacting the local Better Business Bureau or consumer protection agency. If the hotel is in the United States, you can try writing to the American Hotel & Motel Association, although it will only forward a copy of your letter to the property and request a response.

If the hotel is in another country, it may belong to a trade organization or marketing group you can contact (Leading Hotels of the World, for instance, or Relais & Châteaux). If not, seek help from the country's tourist board.

Learning to Speak Brochurese

After spotting ads in a glossy travel magazine for a new luxury resort in Ocho Rios, Jamaica, Robert and Hollyann Burmeister of Stillwater, Pennsylvania, plunked down $2,700 for a week's vacation there. When they arrived, they did not see the "20 breathtakingly beautiful acres of tropical gardens" promised in the ads. Nor the "10,000 plants, flowers, birds, and exotic fish . . . [and] waterfalls cascading into natural swimming pools." What they saw were truckloads of cinder blocks and a construction site. (The hotel has since been completed and, we understand, is quite popular.)

The biggest avoidable gripe we hear about resort vacations is that the information given in the ads, the brochure, or the travel agent's or tour operator's description of the property doesn't match the reality.

If an ad says a hotel is "on the island's south shore" and shows photos of sand and surf, don't assume it's on the beach; it could be a 15-minute drive inland. If a brochure says a hotel is "just minutes from the theaters and cafés of London's fashionable West End," don't assume that means by foot; it might be a $10 cab ride away. Promotional materials might show photos of people playing golf, implying that a resort has its own golf course, when guests actually tee off at a public course 20 minutes away; or pictures of tennis courts that actually belong to a private home across the street; or photos of a lush beach that was washed away in a hurricane several years ago.

Hotel ratings can also be misleading, so beware of terms like "first class" or "five-star," which are thrown around with abandon, not only in brochures but also by travel agents and tour-company representatives. Hotel ratings vary from place to place: What is considered "five star" in one country might be considered "two star" here. And some countries have ratings higher than "first class."

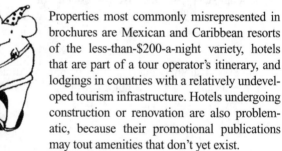

Properties most commonly misrepresented in brochures are Mexican and Caribbean resorts of the less-than-$200-a-night variety, hotels that are part of a tour operator's itinerary, and lodgings in countries with a relatively undeveloped tourism infrastructure. Hotels undergoing construction or renovation are also problematic, because their promotional publications may tout amenities that don't yet exist.

I booked a stay at the Playa Blanca Club Med because the scuba diving and horseback riding sounded terrific and the brochure promised fitness equipment that was "plentiful and second to none." Representatives at 1-800-CLUB-MED assured me that the health club had Lifecycles and StairMasters, and the brochure said that "health experts and exercise instructors are on hand in the enhanced fitness center to lead you in work-outs, and help set up a program you can follow."

I arrived at the resort to find that torrential rains had caused the scuba diving and horseback riding to be canceled, that there were no weight-lifting instructors, and that the "fitness center" had only three old stationary bikes, one Universal, and some free weights. Miserable, I asked Club Med to let me leave and come back another time, but I was told that if I left, my $2,039 payment would be forfeited. So I stuck it out. Back home, I wrote to Club Med demanding a refund. It answered that it could not "be held responsible for any acts of God" and offered a $200 refund and a 15% discount on a future stay, which I find unacceptable.

—*Lynda Bockler, Calgary, Alberta*

 Club Med eventually promised an additional $200 and a 30% discount. Consumer affairs manager Amy Lampert Pfau told Ombudsman that the health club had been scheduled for renovation when the winter brochure was produced and that the new fitness equipment had been delayed by Mexican customs officials. Because of the heavy rains, staffers "who were usually involved with guest programs . . . were commandeered to perform cleanup and safety tasks." Also, as the brochure warns, "activities and programs are subject to change, modification, cancellation, and so on." Although Lampert Pfau called Bockler's experience an "isolated incident," Ombudsman has received a number of complaints from Club Med guests who say their vacations were ruined because of a lack of promised facilities and services.

You can usually get to the truth by looking up the hotel you're considering in a reliable and comprehensive guidebook that includes a map or by calling the hotel directly and asking detailed questions about its location and about the facilities you want to use.

If you book your vacation through a tour operator or airline that is selling the airfare plus the hotel stay as part of an economical travel package, be extra careful about what's promised. Some tour packagers use the old bait-and-switch trick. The brochure touts a desirable hotel—while the fine print notes that accommodations may be in one that is "similar." There is no guarantee of where you will be staying. If the tour packager switches you to a less appealing hotel upon arrival—and some consistently do—there is little you can do about it.

Wait! Stop! Don't Pay Yet

If you are not familiar with a property, make an effort to check it out before paying in advance. If you're considering a little-known eco-resort in Belize, for instance, find out how long it has been in business. For U.S. properties, ask the local Better Business Bureau or the state attorney general's consumer protection office whether there are any complaints on file and, if so, of what nature. For overseas hotels, contact the country's tourist board.

If you must make a nonrefundable advance payment, use a credit card; if you don't get what you paid for, you can request a chargeback. And pay the absolute minimum possible. If the hotel requests payment for all seven nights of your planned stay, for example, ask if you can cover only three. If a large nonrefundable payment is required and you fear your plans may change, consider buying trip-cancellation insurance.

Or, if you're like me—you prefer off-the-beaten-path hotels whose reputations are unclear; flexibility in your itinerary is important; and insurance is too big a hassle for just a few nights' lodgings—avoid hotels that demand advance payment. I prepay only if I will be arriving at night, if the country is far-flung and I don't speak the language, or if I'm traveling in peak season, when rooms are scarce.

Booking the Right Room

So the "penthouse" you reserved at that four-star hotel in Madrid turned out to be a shabby attic in a townhouse with no elevator? You insisted on a poolside room for your Caribbean getaway, only to be kept awake at night by the dance band that moved outdoors for after-hours fun? You arrived at the famed Hotel Danieli in Venice for a once-in-a-lifetime vacation splurge, asked for a room on the lagoon, and found yourself on the ground floor, looking out at mobs of sightseers looking in at you?

You're not the first person this has happened to. In fact, right now, in just about every fine hotel in the world, some luckless sod is having a miserable time.

At many hotels, no two rooms are quite alike. Nor are any two travelers' tastes. While one person heading for a large ski resort might like to be in the main lodge near the nightlife, another might prefer a secluded wing nestled in evergreens, and yet another might require a view of the ski slope with a private balcony for seeing and being seen. Meanwhile, the primary concern of a family with four children might be proximity to the ski storage area, to ease the elaborate morning routine of getting clothed, geared up, and onto the slopes.

Figuring out which room or room type best suits your particular needs can be tricky if you've never visited a property before, since every hotel is so different. If your foremost concern is the view, for instance, you might typically request a top-floor room. This strategy may work with modern high-rises but can fail you at a European palace hotel, where top-floor rooms often have low ceilings and small, recessed windows (they used to be the servants' quarters). Or let's say your primary concern is peace and quiet. You might typically ask for a room "in the back," away from street noise. This tactic might pay off in the French Quarter of New Orleans, where such rooms frequently face a tranquil magnolia-filled courtyard. But it may not work at an historic big-city property, where windows "in the back" often overlook courtyards filled with machinery that whirs and clanks all night.

Getting the right hotel room is an art, but with a lot of science. Some advice for navigating the architectural and managerial maze at fine hotels:

- **Be choosy.** It's better to make requests than not to. Many travelers are afraid of seeming too demanding, but the management at any well-run hotel actually *prefers* choosy guests. The goal, after all, is to meet your expectations; the more information a hotel has about your needs, the easier it is to fill them. Also, at many hotels, guest rooms are meted out in a way that leaves the meek to inherit the worst. First dibs on room assignments go to guests who have specific requests: the couple who honeymooned in No. 753 and for whom no other will do. Next come the guests whose demands are categorical: a patio room, please, *and* a king-size bed. Smokers and adamant nonsmokers must, of course, be accommodated. And the regular patrons. Which leaves you. If you make no request at all, you'll get the leftovers.

Furthermore, making requests may actually increase your chances of an upgrade. Say you ask for a room on a high floor. If some superior top-floor rooms become available—thus allowing the front desk to hand out complimentary upgrades—you'll be among the first in line.

- **Call the hotel directly.** Don't use a toll-free reservations number unless it rings at the hotel itself. On-site reservations agents typically are more familiar with the property's layout, and have more up-to-date information about which rooms are still available. An 800 or 888 number can lead you to some booking agent in Omaha who's never even *seen* the property.

- **Time your call.** Front desks are busiest in the morning and midafternoon: check-out and check-in. Call during down times, and take time zone differences into account.

- **Get a name, and be friendly.** Strike up a relationship with the reservations clerk or, better yet, the reservations manager. Each time you call the hotel to ask a question or confirm your reservation, ask to speak to that same person. You are more likely to be remembered and treated well.

- **Request a property map or floor plan.** The more historic or unusual a hotel, the less predictable the accommodations. Rooms vary considerably in older European hotels, for instance. Their elaborate facades mean that on one corridor with the same view, one room might have a balcony, another three windows, and a third a projecting portion that adds several feet to the length of the room. So ask the reservations desk to fax you a map or cross-sectional floor plan—something that indicates the different views you can get and the rooms' relative size and shapes. With it, you can gauge which rooms are balconied, which are secluded, and which are both; which rooms are near the lobby, the bar, the pool, the elevators, the stairs, the ice machine—whatever you want to be near for the convenience or to avoid because of the noise.

- **Think about the room features that matter to you.** A view? Windows that actually open? Closet space? A whirlpool? Double sinks? Modern decor, or traditional? And the bed? Ask for a king-size if you want, but avoid the ugly-American tendency to demand what doesn't exist: King-size in Europe may be a mere double by U.S. standards.

- **Beware of confusing lingo.** "New" wings are often drearily utilitarian—particularly in Europe, but also in the United States. While old architecture frequently has more charm, new may have better plumbing and less noise. And know what a "series" is. If room 1506 has a view to die for but isn't available, you may be offered 1505 or 1507, next door—which may mean around the corner. In terms of views, neighboring floors are often better alternatives, so ask about other 06 series rooms, above or below the fifteenth floor—1406 or 1606. Also, remember that "ocean view" does not mean "ocean front." In an "ocean view" room you may need to stand on the air conditioner and crane your neck just to glimpse the water. And ground-level "oceanfront" views may be obstructed by beach shops or cabanas. Ask exactly what will fill your line of sight.

- **Think about noise.** Light sleepers should avoid rooms near or above lobbies, restaurants, bars, and discos. Top floors are quietest—no footfalls overhead. Families like poolside rooms, which means daytime splashing and shrieking. Ask about renovations, both on-site and nearby—especially in developing cities, where jackhammers can go all night. Ask if windows are double- or triple-glazed—particularly in Europe and in cities where mopeds buzz past.

- **Ask the reservationist which rooms are popular and why.** If the clerk can't answer the question, speak with the reservations manager. Ask for the pros and cons of several room types. If no descriptions gush forth, try a more direct approach: Ask the manager to tell you his personal favorite, and why.

- **Celebrate something.** If your honeymoon or anniversary is the reason for your visit, say so. Hotels want to make such occasions memorable so you'll return for future celebrations and send other guests their way. They often grant upgrades, too. So whatever you're celebrating—even your birthday—mention it.

- **Confirm your request.** Have the hotel confirm your request for a particular room or room type in writing, and have that piece of paper in hand when you arrive at the front desk. Or ask the reservations manager at what point rooms get assigned—usually a day or two ahead, but often a week or two in advance at resorts—and call on that day to confirm your room request and the rate.

- **See the goods.** When you arrive, ask to see your assigned room before you check in, particularly in Europe, where some hoteliers fill their poorest rooms first—and with unfamiliar foreign faces. If you don't like the room, politely explain why ("This room is so dark. Do you have something with more light, or facing south?").

- **If the room you've been assigned is a lemon, try on-site reconnaissance.** Follow maid's carts down the corridors, and peek into rooms being cleaned. Ask the front desk to show you some other available rooms.

How to Get a Room at a Sold-Out Hotel

Okay, now you've found the perfect hotel *and* the perfect room. But when you try to reserve it, you're told the property is fully booked. Before taking no for an answer, consider these strategies.

- **If you called the toll-free number, call the hotel directly instead.** Toll-free operators (who tend to be at regional offices) often have outdated information about room availability.

- **Ask when cancellation penalties set in, and call on that day.** At what point do guests pay a fee if they cancel their reservation? Three weeks before arrival? Three days? Note the date, then call the morning of that day to see if rooms have opened up as people cancel at the last minute to avoid being charged. Even if you're not first on the waiting list, you may be the first to call. At city hotels in particular, availability fluctuates by the hour, even by the minute. If penalties set in at 6 PM, call between five and six.

- **If the hotel has a deal with a wholesale tour packager, call the wholesaler.** Some hotels provide an allotment of rooms to wholesalers such as Go-Go Tours, Delta Dream Vacations, or Adventure Tours. These companies are given a certain number of days in which to sell those rooms or return them to the hotel's inventory.

- **Call early in the morning on the day you hope to begin your stay.** If a room was held for someone who didn't show up the night before, you could nab his reservation—which may have been for several nights.

Paying the Lowest Possible Rates

- **Call direct.** A hotel's on-site reservations desk will often cite a better rate than a toll-free operator (unless the 800 number rings at the hotel itself), who may not be aware of all the latest deals. Better yet, call both and compare. Don't necessarily trust a travel agent's computer reservation system to provide the best rate; some larger chains include independently owned, franchised locations that run promotions that don't show up on the computer screen.

- **If your travel schedule isn't firm yet, ask about seasonal changes in rates and occupancy.** Low season promises better prices, a better choice of rooms, and a better chance of a free upgrade.

- **Request a rate card.** This lists the different room types and the range of costs, from single to presidential suite.

- **Don't accept the first rate you are quoted.** Higher rates are usually quoted first, of course, so haggle. Start by letting the agent know that you're on vacation, not on an expense account (calling the hotel on a weekend helps to send this message). Ask if any special deals are available—weekend rates (particularly common at city hotels), package deals (for two- or three-night stays, for example), seasonal specials, one-night rates that include breakfast and some other amenities. Also ask about discounts available to members of organizations such as AAA. Be persistent.

- **Use the right travel agent.** If you're going to splurge on a luxury property, use an agent who gets preferred rates through membership in a sales organization, such as Leading Hotels of the World, or in a consortium such as API Travel Consultants, a network of top travel agencies. If you use a first-rate travel agent who has developed relationships with the finest properties and chains around the world, and sends a lot of business their way, you boost your chances of getting an exceptional room at a good rate. Call API (☎ 817/870–0300) for a referral to such an agent.

- **Contact a hotel consolidator.** If you need a room—any old room will do—in a more mainstream hotel, particularly in urban areas, these brokers can often get you steep discounts, although rarely at peak periods or at the most popular hotels:

Capitol Reservations (☎ 800/847–4832): Washington, D.C., and suburbs.
Express Reservations (☎ 800/356–1123): New York and Los Angeles.
Hot Rooms (☎ 800/468–3500): Chicago.
Hotel Reservations Network (☎ 800/964–6835): Most major U.S. cities, London and Paris.
Hotels Plus (☎ 800/235–0909): Major European cities.
Meegan Hotel Reservation Services (☎ 800/332–3026): Boston.
Quikbook (☎ 800/789–9887): Major U.S. cities.
Room Exchange (☎ 800/846–7000): Lisbon, London, Paris, Zurich, and elsewhere.
San Francisco Reservations (☎ 800/677–1550): San Francisco.
Travel Interlink (☎ 800/477–7172): Asia and the South Pacific.
Vacationland (☎ 800/245–0050): Asia.

You can find a hotel consolidator for a region you're traveling to by calling the country's tourist board or, for the U.S., the local convention and visitors bureau or chamber of commerce.

- **Play the dollar.** In countries where the dollar is weak, consider paying in advance in U.S. dollars, an option that is generally available through hotel chains with foreign properties (e.g. Forte Hotels and Inter-Continental). It's a slight gamble, but if the dollar remains weak, and especially if it dips further, then charging your room in advance will be cheaper than paying the foreign-currency rate on site.

When You Have to Cancel

I sent a $70 room deposit to the Hôtel Le Clément in Paris, then called up and canceled the reservation. Almost a year later, the hotel still hasn't returned my check. The French Government Tourist Office in Beverly Hills won't help. Can you?

—*Keith K. Anderson, Santa Fe, New Mexico*

But of course. Ombudsman asked the ministry of tourism in Paris to speak to the hotel manager, who promptly sent Anderson a $70 check. He offered what Ombudsman regards as a feeble excuse—he had not known the best way to reimburse someone in the United States. He also told the ministry that cancellations should be in writing, but three reservationists at the hotel assured Ombudsman over the phone that verbal cancellations are fine.

We receive many complaints about French hotels that keep deposits improperly. Unfortunately, travelers who pay by check rather than by credit card or who cancel by phone rather than by letter often have little recourse.

Many hotels impose cancellation penalties. Sometimes you can cancel without charge just a few hours before your scheduled arrival; sometimes, especially at island resorts, you must cancel several weeks in advance. Unfortunately, incompetent hotel reservationists and travel agents may neglect to mention such fees when you book your room. So, whenever making a reservation, find out the latest date you can cancel without cost.

If you cancel within the penalty period, a hotel might keep an amount equal to one night's stay. Or it might hang onto the full amount you paid. If a property failed to stipulate its cancellation policy—especially if it never sent written notice—dispute any cancellation charge with the hotel and, if you gave your credit card number, with your card issuer.

What if you pay in advance for your stay but, upon arrival, are so disappointed that you want to clear out and try to salvage your vacation by going elsewhere? The hotel says that if you do, you'll forfeit everything you've laid out. Should you stay or should you go?

It's frustrating, but if you prepaid with a credit card, don't assume you will get your money back. The card issuer's decision whether or not to reimburse you will depend on how seriously misled you were and whether the hotel admits it was at fault. If you want to leave simply because the place does not match the picture that was painted in the brochure, don't expect a refund. If key elements were promised but not delivered and you have documentation of everything, you may be able to retrieve some of your outlay. American Express is more likely than other companies to swallow a portion of your bill, as a gesture of goodwill—if you are a "valued cardmember," of course. Only if the hotel cannot provide you with any room at all is your credit card issuer obligated to reimburse you for a prepayment.

If you prepaid in cash and opt to leave early, chances are even fewer that you will ever see your money again. A hotel's refusal to accept credit cards should serve as a blinking yellow light: it may be an effort to keep you from refusing to pay via a charge-back.

When the Hotel Cancels on You

What if your "guaranteed" room turns out not to be? This is, of course, particularly annoying if you have flown thousands of miles and don't speak the language, and no other lodgings are available.

When I arrived in Lagos, Nigeria, L'Hotel Eko Meridien was fully booked and would not honor my confirmed reservation. I told the manager that clients expected to meet me there, but he said there was nothing he could do. When I asked if there was a phone I could use to find other lodgings, he said the only phones were in the rooms and, therefore, unavailable. The other hotels I found were either fully booked or did not accept credit cards. Luckily, a man I had met on the plane let me sleep at his house. I flew home the next day, because, with no room or phone, I was unable to conduct any business. Meridien Hotels has offered to compensate me with a week's stay at one of its properties, but my company, which is out more than $4,000, finds this unsatisfactory.

—*Ernesto Aponte, Fountain Valley, California*

We persuaded the hotel to reimburse $4,080, covering Aponte's airfare and other expenses. It told us it did not receive his booking through the chain's international reservations system. According to a spokesperson for the chain, which has now become Forte Le Meridien (and which no longer has a property in Lagos), the company's policy toward guests whose confirmed reservations cannot be honored differs in different parts of the world. But in general, an overbooked Meridien *will pay for the guest's accommodations at a similar hotel and for a cab to get there.*

Overbooking is more common at big-city or suburban hotels than at vacation resorts. Lodgings catering primarily to business travelers accept reservations from an estimated 5% to 15% more people than they have space for.

Whenever arriving at a hotel to check in, have with you any confirmation notice the hotel may have mailed you or your confirmation number. This should help if the front-desk clerk claims your reservation record isn't in the computer. Membership in a hotel's frequent-guest program should help as well.

If the hotel bumps you anyway, your recourse depends on regional law and company policy. Many establishments find accommodations at other hotels for would-be guests.

In fact, if you guaranteed your booking with a credit card, the hotel is required—by its contract with the card company—to find you a room at a comparable nearby hotel, to provide free transportation there, to give you a free three-minute phone call so you can let your family or office know of your whereabouts, and to forward all messages and calls to you at the new hotel. The overbooked property is also required to swallow the cost of the night's stay. (This is only if the hotel cannot find any room for you whatsoever—not if it is simply unable to comply with a special request—say, it promised a king-sized bed but can only provide a fold-out). If a hotel fails to do these things, report it to your credit card issuer.

What if you guaranteed your booking not with a credit card but by check? After all, many overseas hotels accept deposits only in cash. If a hotel bumps you and refuses to return a prepayment, contact the country's tourist board. Sometimes local law is on the traveler's side. In France, for instance, if you have prepaid for a room but none is available when you arrive, the hotelier is required by law to refund double the amount of your deposit.

Some resort hotels actually overbook as part of a bait-and-switch scheme. Whether they have space or not, they sell rooms to every traveler who calls up requesting one. Then, when the guest arrives to check in, they consistently direct the overflow to an inferior hotel in the same area—and collect a commission from the lesser resort for each "referral."

THE HOTEL FROM HELL

The Hotel from Hell

I've heard it all: Swimming pools closed for repairs, broken toilets necessitating walks to the lobby rest room at 4 AM, cockroaches in the bed, sidewalk drilling that serves as a daily 6 AM wake-up call, herds of drunken college students turning the place into Animal House. . . .

Planning a trip to Grenada when my wife was five months pregnant, I called the Grenada Renaissance Resort to make sure the physical layout, climate, and other conditions would suit my wife's state. Assured that they would, I booked our room.

Upon arriving, we learned that the island was experiencing a severe water shortage and that the hotel could provide water in our rooms only from 5 to 7 PM. At 5, the front desk said the water would be turned on at 7. At 7, I was told it would be available from 10 to 10:30. I was also told that it was my responsibility to check with the front desk throughout each day for the latest water schedule.

We finally got hot water at 10:10. We had time to shower but not to brush our teeth or use the toilet. Later, when my wife started vomiting from morning sickness, there was no tap water to rinse her mouth or the sink, and we couldn't flush the toilet. The situation was intolerable, so we left the next morning. Not only did we have to spend an extra $356 to change our plane tickets, but the hotel manager also refused to cancel the cost of the night's stay. I am outraged that the resort did not warn me about the problem in advance.

—*Marc Saitta, Alexandria, Virginia*

Ombudsman was outraged too—by the hotel's response to the complaint letter Saitta sent. The manager refused to send any compensation, because the water shortage was "not a direct result of the resort or its facilities." But several of the island's resorts had installed desalinization plants so that they could use ocean water. The Renaissance, Grenada's second largest hotel, had no such facility—which could be why The Grenadian Voice reported at the time that the Renaissance was "the hardest hit" by the shortage.

Fortunately, when we asked Renaissance Hotels & Resorts to reconsider, it promised the Saittas a complimentary five-night stay at any of its Caribbean or Latin American resorts. The resort has since built a desalinization plant.

Even if you risk the loss of an advance payment, you may be wiser to bail out if a hotel cannot remedy a lousy situation. If you plan to write to the corporate customer relations office later to ask for a refund, your case will be stronger if you leave early than if you stick it out—what better proof that the situation was intolerable?

Remember, though, that some customer relations departments are more generous than others.

At dinner on my first night at Club Med in Martinique, I was concerned to see perishable foods sitting in the heat, without ice, on the outdoor buffet tables. I chose a dish that looked relatively safe: chicken tacos. Unfortunately, I contracted food poisoning that night and remained so ill for the next six days that I could tolerate only bread, bananas, and water and could not participate in any activities. There was no doctor, merely a nurse who distributed diarrhea pills until she ran out on the second day. My vacation, which cost $1,279, was ruined, and the only refund Club Med would offer was $104, representing the cost of a night's stay.

—*Marie Henseler, Boston, Massachusetts*

Ombudsman wrote to Club Med several times pleading Henseler's case, but the company, while acknowledging that 30 people became ill from the chicken tacos, wouldn't offer further compensation. It advised Henseler to file a claim with its insurance company, but the most she could get from doing so was reimbursement for medical bills not covered by her personal health care insurance. Others who have complained to Ombudsman about food poisoning at Club Med resorts have received similar treatment—about $100 in compensation and a referral to the insurance claims administrator.

How Safe Are You?

The growing number of lawsuits involving robberies and assaults at U.S. hotels reflects their increased liability for failing to take adequate security measures. State and city laws require hotels in this country to provide a level of security tailored to the level of criminal activity in the immediate environment. Not so with all foreign hotels.

A thief grabbed my wife's purse in the lobby of the Best Western Regina in Barcelona. She held on to the purse, and the thief dragged her through the plate-glass front door. The door shattered, and she ended up on her back on the sidewalk, surrounded by glass, her purse gone. Fortunately, she was not badly injured. The stolen purse contained cash, our passports, airline tickets, and other valuables totaling $1,321. Perhaps most shocking is that the incident occurred in full view of the front desk. The hotel did not appear to have had any security staff.

The Regina's insurance company denied our claim, alleging that the incident took place in the street, not the lobby. A translation of the police report could be interpreted that way, but the police spoke no English, and we no Spanish, so all their information came from the Regina. The hotel's claim that the robbery occurred in the street makes no sense to me. What purse snatcher would drag a victim up to a hotel's front door and then push her through it?

We're unsatisfied with Best Western's response. We would also like to warn travelers in Barcelona to beware of street thieves.

—F.W. Albers, Fallbrook, California

When Albers filed a suit in small claims court, Best Western settled in full. The Regina's manager told us he did not see the need for security personnel in the lobby. But Ombudsman has received similar complaints from victims of street crime in Barcelona—as well as in Madrid and Seville—and the State Department's Bureau of Consular Affairs says crime is increasing throughout Spain, particularly in port cities and tourist areas. The bureau's Spain desk advises tourists to leave passports and valuables in a hotel safe, not to carry a purse, to carry only enough cash for the day's needs, and to keep a separate record of passport, traveler's checks, and credit card numbers.

Travelers are usually less vulnerable at vertical, business-oriented hotels than at spread-out resorts where they spend a lot of time outdoors—especially properties with individual cottages.

Two friends, my husband, and I paid more than $8,000 for a week in a villa at Ciboney Ocho Rios, a Radisson resort in Jamaica. One morning at about 4:30 we awoke to a loud crash and two shotgun blasts so close that we could see the flash. My husband and I hit the floor, pressed the security button near the bed, and were told by security that a prowler had been caught.

The next day the hotel refused to tell us anything more. The management did not apologize for the inconvenience or even seem concerned about the impact of this incident on our vacation.

—*Ann Jones, Short Hills, New Jersey*

Actually, Radisson was much concerned. It promptly offered the two couples a complimentary seven-night stay at a Radisson resort of their choice. The company told us that security guards and local police fired warning shots before arresting a suspected burglar at 4:45 AM near the couples' villa. Officials did not answer Jones's questions about the incident because they were told not to discuss it until the police investigation was over. We sympathize with Jones's distress, but think she should be thankful that the prowler was caught.

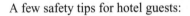

A few safety tips for hotel guests:

- **Make sure your room has a deadbolt or chain lock and a peephole.** Electronic card locks are safer than key locks.

- **Be wary of unexpected deliveries and service calls.** Call the front desk to make sure the delivery person is legitimate. If you order room service, ask that the receipt be slid under the door before you open it.

- **Avoid rooms in remote or insecure spots.** Book one near an elevator, concierge desk, or other busy area if hallways are long and dimly lighted. Avoid ground-floor rooms, where intruders can more easily break in.

- **Be careful what you tell strangers.** Don't give out your room number when you meet strangers in the lobby, bar, or elsewhere.

- **Don't draw attention to yourself.** Avoid displaying large amounts of cash or expensive jewelry.

- **Leave a light on when you leave your room.** Then you'll be able to see when you come back.

- **Exercise caution when returning to the hotel late at night.** Use the main entrance.

ESPECIALLY FOR WOMEN

Women staying in hotels alone are sometimes vulnerable in ways men are not. Some extra safety measures that women can take:

- **Choose a secure hotel in a well-lighted location.** That includes the surrounding streets and the parking area. A hotel where everyone must enter through a lobby is preferable to a motel whose rooms open onto a parking lot. Atrium hotels are a good choice, because each hallway is within sight of the lobby security guard.

- **Use valet parking.** Drive up to the front entrance and have hotel staff park your car if possible.

- **Keep a low profile when checking in.** Ask the front-desk clerk not to announce your room number when handing you the key, lest the wrong people overhear. And use an initial rather than your first name when filling out the guest-registration card.

How Safe Is Your Property?

My briefcase containing irreplaceable documents and more than $10,000 worth of valuables was stolen from my room at the Crown Sterling Suites Hotel in Phoenix. I immediately reported the theft, and the police came and filled out a report. The hotel referred me to its insurance company, which decided not to reimburse me. The police eventually found the briefcase and about $7,500 worth of my property in a dumpster, but I have been unable to get the hotel to compensate me for my losses.

—*Steven N. Gabelman, Atlanta, Georgia*

We were very pleasantly surprised when Crown Sterling Suites changed its tune and sent Gabelman a $1,500 goodwill check. Jack Roberts, Jr., the company's vice president, emphasized that the hotel was not "legally or even morally liable" and that it assumed responsibility for valuables only when they are placed in the hotel's safe deposit boxes. Crown Sterling Suites's generous spirit was extraordinary.

Ombudsman rarely sees hotels or insurance companies reimburse victims of hotel-room burglaries.

───

Theft of personal property is one of the most common hotel-related complaints we receive. And one of the most frustrating, because there's typically little we can do to help.

I've heard tales of robberies occurring while guests stepped out of their room just for a dip in the pool or for a cup of coffee. There was even the Rolex watch pilfered while its owner took a shower. The stories have made me so paranoid that whenever I stay at a hotel I automatically stash my electronic organizer in the room safe and my laptop in the lobby vault. All expensive jewelry gets left at home, of course. It helps that I take only carry-on luggage; it means never having to relinquish valuables to a bellhop who might let my suitcase linger perilously in the lobby.

The liability of a hotel in cases of theft differs from state to state and country to country. But in general, if a U.S. property gives adequate

notice that there is a safe in which to place valuables, and a guest chooses not to use it, then the hotel is not liable. Only if it is determined that the hotel was negligent (which is difficult, especially if the accused thief is an employee) can the establishment be held liable, and even then, its liability is limited.

In Colorado, for instance, a hotel's liability for theft is limited to $200. In Florida, the limit is $500, although a guest can increase it to $1,000 if he takes his valuables to the front desk and lets the manager inspect them and file an inventory, and the hotel agrees that they are worth more than $500. If the items are then stolen and the hotel is determined to be at fault, its liability would exceed $500 but be no more than $1,000.

HOW SAFE IS THE SAFE?

Although it's wiser to put valuables in a room safe than to leave them lying around, these vaults offer a false sense of security: Hotels typically are not liable for theft from in-room safes. If you intend to rely on one, keep in mind that electronic safes are more reliable than the old-fashioned key kind.

Lobby safes are a better bet, although they, too, do not offer as much protection as you might assume.

Several years ago, at 1:00 PM on December 23, my husband and I placed $4,000 in a safe-deposit box in the lobby of the Sands Hotel and Casino in San Juan. The hotel said it was giving us the only key and had us sign an agreement stating, "I hereby agree that access to this safety deposit box will be obtainable only through this signature and upon presentation of this key in person." When we opened the box at 8:20 PM two days later, the money was gone. One of the managers said that he thought we were pulling a scam, but another gave us a copy of the safe-deposit record, which shows a withdrawal at 8:05 PM on December 23. Whoever made the withdrawal did not sign the "authorized signature" space, a violation of our agreement with the hotel.

The day after the robbery, while sitting by the pool, we happened to start talking to a man who, to our astonishment, told us that $2,000 had been stolen from his safe-deposit box sometime between the evening of the 23rd and the afternoon of the 24th. Upon complaining to the management, he too had been treated like a criminal.

We finally received a $1,000 check from the Sands's insurance company, as did the other victim, but we are still furious about this experience and wanted to warn your readers about the danger of leaving cash in a lobby safe.

—*Marsha Sher, Plainview, New York*

We thank Sher for her advice, but we still think it's better to leave valuables in a lobby safe than in a guest room—and, of course, to carry traveler's checks rather than large amounts of cash.

For almost a year, our inquiries to the Sands' management went unanswered. Finally, we received a letter from Rick Newman, its vice president of operations, stating: "There has never been a duplicate key made for any box at the Sands. This indicates that there is only one guest key available to each safe-deposit box. Once a key is issued to a guest the only way to access the box without physically removing the lock is with a special device, which requires a service call" from the company that maintains the system.

Newman did offer the Shers a complimentary two-night stay at the resort as partial compensation, but he never explained why the hotel allowed a withdrawal without the "authorized signature" specified in the agreement.

⬤

The liability of U.S. hotels for theft from lobby vaults is limited and usually does not exceed $500. A couple of notable exceptions: In Florida, the limit is $1,000, provided the property gives the guest a receipt stating that it is not responsible for any losses exceeding that figure. In Colorado, the liability is no greater than the amount declared by the guest at the time of deposit, and the hotel does not have to accept anything greater in value than $5,000.

Guests at foreign properties are sometimes in better shape than they are here. "If a guest deposits $5,000 worth of valuables in safe custody at a hotel in New York and the valuables are stolen, the guest can only recover $500," points out Judge Thomas A. Dickerson, author of *Travel Law,* the industry's standard legal reference. "If the same goods are deposited in safe custody in a hotel in Australia or in the United Kingdom, the full value of goods can be recovered." There are cases, Dickerson says, where travelers have taken a U.S. hotel to court and overridden liability laws.

When entrusting valuables to a lobby safe, inquire about the hotel's liability limit. If your belongings are worth more, ask if the management can assume a greater liability. Most hotels won't, but some will, as a courtesy to their guests—especially those with a well-heeled clientele. Bring your valuables to the front desk and let the manager take a look. If he consents to a liability increase, come up with an agreed-upon value of the items, and put it all in writing. If the manager is unhelpful and you've got something with you that is extremely valuable, contact hotel security.

The best way to make sure you recoup any loss at a hotel is to make sure you're covered by a proper homeowner's insurance policy.

WHAT ABOUT LUGGAGE AND CARS LEFT WITH THE HOTEL?

⬤

When my husband and I arrived at the Drake Hotel in New York for a brief holiday visit, the bellman took our Louis Vuitton bags from the taxi and placed them on his cart. We checked in, then proceeded with the bellman toward the elevator. At this point we noticed that only two of our four bags were on the cart. The bellman asked that we go to our room, saying he would return with the remaining luggage.

We did, and were eventually informed that the two bags had been stolen from the cart and that the security guard on duty had been a witness. His attention had apparently been diverted by a passerby while the perpetrators made off with the luggage.

The police were called, and we lodged the appropriate complaint. The license plate number of the alleged thieves' vehicle was provided by the security guard, and the hotel gave the police a videotaped recording of the lobby at the time of the incident.

The hotel forwarded our claim to the insurance company, which told us it was not liable for valuables that hadn't been stored in the hotel's safe. We are out some $3,500. Can you help?

—*Christine and Donald Brooks, Washington, DC*

We thought the Brookses deserved some compensation, and the Drake Hotel eventually agreed, offering them $1,800. Hotels in New York are not liable for theft of valuables unless they are placed in the lobby vault. According to Judge Dickerson, "If the theft occurs between the street and the lobby, prior to check-in, the hotel might not be responsible at all, because the contract of innkeeper and guest must be established."

When arriving at a hotel, stick close to your luggage. Stay with the bellman until you're well inside. If you must part company with your bags, get a receipt for them. And remember: Expensive-looking suitcases can attract a thief's attention.

Hotels deny liability not only for bags left in the lobby but also for luggage stored at a hotel after you check out. It's important to know, though, that just putting a liability disclaimer on the back of a baggage claim check doesn't make it binding. Some courts have declared such disclaimers null and void.

Same with the disclaimers on the back of car claim checks. Still, if a car you leave in a hotel's garage or parking lot is damaged or stolen, you'll most likely be out of luck, unless you can prove negligence.

Exorbitant Phone and Fax Charges

Telecommunications services have grown into a profit center for many hotels in the United States and abroad, and the nickel-and-diming can become dizzying. Even travelers who are well aware of the hole they burn in their wallet by charging long-distance calls to their hotel room may be surprised at just how expensive local calls can be (often 75¢ to $1) and how hefty the service charges are for calling-card, collect, and toll-free calls (the same). Some hotels impose these fees whether or not a call goes through.

Many properties subscribe to local phone companies that charge higher rates than the major long-distance carriers. Some block you from using certain long-distance services, and some won't even connect you to the international operator. Come check-out time, markups can add hundreds of dollars to your bill.

I made a 15-minute phone call to Salem, New Hampshire, from the Hotel Sol e Mar in Albufeira, Portugal, and was billed $125. Finding this charge outrageous, I used my AT&T calling card for my next call to Salem from the hotel. This time, a 16-minute call cost $18.84. I paid the hotel bill with my American Express card and disputed the $125 charge once I got home, but I seem to be getting nowhere.
—*Carol Deroo, Stoughton, Massachusetts*

American Express negotiated with the hotel and credited Deroo's account $100. The credit-card company says that it has no firm rule regarding refunds for overpriced phone calls, but if a cardholder has proper documentation—Deroo was able to provide both the hotel telephone bill and her AT&T bill—it will try to negotiate with the hotel on the cardholder's behalf.

Before picking up the phone in a hotel room, read the rate information, which should be printed on the telephone, listed in the guest services directory or, at the very least, posted at the front desk. U.S. hotels are required to list their rates, name their provider of operator services, and permit use of calling cards and other access-code services for the same price that they charge for a local phone call. The rate explanation should also tell you whether a charge is posted after a certain number of rings, even if the other end never picks up.

Try to use a telephone credit card for long-distance calls. When overseas, use a long-distance service with an access code that connects you to a U.S. operator (say, AT&T's USA Direct, MCI Call USA, or Sprint Express). When staying in U.S. hotels, dial your carrier's domestic access code (10-288-0 for AT&T, 10-222-0 for MCI, and 10-333-0 for U.S. Sprint). Another method is a service called Kallback Direct (☎ 800/959–5255): Customers dial an assigned number in Seattle, let it ring once, and hang up. The computer then calls the customer back, anywhere in the world; by answering, the customer is plugged into a standard U.S. phone line complete with dial tone. Long-distance rates are favorable compared to other major carriers, and there is a $10 monthly service charge.

Consider staying at hotels that have eliminated phone surcharges; large chains such as Marriott and ITT Sheraton have dropped fees for calling-card and toll-free calls. Or simply use the lobby phone.

As for fax communications, some hotels charge for the transmission time even if the fax does not go through. We've had reports from visitors to Europe and the Far East who have been charged up to $15 per fax page. Some hotels even charge you to receive a fax. Check into whether it may be cheaper to send or receive faxes at a hotel's business center or a nearby store.

Other Hotel-Bill Shockers

It's annoying, but many a hotel tab grows larger than anticipated because of a variety of mandatory surcharges imposed on top of the quoted room rate. We hear this gripe most often about Caribbean resorts, which may assess room service charges as well as meal service charges, energy fees, pool and beach charges, and bellman gratuities. All of which, combined with government room tax, can add as much as 21% to your bill. (After checking out, these same Caribbean vacationers grumble their way to the airport only to get hit with a departure tax of up to $15 per person.)

Other surcharges, particularly at big-city hotels, include mandatory valet parking and fees for use of the health club or airport shuttle bus. The Biltmore in Coral Gables, Florida, automatically adds a $5-per-day "incidentals" charge that covers local phone calls and access charges (whether or not they're made) and use of the swimming pool, fitness center, and parking facilities (whether or not they're used).

Some business-oriented hotels also impose fees of $25 or $50 for checking out a day or two earlier than scheduled. (The hotels justify this by saying that they may have turned away bookings because they had figured your room would remain occupied.)

And then there are room taxes, which in some U.S. cities exceed 15% (when you combine both state and local taxes) and which in foreign countries can reach 25%.

My advice here is obvious: Ask in advance about taxes and mandatory surcharges, so that you can budget for them.

One more fee that is particularly annoying—we're happy to say that we've seen it only infrequently—is a surcharge of about 5% levied on guests who choose to pay with a credit card. Such fees are prohibited by credit card companies and should be reported. If at check-out time you're asked to pay such a charge, call your credit card company on the spot. If that's impossible, and you see no choice but to pay up and try for a refund through your card issuer later on, you'll need proof that the surcharge was, indeed, for using a credit card. Ask the front-desk clerk for an itemized receipt indicating this, or have him write "credit card surcharge" on the bill next to the charge. If he won't, then you write "credit card surcharge accepted under duress" on his copy of the bill.

What if there's a mistake on your tab that you don't notice until after you've checked out? Some travelers are in such a rush to get to the airport that they don't scrutinize their bill properly before signing. If you don't realize you were incorrectly charged until you receive your credit-card statement, make sure to dispute the charge within 60 days of the billing date.

When my wife and I checked into Le Deck Hotel and Beach Club in Providenciales, Turks and Caicos Islands, the hotel asked for my credit card so it could make an imprint. A few days before checking out, I told the manager that I planned to pay in cash, and he said that the hotel had already billed my Visa card, but that he would cancel the charge.

When the $4,510.35 charge that I had paid appeared on my First Card statement, I contacted the manager, who promised to credit my account or send a check. No refund appeared, so I wrote to First Card, which said it would try to help but would not give me a temporary credit because I had failed to dispute the charge within 60 days of the billing date on my statement. I had not disputed it earlier because we knew the manager well—we were repeat guests—and had trusted him. So I am now paying interest on a charge I do not owe, First Card has made no headway, and Le Deck won't return my phone calls.

—*Anthony Assini, Martinsville, New Jersey*

With some help from First Card, we finally got the hotel to pay up, but this one gave Ombudsman a splitting headache. First, the manager told us that he had sent a refund check but that it had come back in the mail, and he promised to send another. It never arrived, so we wrote again. This time, the owner responded that the hotel did not owe a refund because it had neither charged nor been paid by First Card. So we wrote to First Card, which insisted that it had indeed paid the hotel and convinced Le Deck to send a $4,510.35 check.

The owner also promised to reimburse the approximately $900 in finance charges that Assini owed Visa. Then, two months later, he reneged . . . until we faxed him a copy of what we planned to print in the magazine. Within the hour, he had written Assini a $900 check.

The moral of the story: If you do not owe a charge on your credit-card statement, dispute it immediately, even if you plan to resolve the matter directly with the merchant.

Rentals: Villas, Cottages, *Gîtes*

Do-it-yourselfers who prefer to live like the locals rather than insulate themselves in a hotel may consider renting a private house or apartment. Rentals aren't for those who want to be pampered; they don't normally come with daily maid service. What they offer is greater privacy, more local color, and a more affordable price. Having a kitchen allows for saving on meal costs, too.

Keep in mind, though, that there are no quality standards for vacation rentals. What you get depends on the rental agency you use. You typically have to pay the full rent in advance, and many rental companies don't accept credit cards. If on arrival you discover that the place is a dump and want to cancel, it may mean forfeiting your entire payment, especially if you paid by check and thus can't seek recourse through your credit card issuer. Your only choice may be to sacrifice the money and move.

I asked the British Virgin Islands Tourist Board about villa rentals on Tortola. The tourist board's description of Paradise House—a brand-new two-story villa with pool and daily maid service—sounded lovely. The reservations manager said he'd examined the site himself after construction was finished and he handed me a photo brochure displaying a fully furnished house. I paid the $900 fee and booked the property for the week of December 24.

My girlfriend and I arrived in Tortola only to discover that Paradise House was an uninhabitable construction site. We left to spend the night at a nearby hotel and returned the next day to take photos of the cinder blocks and rubble. We complained to the tourist board and spent the rest of the week at the hotel. First the tourist board promised to reimburse our $900 fee. Then it decided to refund the difference between the villa rental fee and the cost of our hotel stay. Six weeks later, I've received no money whatsoever, and the tourist board won't return any of my phone calls. Perhaps it will return yours.

—*Mark Rudnitzky, New York, New York*

Once Ombudsman reported this incident to the governor of Tortola, the tourist board reimbursed the entire $5,160 cost of Rudnitzky's vacation, airfare and car rental included.

But Rudnitzky wasn't the only victim. Ombudsman discovered that the tourist board had rented Paradise House—described as a "private luxury villa"—to J. Raymond Lewis and his family for the same week that Rudnitzky was to stay there. The tourist board gave Lewis's travel agent the same photo brochure that Rudnitzky received. When Lewis arrived at the property, he, too, took snapshots and left for a hotel. After our intervention the tourist board refunded Lewis's $3,000 villa payment as well as his $3,998 hotel bill.

M.E. Georges, then the acting governor of Tortola, expressed "considerable alarm" over the incident and assured Ombudsman that the director of tourism corrected this breach of established procedures.

How to protect yourself from rental hell?

- **Do your homework.** Ask people you know who have rented houses to recommend a rental agent. If you must rent blind, stick with a large complex used mainly by short-term renters.

- **Approach brochures with skepticism.** Glossy photos taken with wide-angle lenses can make a broom closet look like a bedroom. And the word "villa" can describe a variety of private dwellings: Apparently "cottage," "apartment," and "condo" sound too prosaic.

- **Ask to see a video or CD-ROM of the property as well as photos.** More and more rental companies are putting these out, and they make misrepresentation less likely.

- **Check up on both agent and owner.** Contact the tourist board of the country where you want to rent to find out whether complaints have been filed against either one.

- **Don't rent sight unseen.** If you're particularly cautious, hold off until you get to your destination. Start out in a local hotel while shopping around for the right rental. Be prepared, though: Pickings can be slim in peak season.

Home Exchanges

An even more affordable way to absorb the flavor of a foreign place is to exchange your own house for someone else's. Several agencies—among them Vacation Exchange Club (✉ Box 650, Key West, FL 33041, ☎ 305/294–1448 or ☎ 800/638–3841) and Intervac U.S. (✉ Box 590504, San Francisco, CA 94159, ☎ 415/435–3497)— publish directories listing people interested in exchanging their homes. These agencies stress that home exchange is for people who tend to trust other people and can make arrangements by phone.

But what if the house you end up with more closely resembles a pigsty? Or the other family cancels out of the deal at the last minute? Or you arrive back home to find your antique Chinese vase missing?

- **Talk to the home owners you're exchanging with at length.** Confirm information about facilities, exchange photos of the major rooms and the property, and ask for references from people they've exchanged with before.

- **Meet them first if you can.** Consider arriving a day before the exchange begins—spend the night at a nearby hotel—so you can get to know them. Have them show you around the house, eat dinner together, discuss what you're going to see and do. Friendship serves as a type of insurance.

- **Draw up a written agreement.** It doesn't have to be legally binding—just an agreement that clarifies and confirms what you and the other party have already discussed on the phone. This is particularly important if there is a language barrier. You might want to put in writing rules concerning maintenance of the property, care of the pets, use of the car, which items shouldn't be touched, where smoking is or isn't allowed, what to do in an emergency, and so on.

- **Come up with a contingency plan.** If one party cancels, what happens to the other? Don't exchange with anyone who won't agree to a contingency plan.

- **Buy homeowners' insurance if you don't have it already.** It protects you against damage and theft. If you plan to swap cars, make sure that your coverage will apply.

No governmental agency or industry association oversees home exchanges, so unless you are a victim of fraud, your recourse is minimal. If the exchange is a disaster, notify the publisher of the directory that listed the house; it might intervene on your behalf by threatening not to include it in next year's catalog.

Time-Share Traps

Vacationers in popular U.S. tourist spots (particularly Florida and Hawaii) and in Mexico and the Caribbean may find themselves lured, through offers of free tickets to a nearby attraction or a free sightseeing excursion, into spending an hour or two attending a sales presentation hosted by a local time-share developer.

These high-pressure sales spiels explain how, for a very reasonable price, you can "own" a time-share—a condo unit that is used throughout the year by many "owners," each of whom has bought an annual one- or two-week time slot—and how you can exchange it for a week or two at any of thousands of other time-share resorts around the world. They tell you how flexible and easy it is: Not only are you not locked into one particular locale but, because many developers sell floating time slots rather than specific weeks, you're often not locked into one particular week either. They tell you what a good investment it is: It's a relatively inexpensive way to guarantee the quality of vacations you take for years to come. Indeed, because you can pass ownership on to your children, it is an investment in your children's future as well.

Be warned that if you succumb—and the time-share industry has grown because so many people do—you may find out too late that what you purchased isn't what was promised.

A year after I bought a time-share in Cancun, I arrived for my first week and was placed in a street-side unit—not the oceanfront one the salesman had promised. The management refused to move me to an oceanfront unit without additional money, arguing that the unit number specified in my contract is on the street side. But they admitted that the salesman I dealt with has a history of misleading clients. Can anything be done?

—*Mark Montgomery, Lake Mary, Florida*

Unfortunately, Montgomery's contract stipulates that "any verbal offers made by our sales representatives that are not included in the contract are not valid."

Ombudsman has received quite a few complaints from vacationers misled by time-share salespeople. Travelers who attend a time-share sales presentation and decide to buy should take the contract home and scrutinize it before signing. Anyone whose arm is twisted into signing the contract on the spot should make sure it includes a rescission period.

Time-share salespeople tell you a lot of things. They may tell you that the purchase represents a good financial investment. Real-estate experts galore will tell you it does not. Time-share salespeople may tell you that the purchase is entirely or largely tax-deductible; what they ought to say is, "Everyone's tax situation is different. I suggest you consult your tax advisor." They may tell you that, should you ever become tired of the property, it will be easy to resell and, in fact, they will help you do it. What they don't tell you is that the time-share resale market stinks, that the developer's first priority is to sell all its still-unsold units, and that, if they do manage to resell your unit eventually, they'll keep something like a 25% commission.

Additionally, many time-shares are fraught with unanticipated problems two or three years down the road. Some of the most common gripes:

- **Extra costs add up over time.** In addition to the purchase price, you pay annual maintenance and cleaning fees, which can rise substantially, especially if a disaster such as a storm strikes. Also, to exchange your time-share for a week at another property, you must pay to belong to an exchange network (both an initial membership fee and a yearly fee thereafter).

- **The property deteriorates.** A lot of time-shares get run-down after a few years, especially after the developer sells all of the units and puts a different management company in charge of the upkeep.

- **Exchanging can be a hassle.** Numerous time-share owners say they never seem to be able to exchange into the resort or country of their choice during the season they want. In fact, they can't exchange into anything decent unless they arrange it more than six months in advance.

What if you decide that, despite the possible pitfalls, a time-share suits your vacation lifestyle?

- **Talk to your lawyer and tax advisor before buying.** Show them the contract and discuss the tax implications.

- **Make sure you like the time-share resort you buy into.** Will you enjoy returning there repeatedly? Don't buy just for the exchange opportunities, because the exchanges you request may rarely be available.

- **Consider buying a used time-share.** They are often in just as good shape as new ones, and you can get them for a fraction of the price.

Where to Turn for Help

IF YOU HAVE A COMPLAINT ABOUT A U.S. HOTEL

American Hotel & Motel Association
✉ 1201 New York Ave. NW, Suite 600
Washington, DC 20005-3931
☎ 202/289–3100
FAX 202/289–3199
This trade association representing the U.S. lodging industry will not mediate disputes, but if you write to it about problems you are having with a property (whether or not it is a member), it will forward a copy to the hotel and request a response.

FOR HOTEL-RELATED LAWS

Travel Law, by Thomas A. Dickerson, a comprehensive legal reference, discusses a vast range of hotel problems, a hotel's liability in a variety of circumstances, and court cases in which liability limits have been overridden. Available from Law Journals Seminar Press (✉ 345 Park Ave. S, New York, NY 10010, ☎ 212/779–9200; $98).

FOR HOTEL DEALS AND TRENDS

Consumer Reports Travel Letter (subscriptions ☎ 800/234–1970; $39 annually, $5 per back issue) is a superb overall resource for anyone who travels frequently and wants to do it economically.

COMPLAINTS ABOUT EXCESSIVE PHONE CHARGES

Federal Communications Commission
Informal Complaints and Public Inquiries Branch
✉ Mail Stop Code 1600 A2
Washington, DC 20554
☎ 202/418–1500
http://www.fcc.gov
Include a copy of the phone bill and the exact phone location. Call for the free fact sheet **"Know the Phone Facts Before You Hit the Road"** and other consumer brochures.

INFORMATION AND COMPLAINTS ABOUT TIME-SHARES

American Resort Development Association
✉ 1220 L St. NW, 5th floor
Washington, DC 20005
☎ 202/371–6700
This organization of time-share developers has a code of ethics and distributes brochures for consumers who are considering buying time-shares.

CHAPTER 4

Travel Agents and Tour Operators

Most travelers fall into one of two groups: Those who swear by their travel agent, and those who've sworn off theirs. The first group wouldn't dream of booking a trip without their trusty guide. The second sees no need for a middleman programmed to do what's in his own best interest.

This is because some agents deliver far more value than others. The best can find you air and cruise fares far below the advertised rates. They can negotiate free upgrades. They can obtain rooms at supposedly fully booked hotels and seats on "sold-out" flights. When Kenneth Johnson of Alpine, New Jersey, asked Stratton Travel if it could finagle tickets to the sold-out Papal Mass at Giants Stadium, the Franklin Lakes, New Jersey, agency got him four tickets in the front tier and V.I.P. parking passes. When a flight delay en route to a cruise prompted Naples, Florida, resident Charles Iannitto to notify his agency that he was going to miss the boat, Betty Maclean Travel, also of Naples, faxed the ship's captain and persuaded him to hold the vessel in port. When Ed Connor of Carmichael, California, lost his driver's license in London, the day before he was to rent a car for a three-week journey, Wood's World of Travel in Sacramento got the Department of Motor Vehicles to issue a temporary license and send it to him via Federal Express.

Then there are the agents we hear about in the Ombudsman department—the liars, the procrastinators, the bunglers. When Maria and Bernard McCue of Fort Lauderdale, Florida, asked an agent to send them to a tropical paradise in the Caribbean for their honeymoon, she said she'd found the ideal spot: the tiny island of San Andres, off the coast of Nicaragua. When the McCues arrived on San Andres, they found streets strewn with garbage, a wreck of a hotel undergoing renovations, a "deluxe" room in which the lights, television, and bed were all broken, and military men parading around with machine guns.

And there are the agencies that go out of business—hundreds of them every year.

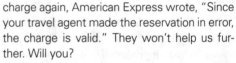 My wife and I asked our travel agent to find us a Christmas hotel-and-golf package in Cancun. She suggested the Tryall Golf, Tennis & Beach Club in Jamaica instead. We said we weren't interested in such an expensive vacation and found a more reasonably priced Cancun package on our own. Later on, we were shocked to discover two charges by Tryall totaling $5,966 on our American Express statement. The travel agent had given Tryall our credit card number against our wishes. She promised to straighten the matter out with American Express, but the next time we called her, the phone was disconnected and the agency had gone out of business.

So I disputed the charges, and American Express got Tryall to reimburse everything but the $1,803.45 three-night deposit. When I disputed this charge again, American Express wrote, "Since your travel agent made the reservation in error, the charge is valid." They won't help us further. Will you?

—James H. Watson, Woodstock, Vermont

You bet. When we asked American Express why a cardmember should have to pay $1,803.45 because his travel agent gave out his credit card number without his permission, the company credited the amount to Watson's account. American Express said that the charge was valid but that it decided to absorb the bill anyway to show how much it values Watson's membership. We also pointed out Watson's predicament to Tryall, which offered him a complimentary three-night stay as a gesture of goodwill.

Watson's travel agent, now at a different agency, told Ombudsman that she gave the hotel Watson's credit card number with instructions not to confirm the reservation until she had checked with him. But Tryall said that by supplying Watson's credit card number, the agent had confirmed his reservation, which is standard industry practice.

Watson was lucky. When travel agencies go under, clients often have to kiss their money good-bye.

⬤

The rules that apply when choosing and using a travel agent are similar to those that apply when dealing with tour operators. The term "tour operator" does not just mean companies that run escorted group tours. Some tour operators arrange customized trips for individual travelers. Some put together "travel packages" that include, say, round-trip airfare and several nights at a hotel. In other words, they often do the same things travel agents do. Thus the same precautions apply.

How Do You Find a Good Travel Agent?

Most people find an agent they like through word of mouth. But this method is not infallible. There are different types of agencies for different travel needs—destination specialists, adventure specialists, cruise specialists, corporate agencies, rebating agencies—and an agent who suits one traveler may not suit another. So consider these factors when auditioning an agent:

- **How experienced is the agent?** Usually someone who's been in the business for years is a lot more knowledgeable than someone who hasn't. On the other hand, you don't want an old fogey who won't take advantage of the latest technology to book trips and procure information.

- **How knowledgeable is the agent about the type of trip you're planning?** How much has he traveled to the places where you want to go? How often does he send clients on similar trips?

- **Does the agent ask questions about your travel habits and preferences?** You can't expect an agent to lavish this kind of time on you if all you're buying is a cheap airline ticket. But if you're a repeat customer, or you have an expensive trip in mind, a good agent should get to know your likes and dislikes.

- **Is the agent a CTC?** The Institute of Certified Travel Agents (ICTA), a non-profit group in Wellesley, MA, confers the title "certified travel counselor" on professionals who have at least five years' experience and training in travel management. There are competent agents who are not certified but, if your agent is a CTC or works for an agency that employs CTCs, it's a good sign.

- **Does the agency belong to a consortium?** A consortium negotiates preferred rates with travel suppliers. Large chain agencies do such a huge volume of business that they can negotiate discounts on their own; smaller, independent agencies join consortiums in order to offer competitive prices. You may want to ask a prospective agency if it belongs to Giants, one of the biggest and best-known consortiums. My favorite is an exclusive group called API Travel Consultants. Although it has only about 200 member agencies, they are among the nation's very best and really know how to pull strings. They specialize in luxury travel and cruises, so don't even think about using them if you book only low-budget trips.

- **Does the agency use a consolidator?** Consolidators sell discounted airline tickets, often at rates far below the lowest advertised price (☞ Buying Tickets from Consolidators *in* Chapter 2). A savvy agent concerned about getting the best deals works with at least one reliable consolidator.

- **Is the agent skilled at using computer reservation systems?** You want an agent who can use the computer to survey your range of flight, room, and rental car options quickly and efficiently, to find the one that is most convenient and best priced. You also want an agent who is willing to forego the computer reservation system, despite its convenience, when it's in your best interest. Sometimes the biggest airline and hotel deals are not in the computer; it takes a few phone calls to find them.

- **Does your agent have the latest technology?** Some agencies are automated to check airfares around the clock; if fares drop, the computer automatically rebooks you at a lower fare. And some use online services and CD-ROMs to get information.

- **Does the agency have a 24-hour phone line?** Large agencies—especially corporate ones—are staffed after-hours; some smaller ones use a subcontractor's staff.

- **How does the agency protect customers' deposits?** Ask whether it puts payments in an escrow account or has posted a bond. Make sure there's a way to retrieve your money if the agency folds before you take your trip.

A question I'm often asked is whether it's better to stick with a single agency, or to use different specialists depending on the type of trip you want to take. It's a tough call. It generally makes sense to use one agency as much as possible, because loyal customers get the best treatment. On the other hand, asking an agent whose specialty is Italian country inns to book you on an Alaska cruise is like asking an ophthalmologist to perform an appendectomy. If the trips you take tend to be varied but relatively conventional, you might want to use one large agency that employs specialists in areas that appeal to you—for example, cruises and adventure travel. If you tend always to book the same type of trip—say, vacations with the kids—you may want to use an agency that knows family travel better than anything else.

Economy-minded travelers who simply need an order-taker—rather than someone for customized advice and hand-holding—often use so-called rebating agencies that give back about 5% of the cost of the trip. Although it's hard to say no to such a discount, using a rebater may not be in your long-term best interest if you already use a good full-service agency for your more complicated trips. The more business you give the full-service agency, the more likely it will repay you through special discounts, upgrades, and other extras that in the long run can save you much more than 5%.

How Do You Find a Good Specialist?

The mom-and-pop travel agency down the street and the corporate agency you use for business trips may be able to book a conventional fun-in-the-sun beach vacation or Vegas jaunt. But what if you want to go river rafting in Costa Rica or trekking in Nepal? What if you want to cruise to Antarctica or tour rose gardens in England or learn Mayan crafts in Mexico? How do you find an agent who can match you to a group trip that suits your travel style as well as your level of interest and expertise? An agent who knows which travel  suppliers are the most seasoned and knowledgeable in that area? And which are safe and reliable rather than operating out of a basement? The field of special-interest travel is dotted with land mines.

I paid $1,672 to the Foundation for Field Research, a non-profit organization that funds scientific expeditions by recruiting volunteers who share the costs, to participate in a 14-day project in Africa researching tribal medicines. Six other volunteers assembled in Mali—five to study rare elephants and one to track chimpanzees.

Upon arrival, we learned that the elephant project had been canceled months before because of tribal unrest and that the medicine study had been canceled because the project leader had pulled out, as had the chimpanzee specialists. The seven of us had no choice but to work on the chimpanzee project with the elephant specialist. Not only that, but the truck carrying our equipment and supplies had been delayed, and the expedition money had disappeared. We were stuck in an isolated house with no refrigerator, hot water, beds, or furniture, and with nothing to eat but rice, beans, and peanut butter and jelly sandwiches. On the fourth miserable day, in an effort to salvage the trip, I loaned $2,000 to the expedition with the assurance that the foundation would repay me immediately upon my return to the United States. It has paid back only half of the loan, and that only after receiving a letter from my attorney.

—*Maria Ward, Carpinteria, California*

After eight months and several letters from Ombudsman, the Foundation for Field Research finally reimbursed Ward in full. It also issued the seven participants full credit toward another expedition of their choice. The foundation said that two months before the trip, it wrote all the volunteers, informing them that the elephant and medicine projects had been switched to a chimpanzee expedition and that they could cancel and receive full credit toward a future project. But Ward and two other volunteers say they never received such a letter. As for the disappearance of the project truck and funds, the foundation said that they were detained in Ivory Coast because its representative refused to pay bribes to border officials. "Rarely do we have a string of problems like we had here," said Tom Banks, the foundation's director. "It was quite a disaster."

If you are considering a special-interest trip and need help narrowing your options and choosing a reliable and experienced company, determine whether your regular travel agent is up to the task. How many trips of this type has he sold? How many special-interest tour companies of this type has he worked with? How many such trips has he taken himself? If you're computer-savvy, compare the information your agent gives you with what you can find on the Internet and via America Online, where hundreds of special-interest travel companies post information and thousands of travelers who have taken such trips discuss their experiences. In particular, check out America Online's travel area, especially "Outdoor Adventure Online" and "Ultimate Adventures," and the Adventure Travel Society's World Wide Web site at http://www.adventuretravel.com/ats.

If you decide you need a specialist, ask friends who have taken a similar trip whether they would recommend their agent, ask a special-interest tour company with expertise in that area for a recommendation, or contact the Institute of Certified Travel Agents, the American Society of Travel Agents, or API Travel Consultants (☞ Where to Turn for Help, *below*).

Keep in mind that a specialist should:

- **Know world geography.**

- **Have the resources to research places you might want to visit.**

- **Be able to discuss specifics about your chosen destination.** (Even if what you want to talk about is the Monteverde cloud forest.)

- **Ask about your level of physical fitness and skill.** A specialist should make sure your ability and expertise are suited to the demands of the trip.

- **Have you speak directly with the tour operator.** This helps make sure you're matched with the right trip.

- **Provide details about practical matters.** That includes immunizations, health issues, immigration documents, and travel insurance.

- **Charge a service fee only if booking a customized trip.** None should be assessed if you buy a package already assembled by the tour company.

- **Call to get your feedback after the trip.**

How Do You Find a Good Tour Operator?

Whether you use a travel agent or book the trip yourself, a company that runs tours—especially adventure and educational trips—should be asked the following:

- **How long have you been in business?**

- **Do you run your own trips or subcontract them to another company?**

- **Are your group leaders trained?** What are guides' qualifications, language skills, safety and first aid training, and experience leading trips such as yours?

- **What is the ratio of guides to group members?**

- **How long have most guides been with the company?**

- **Is your company's president involved in field research?** Does he or she ever lead trips?

- **Do you carry liability insurance?** May I see a copy of the policy? (If the trip that interests you is an outdoor adventure in the United States, you or your travel agent should ask for copies of the company's permit for operating on federal lands and its annual insurance certificate.)

- **How do you protect customers' deposits?** Are you bonded? Do you have an escrow account?

- **What percentage of customers has either traveled with the company before or been referred by past guests?**

- **Will you provide two or three client references?**

Especially for outdoor adventure trips, a good tour operator should question you closely about your physical ability, expertise, and attitude to make sure they are comparable to those of the other participants. He or she should also brief you on any physical risks involved.

I took a Hawaii tour sponsored by the Institute of Noetic Sciences in Sausalito, California. The point of the trip, the brochure said, was to "experience the true Hawai'i of native Hawaiian people. They will take us into their world of *wahi pana,* the cornerstone of Hawaiian spirituality, which loosely translates as 'sacred place.' Our agenda for the second day of the trip was a "hike to a secluded waterfall for a swim and more learning about *wahi pana.*"

The hike required trekking down a mountain to the waterfall and back up again. When I saw the mountain's steep incline and muddy condition, I balked—I am 63, weigh 250 pounds, and am not outdoorsy—and told the tour leader I would wait until the group returned. She said that I must come along, since this place was her personal *wahi pana* that she wanted to share. When I declined again, she said that the point of the trip was to push us to our limits. Not wanting to miss the whole reason I was there, I gave in. The descent went well. But the tour leader had not considered how difficult the ascent would be. When I slipped, the guides wrapped a rope around my middle. One of them threw the rope around a tree, tied it to his hips, and started down. Suddenly hauled upward, I lost my footing, fell, and lay there on the mountainside, hanging from the rope, until they helped me up again. By the time I got to the top, I had a rotated hip, a lumbar sprain, and other injuries.

At no time were tour participants asked about our physical condition or warned about potential hazards. I've considered taking legal action against the Institute, but my talks with attorneys have convinced me that it would be too expensive and time-consuming. I just want to put this fiasco behind me so I can return to Hawaii and, this time, enjoy it.

—*Katherine Stadler, Thousand Oaks, California*

Good news. The Institute ultimately gave Stadler a free plane ticket back to Hawaii and a $500 refund. Winston O. Franklin, the executive vice president, said that if the Institute ran such a tour again, he would advise against using the rope tactic that Stadler says caused her injuries. The Institute should have had a staff member accompany the tour, he added, especially because it had not worked with the Hawaiian tour leader before.

Nonetheless, the Institute denied responsibility for the accident, because it was Stadler's choice to join the hike. "Any of us who have ventured into unfamiliar cultures have faced similar instances where we are expected . . . to do things that seem inappropriate, yet would be offensive to our hosts if we refused," said Franklin. "However, [the hike] was described in detail the night before, and [Stadler was] given a clear choice of participating or staying at the hotel." Though she may have felt pressure from the tour leader, she was "ultimately responsible for the decision to participate."

Still, this incident shows how important it is to be as clear as possible with tour-goers about exactly what a trip will entail, said Franklin, adding that the Institute's future brochures would point out potential hardships more explicitly.

Before You Spend a Nickel

Travel agencies go out of business all the time, taking customers' advance deposits with them. And every year a couple of big-name tour operators collapse as well, leaving travelers with neither their trip nor their money and stranding them in places like Beijing. And each time the Ombudsman department gets flooded with letters. Unfortunately, there's usually little we can do to help after the fact. So get ready for an earful about what to do up front to check out companies and protect your payments. It's not sexy stuff, but it's vital if you're planning to hand over thousands of dollars to total strangers.

The protection you have against the failure of a travel supplier partly depends on where you live. In some states, anyone who sells travel must register with the state and provide proof of some degree of financial security. In Florida, for instance, sellers of travel must sign up with the Florida Department of Agriculture and Consumer Services, and some must post a $50,000 bond. In California they must register with the state attorney general's office, and the registration fees go into a restitution fund that reimburses travelers in case a registered agency or tour operator fails.

But this doesn't mean that Floridians and Californians have nothing to worry about if a company folds after they book a trip with it. In California, you're not protected if you buy a ticket directly from an airline or a cruise line that goes under. Nor are you protected if you buy through an out-of-state travel agent. And even if you buy from a registered, California-based agency, you're not protected if it uses an out-of-state tour operator that fails.

How can you be reasonably certain, then, that a travel firm you're eyeing is a good bet?

- **Ask how your payment is protected if the firm, or a travel supplier it uses, collapses before you've taken your trip.** Does it belong to a trade association such as the U.S. Tour Operators Association, which requires members to post a bond? Does it maintain an escrow account? What is the name of the bank and the account? Check it out.

- **Check out the firm with the appropriate government agency.** If a company you're considering buying from is based in a state where sellers of travel must register, verify that the company is indeed registered and has complied with all the requirements. If you're not sure where to call, try the state attorney general's office.

- **Look into the company's history.** Check with the state attorney general's consumer protection office and the local Better Business Bureau to see whether there is a record of complaints about the company on file. Call any trade associations to which the company might belong—the American Society of Travel Agents, for instance—to see if it has received a string of complaints.

What else can you do to protect yourself?

- **Pay with a credit card.** If you don't get your trip, you can ask your credit card issuer to remove the charge.

- **Use a travel agency close to home.** Should something go wrong, you'll have more recourse through state laws, and you can use small claims court if need be.

- **Try to withhold payment for tickets until they're in your hands.** If it's feasible, tell the travel firm or your credit card issuer that you're not going to pay until you've actually received the tickets.

What if a company you've paid goes belly up? How can you get your money back?

- **If you've paid a travel agent who has gone under, contact the trip supplier.** If you bought a tour or cruise or travel package, ask the tour operator or cruise line whether the agent ever forwarded your payment.

- **If you used a credit card, contact your card issuer and request a chargeback.**

- **Call your state attorney general's consumer protection office.** This organization or other appropriate consumer agency can give you advice.

Travel Scams

My son's wife filled out a travel questionnaire at the supermarket and later received a phone call from American Global Travel Division saying that her participation in its marketing survey had made her eligible to receive travel vouchers. For $498, she could get vouchers good for 24 round-trips on all major airlines. They would be valid for three years, and there would be no blackout periods. The offer sounded too good to be true. Do you think it's legitimate?

—Carole M. Logan, Salem, Massachusetts

Ombudsman checked out the offer and advised the Logans to steer clear. When we called American Global, it said that the vouchers came from Worldwide Travel & Tour, a South Florida travel agency that had "been in business for 10 or 11 years," was "approved" by the local Better Business Bureau, the state attorney general, and the Florida Department *of Agriculture and Consumer Services (with which all Florida-based sellers of travel must register), and had "a $6 million bond backing it."*

But the Better Business Bureau told us that Worldwide was under investigation for unfair and deceptive business practices. And the Florida Division of Consumer Services, which had received more than 70 complaints about Worldwide at the time, said that the company was backed not by a bond but by a liability insurance policy. Although a consumer who is owed money by a bonded company can get it without going to court, his only option with a company backed by a liability insurance policy is to sue the insurer.

Anyone considering doing business with a Florida-based travel firm should check it out with the Division of Consumer Services. Worldwide's registration was eventually revoked, by the way, and the company no longer exists.

───

Some vacation offers that come over the phone or via a postcard are legitimate. But many aren't, and these scams are becoming increasingly sophisticated.

In a common scenario, you're given a certificate—through a department store promotion or in exchange for participating in an event—that says you've been "specially selected" to receive what looks to be a free trip to Hawaii or another popular spot. You call the toll-free number on the card and learn that, actually, you have to pay for the hotel, but the rest is indeed free. A professional-sounding voice at the other end of the line assures you that you can take the trip at your convenience anytime within the next 18 months. It won't be available much longer, though, so you'd be wise to give your credit card number today and call back with your travel dates. The charge—which includes a processing fee—is placed on your credit card. When you receive the booking instructions, you learn there's a reservation fee. And several other incidental charges. By now you're paying more than if you'd booked the trip through a reputable travel agent. When you call back with your travel dates, they aren't available. You call back a few days later with different dates, and those aren't available either. Next time you call, the phone has been disconnected and the company has disappeared.

There are dozens of variations on the theme, including the one where you get a call from a representative of an official-sounding government organization or consumer protection program. For a small fee, he says, he can recover the money you lost when you bought that Hawaii trip that never materialized. It's the same guy who ripped you off last year, trying to do it again this year.

WARNING SIGNS OF A SCAM

- **The price is unbelievably low.** Few legitimate businesses can afford to undercut everyone else's price substantially. A $79 airfare to Europe simply is not going to happen.

- **You're pressed to give your credit card number over the phone.** Sometimes all they want is your card expiration date, "to verify that you're a winner." Don't think you're safe giving only the expiration date; it means they've already gotten your credit card number through some other fraudulent means.

- **You must decide NOW.** Legitimate companies let you look over the details in writing before you make your purchase.

- **The caller says you can't leave on your trip for at least two months.** They do this because the deadline allowed by law for disputing a credit-card charge is 60 days.

- **The caller won't provide his full name, street address, and phone number.**

- **The caller won't give you specifics.** He identifies the airline being used as "a major airline," or he offers a collection of airlines but won't say which one you'll be flying.

- **He won't send information in writing.** And if he does, it bears little resemblance to what you were told on the phone.

HOW TO SIDESTEP A SCAM

- **Ask detailed questions about the cost of the trip.** What specific components are included in the price? What extra fees—service charges, taxes, processing fees, port charges—will there be? Determine the complete cost of the trip, in U.S. dollars.

- **Ask for names of specific hotels, airlines, and other companies being used.** Contact them yourself to verify the arrangements that have allegedly been made.

- **Get details in writing.** Look over the written materials, including the restrictions and exclusions in the "terms and conditions" section, and the refund and cancellation policies. Do they confirm everything you were told on the phone?

- **Get a confirmed departure date in writing.** And make sure it's earlier than your credit card issuer's deadline for disputing a charge, which is usually 60 days after the posting date (when your credit card processes the transaction) or the billing date (when your statement is mailed).

- **Check out the company.** Contact the appropriate government agencies and trade groups (☞ Where to Turn for Help, *below*). Don't limit your research to the local Better Business Bureau, because con artists change the names of their businesses frequently to avoid detection. There may be no complaints filed under the operator's current name but there could be 50 filed under the name used a week ago.

- **Do not send money by messenger or overnight mail.** Some scam operators offer to send a messenger to pick up a check or money order. They say he will hand over written materials in exchange for your payment. This means you won't have time to read them before paying. Any transactions should go by regular mail, so that if you're conned the scam falls under the jurisdiction of the U.S. Postal Service and the Postal Inspector can investigate the operator for mail fraud.

- **Once you're satisfied that an offer is legitimate, pay with a credit card.**

When Travel Agents Charge Service Fees

I asked American Express's Platinum Card Travel Service to book rooms for me at five hotels in Argentina. The agent charged a total of $1,332 but would not itemize the costs. During my trip, I wrote down each hotel's posted room rate and discovered that if I had walked into the same hotels without reservations and stayed for the same time, I would have paid only $906.

When I asked for an explanation of the $426 difference, an American Express customer-service agent wrote: "The pre-paid tour price . . . may include administrative costs, rate of exchange fluctuation and allowance, taxes as required, local surcharges, telephone and telex costs, as well as a reasonable profit." American Express apparently charged a hefty booking fee.

—*Debbie Carstens, Telluride, Colorado*

For months American Express denied Carstens's claim. Only when we pressed did it finally determine that she'd been mistakenly charged a $174 commission. Later, when the company knew we planned to publish her letter, it decided to refund the entire $426. Even so, it insists that Carstens would not have paid just $906. A company spokesman told us that the figure did not include the local taxes, surcharges, and Continental breakfasts that—along with the guarantee of a specific dollar rate—were part of the American Express package. He added that the Travel Service does not make a profit at its cardholders' expense. Sometimes it imposes booking fees because the tour packager has levied a charge, but it does not do so across-the-board.

More and more travel agencies impose fees these days. Usually, the less you spend (if you're buying only a cheap plane ticket, for instance), and the more work you require (say, a personalized itinerary that will take hours to plan) or the more telephone, fax, messenger, and other expenses incurred in booking your trip, the more likely it is that your agency will levy a fee. It should not charge a fee for booking cruises, tours, and other expensive trips that come prepackaged.

When You Have to Cancel

If you're laying out a huge non-refundable advance payment, consider buying trip-cancellation and trip-interruption insurance, in case you must call off your trip or cut it short. Companies waive cancellation penalties only in extraordinary circumstances.

Himalayan Travel, a tour operator in Connecticut, booked the land portion of a trip to India for my husband and me. When the State Department advised against nonessential travel to India, we reluctantly canceled. The airline and cruise line refunded all our money, but Himalayan imposed a 45% cancellation fee. This $2,035.80 penalty seemed unfair, so I decided to find out what penalties Himalayan was charged by its suppliers. One of them, the Taj Group of Hotels, with which Himalayan had supposedly booked five of our hotel stays, said it never had reservations for us. I think $2,035.80 is a high price to pay for such questionable service.

—June Schwartz, San Francisco, California

Himalayan sent a $1,535.80 refund, which represented the penalty minus a $250-per-person "basic cancellation charge." But the company claims that Schwartz's trip was completely booked and that the 45% penalty was fair. Himalayan's cancellation policy is "clearly detailed in our brochure for approval by our clients prior to booking," the company's president, James Faubel, told us.

He insists it would have been safe for the Schwartzes to travel despite the State Department advisory. "Our trips to India were operating without incident at the time [they] canceled. In the 18-year history of Himalayan Travel, we have not had one person harmed . . . due to political unrest in India."

⬭

Before buying big-ticket trips, then, read the cancellation policy and make sure you can live with it. If you can't, buy insurance (☞ Travel Insurance *in* Chapter 8).

The Travel Agent as Safety Net

I think one reason people use a travel agent is to have someone to blame if something goes wrong. Which isn't such a bad idea.

When plans go awry and it's not clear who's at fault—the agent? the tour company? the airline?—it's best to request restitution from the party you paid, even if it looks as though someone else is responsible, because that's the party with whom you had a "contract."

⬭

I paid Carlson Travel Network $2,325 for a trip to Costa Rica for three. Four friends also booked the same trip. When two of them told Carlson that they had to cancel, somehow all seven reservations were canceled by mistake. I never got my trip, and after 33 phone calls and letters trying to retrieve my money, all I have to show for my efforts is a huge stack of documents and an enormous amount of frustration. Carlson says that the tour operator, Design Tours of Miami, erroneously canceled my reservation and is responsible for my loss, since it currently holds my money. But Carlson is the only company I dealt with. The way I see it, it's Carlson that took my money, so it's Carlson that owes me a refund.

—*Geoffrey K. Booth, Tiburon, California*

We saw it that way too, and eventually Carlson came around. It told us that Design Tours was the proper party to issue the refund, but it decided to reimburse Booth and pursue the tour operator itself. "Design Tours, a company we have not dealt with extensively in the past, is not one that we normally recommend to travelers," a Carlson official told us, adding that Carlson used the company this time because Booth specifically requested it.

When foul-ups occur, some travel agents try to make it up to their client (especially if he or she is a loyal customer), some don't care, and some try to reach a compromise and split the cost of the damages.

My wife and I paid Abercrombie & Kent for an expensive trip custom-designed to satisfy our lifelong wishes—hers to see Africa, mine to scuba dive off Seychelles. When we arrived in Nairobi, Abercrombie & Kent confirmed our Kenya Airways flight to Seychelles two weeks later.

Upon checking in for the flight, we learned that it had left two hours early. Since the next flight was almost a week away, we had to abandon our Seychelles plans and return home. Abercrombie & Kent says Kenya Airways never informed it of the schedule change. But any experienced traveler knows that reservations on international flights must be reconfirmed 72 hours before the flight. Abercrombie & Kent apparently did not reconfirm ours. We would have done it ourselves had the company not reassured us that it had done so. Because of Abercrombie & Kent's mistake, we missed out on half of our trip, and all we received as compensation was a refund for the Seychelles arrangements.
—*Bruce L. McNaughton, Tucson, Arizona*

We thought Abercrombie & Kent should consider how much it would cost McNaughton to fly back to that part of the world to see Seychelles, so we contacted the company, and it decided to send a $1,000 goodwill refund. It pointed out, however, that it reimbursed McNaughton for the Seychelles portion even though it was charged a 100% cancellation penalty. And it told us it did indeed reconfirm the flight 72 hours in advance. The airline either gave incorrect information or changed its schedule after the company called. Had McNaughton himself called to reconfirm 72 hours beforehand, Abercrombie & Kent said, he would have received the same information. Kenya Airways used to be a difficult air-

line to work with but, according to the tour company, it has since come under new management and its service has improved considerably.

―

What about screw-ups where several middlemen are involved? We've seen cases where the travel agent blames the tour company, the tour company blames the wholesaler, the wholesaler blames the local subcontractor, the local subcontractor blames the guide . . . and the customer is forced into a wild goose chase. Again, when several different travel suppliers are involved, seek remuneration first and foremost from the company you paid. If it refuses, and you can document exactly what you were promised and what you got that was inferior, consider settling the matter in small claims court.

This is why it's a good idea to use a travel agent when buying a tour or travel package, says the author of *Travel Law,* Judge Thomas A. Dickerson. You can't sue a tour operator in small claims court if the company has no local branch in your area, but you *can* sue a local travel agent. Even if your agent doesn't appear to be the party at fault, the agency is in

a better position than you are to negotiate a resolution to the dispute with the tour operator or, failing that, to sue him in turn.

Frequent Foul-Ups

WHEN YOUR LODGINGS ARE CHANGED

So the "beach resort" that was supposed to offer "an array of water sports" turns out to be five blocks from the ocean and provides only some shabby snorkeling gear. Or the charming turn-of-the-century hotel in the heart of Prague's Old Town gets switched for a modern skyscraper half an hour away. Such a change of accommodations is one of the most common situations to poison a group tour or an individual travel package.

It can be the result of an honest oversight or it can be part of a bait-and-switch scheme practiced by sleazy tour operators: A hotel is described and pictured in the brochure, with fine print stating that one that is "similar" may be substituted if rooms here are not available. The tour operator sells many more travel packages than there are rooms available at the advertised hotel. The overflow gets sent to the alternate hotel, which turns out not to be "similar" at all. It is less convenient and offers fewer facilities.

If you're stuck in lousy substitute accommodations, kick and scream if it will help. But don't forget to gather documentation of just how inferior it is: Take photos of the substitute hotel, and collect written materials describing it, so you can fashion a powerful letter of complaint to the tour operator when you get home. The company may send a robotic response reminding you that its brochure warns that it reserves the right to substitute different accommodations. Such disclaimers fly in the face of certain state consumer protection statutes, says Judge Dickerson, and may be overridden if you take the complaint to small claims court.

Sometimes the substitution of inferior lodgings is completely beyond a tour operator's control, especially in locales with less developed infrastructures.

Arriving in Paro, Bhutan, as part of a "Himalayan Kingdoms" tour run by Distant Horizons, a Boston tour company, we learned that we were to be housed in tents. Bernardo Bertolucci, the Italian director, and his crew were shooting a film there, and the king had put them into the hotel booked for us. Staying in tents seemed like an adventure at first, but by bedtime it had stopped being fun.

I am 81 years old, and my tent was a good city block away from the pit toilets, which made them difficult to find and use in the dark. The chilly weather caused many of us to shiver throughout the night, and the climb to the shower near the river was too steep for me to make. Bhutan is a beautiful country, and its people are charming, but I think $250 a day was a pretty steep price to pay.

—*Virginia Heily, Bellingham, Washington*

By the time Ombudsman contacted Distant Horizons, it had persuaded its suppliers and the Bhutanese government to arrange a refund of $90 a day for every member of the group. The remaining $160 a day covered meals and sightseeing expenses, said Janet Moore, the company's president. "Whilst I was extremely upset by the inconvenience caused to our group," she added, "this is somewhat the price one pays for traveling to more remote parts of Asia. We warn people that in countries where limited hotel space exists, one does have to be prepared for state visits and unforeseen circumstances that result in this kind of *experience. Recent changes in Bhutan mean that private companies can now organize travel there. I hope, with the opening of new privately owned hotels . . . we will be able, in the future, to avoid the situation that Ms. Heily was forced to experience."*

WHEN YOUR ITINERARY IS CHANGED

So you didn't get to see what you were supposed to see—sights you traveled thousands of miles and spent thousands of dollars to see. Again, to get out of having to make it up to you, the company may rely on small-print disclaimers in its brochure, stating that it reserves the right to alter itineraries.

A countermeasure—which may or may not work—is to note on the reservation forms that you submit to the tour company that you consider a particular stop or region an essential feature of the tour and the primary reason you're buying it. This could be viewed as an amendment to the "contract" between you and the tour company, and could increase your chances of a refund if that portion of the trip is eliminated.

The less developed the tourism infrastructure in the country you're visiting, the greater the chance that itinerary changes will occur and will be outside the tour operator's control.

My wife and I booked an 18-day tour of China, including a 5-day Yangtze cruise, through Intertour of America. Once there, we learned that the tour had been cut to 15 days. We missed the Children's Palace in Shanghai, the mountaintop temple in Wanxian, the 2,000-year-old mummified man in Shashi, the caves carved into the mountainside in Chongqing, the Three Gorges, and the Lesser Three Gorges (which, according to the brochure, are "generally considered the highlight" of the cruise), the Chengdu Zoo's giant pandas, and much more. We had been to China twice before and had chosen this tour specifically for these sights. When I complained to Intertour, it promised to contact its Chinese suppliers and get back to me. Now it won't answer my letters.
—*Elmer N. Wolf, Melrose, Massachusetts*

Intertour answered ours (although it took almost three months) and sent a $500 refund. "In spite of much communication with China, *we have yet to receive a response that we feel is satisfactory," an Inter-tour official told us. "It is our experience that the Chinese distance themselves completely from problems; we have found it difficult to recover funds in the form of credits or refunds for any clients who choose to register dissatisfaction." Ombudsman hopes this will serve as a warning, for we too have rarely been able to help travelers who encounter trouble in China.*

WHEN THE TOUR GUIDE IS CHANGED

For some tours—usually education-minded ones run by universities, cultural institutions, or tony operators like Abercrombie & Kent—the primary draw is the guide or lecturer. What if an expert or celebrity set to accompany a group falls ill or for some other reason can't go? Some tour operators consider it their responsibility to warn travelers in advance, some don't. Some allow you to bow out, some won't. What if you don't find out until the trip is underway? Furious tour participants may demand a refund, on the basis that the substitution degraded the quality of the tour. The company may disagree, claiming that the essence of the tour was maintained.

Again, a precaution to take when you book the tour is to write on the reservation form, perhaps under "special requirements," that you are booking it primarily for the lecturer. If he drops out, this might be viewed as a valid emendation of the "contract" and could help you procure some sort of compensation.

As for more mainstream tours—where the guide is not a star lecturer but more of a combination mother hen and troubleshooter—there's not much you can do if he turns out to be incompetent, short of a mutiny.

The trip I took from Borneo to Myanmar, organized by Mandala Tours, was thrown off course several times because the tour guide lacked the proper travel documents. First, he could not accompany us from Malaysia to Indonesia because he didn't have the right visa, so we toured Sumatra for three days without him. On our way to northern Thailand, he was again detained for lack of credentials, so we missed our Chiang Mai expedition. And although we had prepaid for Myanmar visas, Mandala did not procure them in enough time for our flight to Rangoon. We had to stay in Bangkok an extra three days waiting for them. Our visas finally materialized, but the guide's didn't, so we went to Myanmar without him. Of course, we could spend only two days there, rather than the scheduled five. Please help me get a refund for the missed portions of this disastrous tour.

—*Wanda Brite, Springdale, Arkansas*

After we interceded, Mandala—about whom the Ombudsman column has received many a complaint—sent a check for $466. Its president, Dave Sharma, told us it's not his fault if a country's government is slow to issue visas. He also said that Mandala provides refunds to tour members whenever a guide cannot accompany a group because of problems caused by the local government. This was before Mandala Tours went bankrupt. Ombudsman is very glad that travelers won't be mistreated by the company anymore.

Where to Turn for Help

TO CHECK OUT A TRAVEL AGENCY OR TOUR COMPANY OR FOR HELP WITH A COMPLAINT

American Society of Travel Agents
Consumer Affairs Department
✉ 1101 King St., Suite 200
Alexandria, VA 22314
☎ 703/739–2782
FAX 703/684–8319
http://www.ASTAnet.com
This organization mediates consumer disputes against its 13,500 member agencies and 1,500 member tour operators, who have pledged to abide by a code of ethics; keeps on file complaints lodged against them and against some non-member agencies as well; and publishes **"Avoiding Travel Problems"** and other free consumer brochures.

TO FIND A GOOD TRAVEL AGENT

Institute of Certified Travel Agents
✉ 148 Linden St., Box 812059
Wellesley, MA 02181
☎ 800/542–4282 or 617/237–0280
http://www.icta.com
This group can recommend a "certified travel counselor" near you. There are 14,000 agents who have earned their diploma but only 6,000 have kept their certification renewed, so if you're picky, ask for a referral to an "active member." ICTA can also provide names of specialists in a variety of destinations and in the fields of ecotourism, adventure travel, spa vacations, and sports vacations.

API Travel Consultants
✉ 500 Main St., Suite 400
Fort Worth, TX 76102
☎ 817/870–0300
http://www.apitravel.com
The most knowledgeable travel agents I know tend to belong to this network of about 200 agencies whose forte is deluxe travel and cruises. Call for referrals to agents in your area or for specialists in customized itineraries, cruises, and adventure travel.

American Society of Travel Agents (☞ *above*)
Check its World Wide Web site for names of specialists in senior, family, and special-interest travel.

TO FIND A RELIABLE TOUR OPERATOR

U.S. Tour Operators Association
✉ 211 E. 51st St., Suite 12B
New York, NY 10022
☎ 212/750–7371
FAX 212/421–1285
USTOUR@aol.com
Each of the USTOA's 45 member tour operators must abide by a code of ethics and post $1 million in security. This protects prospective tourgoers in case of bankruptcy or default of a member company. The association does not mediate disputes but will forward complaint letters to members. Publishes free brochure **"How To Select A Tour Or Vacation Package."**

National Tour Association
✉ 546 E. Main St.
Lexington, KY 40508
☎ 800/682–8886 or 606/226–4444
FAX 606/226–4404
http://www.travelfile.com/ntatours
The NTA represents 624 companies based in the United States, Mexico, and Canada that run motorcoach tours worldwide. Each member must abide by a code of ethics and carry $1 million in liability insurance and errors and omissions insurance. A $250,000 consumer protection plan protects customers' deposits in case a member company goes bankrupt. The NTA also mediates consumer disputes with member companies.

FOR A LIST OF SPECIALIST TOUR OPERATORS

Specialty Travel Index
Alpine Hansen Publishers
✉ 305 San Anselmo Ave., Suite 313
San Anselmo, CA 94960
☎ 415/459–4900
FAX 415/459–4974
http://www.spectrav.com
This publication ($6) and Web site list 600 special-interest tour companies by activity and destination.

Adventure Travel Society
✉ 6551 S. Revere Pkwy., Suite 160
Englewood, CO 80111
☎ 303/649–9016
FAX 303/649–9017
http://www.adventuretravel.com/ats
Its Web site lists, by destination and activity, adventure companies that it promises are reliable. It can also send the list by mail.

FOR INFORMATION ABOUT AND ASSISTANCE WITH TRAVEL SCAMS

Federal Trade Commission
✉ 6th St. and Pennsylvania Ave. NW
Washington, DC 20580
To report a scam, call the Division of Marketing Practices Consumer Help Line (☎ 202/326–3128). For the free pamphlet **"Telemarketing**

Travel Fraud," call the Public Reference Branch (☎ 202/326–2000). If the FTC receives a number of complaints about a particular company, it will investigate.

National Fraud Information Center

✉ Box 65868
Washington, DC 20035
☎ 800/876–7060 (hot line)
The hot line is administered by the National Consumers League, which works with federal enforcement agencies to stop fraud.

U.S. Department of Transportation

Office of Consumer Affairs (I-25)
✉ 400 7th St. SW
Washington, DC 20590
☎ 202/366–2220
This is the place to call if the vacation offer involves airline travel (☞ Where to Turn for Help *in* Chapter 2).

Florida Department of Agriculture and Consumer Services

Division of Consumer Services
✉ Mayo Building, 2nd floor
Tallahassee, FL 32399-0800
☎ 904/488–2221
FAX 904/921–2671
This is the place to call if a vacation offer comes from a Florida-based company. It keeps complaints on file, offers advice, and helps mediate disputes between consumers and Florida-based companies that sell travel.

CONSIDERING LEGAL ACTION?

Travel Law, by Thomas A. Dickerson, a comprehensive legal treatise, discusses federal and state regulations concerning travel agents and tour operators, their liability in a variety of circumstances, and related court cases. It's available from the Law Journals Seminar Press (✉ 345 Park Ave. S, New York, NY 10010, ☎ 212/779–9200; $98).

CHAPTER 5

Cruises

C ruise brochures promise a seamless trip to paradise. Stunning views. Gourmet cuisine. Broadway-caliber entertainment. Constant pampering. Travelers planning a cruise build high expectations and make large payments up front. When the reality doesn't live up to the fantasy, they are particularly insistent about remuneration.

For our 25th wedding anniversary, my husband and I took an 11-day cruise from Honolulu to Tahiti on the *Fair Princess*. On the fifth day, the cooling system broke. For three days there was no air conditioning, cold water, or refrigeration. Our cabin became so hot that we could tolerate it for periods of only five to ten minutes before getting sick. We endured burning sensations in our throat, nostrils, and eyes, and I suffered migraine headaches, but the doctors in the makeshift hospital on deck were too busy with the elderly to treat us. We could not sleep in the cabin, so we camped out wherever we could. The ship looked like a homeless shelter. Sharing our sleeping quarters with 890 strangers was not our idea of a second honeymoon.

Not only was everyone's health jeopardized, but we were forced to skip Christmas Island, Bora Bora, and Moorea so we could get to a cool hotel in Papeete as quickly as possible. We paid $5,098 for this lovely escapade and think we deserve more than the $2,205 refund offered as compensation.

—*Joan Roback, San Bruno, California*

We thought so too, so we contacted Princess Cruises, which eventually agreed to full reimbursement. Other passengers expressed

117

unhappiness about Princess's initial offer of a 75% refund of the cruise fare only and a two-for-one credit on a future sailing, and the line handled those complaints on a case-by-case basis. It decided to give the Robacks a full refund because they had become ill.

This was not the first time the Fair Princess's air conditioning system had failed. The ship, Princess's oldest, has now been retired from the fleet.

Unfortunately, cruise passengers have minimal rights when something goes awry. The cruise business is relatively young and unregulated. Most rules governing cruises are based on 19th-century maritime law rather than modern consumer-oriented law. Also, most cruise ships are registered in foreign countries, so if a mishap occurs that you consider to be grounds for legal action, it is the country's law that applies, and many common countries of registry are not known for their emphasis on consumer protection.

On the other hand, cruise lines are desperate to keep past passengers happy—their survival depends on repeat business—so they are typically generous when it comes to compensating travelers whose cruises have gone rotten.

If a cruise isn't all you thought it would be because it doesn't live up to the ads—the food was crummy; the cabins, photographed with a wide-angle lens for the brochure, were minuscule; the entertainment was Vegas-lounge-act disastrous—there's not much you can do about it onboard. But you can write to the cruise line's passenger relations department when you get home. The company is not obligated to compensate you but, as a gesture of goodwill, might just decide to give you a credit applicable toward a future cruise, depending on the legitimacy and severity of your complaint.

On the other hand, if a problem occurs that you *can* do something about onboard—say, your cabin is noisy—contact the purser. Perhaps he can find you another cabin. If not, at least you've documented your complaint and can pursue it later through passenger relations. Be sure to collect as much information and documentation as you can—names, dates, cabin numbers, receipts, claim tickets, photos—because the more evidence you can present, the stronger your case will be. Put your complaint to the purser in writing and keep a photocopy.

When you present your case to passenger relations, don't expect to see your money again—refunds come from cruise lines only in rare cases.

But do expect a letter of apology within six to eight weeks and possibly a discount on a future cruise (typically ranging from 10% to 50%).

The most common cruise-related gripes we hear are from people who ended up on the wrong ship.

The Wrong Cruise

Each cruise line has a different personality and suits different types. But almost all cruises are booked through travel agents, and many agents fail to match travelers to the right vessel.

My family and another family, the Perzows, took a cruise on the *Radisson Diamond*. Our travel agent assured us that the ship would be great for children. It most assuredly was not. The kids were miserable. Bad weather prevented the ship from deploying its retractable marina, so they could not do the promised water sports. Nor were they allowed to play in the pool or ride the elevator without adults. The cruise director even asked us why we had brought children on such a cruise. We spent $25,000 and were sorely disappointed.

—*Zave Aberman, Montreal, Quebec, Canada*

Aberman's travel agent led him astray. "The vessel does not provide the experience the Abermans and Perzows are looking for for children," a Radisson official told us. Children "are not promoted or encouraged by special rate reductions, and in our promotional literature there is no mention of any children's activities." He says that the Aberman and Perzow children were ordered not to ride the elevators alone after they nearly knocked over an elderly guest while doing so, and that they were forced to curtail their pool activities when guests complained about their splashing and ball throwing." Fortunately, Radisson decided to offer the four parents a weeklong cruise at a cost of only $700 per person as a gesture of goodwill.

It is important to use an experienced travel agent who specializes in cruises and really understands the differences between ships. Janet Olczak, president of Seattle-based Cruise Specialists, tells us that she would book Murphy Brown, for example, on a Windstar cruise ("She's casual, she can afford it but isn't trying to impress anyone with her money, she's an interesting conversationalist"); James Bond on Seabourn

("He likes wearing a tuxedo and going to exotic destinations; he'd like their water-sports program"); the Golden Girls on Holland America ("It's sophisticated enough but not so stuffy that they'd feel uncomfortable; they'd enjoy sharing dinner conversation with people in their age group"); Indiana Jones on a Special Expeditions cruise ("He's adventurous, he likes distant lands, he wants to hike through the jungle and slog through swamps"); Roseanne and her television family on Carnival ("She'd enjoy eating six times a day, not having to dress up, shoving Ping-Pong balls down her bathing suit to win a prize"); and Bill and Hillary Clinton on Crystal ("They're Baby Boomers and they're affluent but not superrich").

How to find such a specialist? Look for a travel agent with credentials such as membership in the National Association of Cruise-Only Agencies or accreditation by the Cruise Lines International Association (CLIA). CLIA "Master Cruise Counselors" have a higher level of training than CLIA "Accredited Cruise Counselors." High-end cruisegoers should use one of the specialists who belong to API Travel Consultants, a network of the nation's top travel agents (☏ 817/870–0300); they know luxury cruises inside and out (☞ Where to Turn for Help, *below*).

Look for an agent who has not only toured many different ships but sailed on them. A good agent asks lots of questions about your travel preferences, gives customized advice, makes special arrangements, and prepares you for possible mishaps.

When choosing a ship, consider what facilities are important to you. If a long dinner every night sounds tiresome, choose a ship with a café or pizza parlor, where you can eat more quickly and informally. If you don't want to pay an arm and a leg for laundry service, choose a ship with a laundry room. And consider nighttime entertainment. If you prefer films to musical shows, and educational talks to gambling, choose a ship that schedules lectures in the evenings or that has a movie theater or in-room VCRs.

And by all means consider the clientele.

The Wrong Crowd

On a cruise through the Norwegian fjords on the *Mermoz*, my sister and I seemed to be the only passengers who didn't speak French. The shore excursions, activities, and entertainment were all in French, almost all the passengers were French, and we couldn't understand what was going on. My travel agent says she was never informed that the cruise was for people who spoke French. The way we see it, if Paquet Cruises advertises in the United States, it's valid to assume that its cruises are appropriate for English-speaking passengers.

—*Shirley Spencer, Avon, Colorado*

The way we see it, Spencer's travel agent should have known better. "We make it painstakingly clear that the Mermoz offers a French cruise experience," Paquet's president told us, adding that in the United States the ship is marketed under the banner "Paquet French Cruises." The brochure states, "This is cruising with an accent that is decidedly French." It promises the virtues of French cuisine and entertainment and of having a "unique cultural experience," he said. "Had these passengers seen or been shown our literature they would have been well aware of the kind of cruise they were purchasing." (Paquet Cruises, by the way, no longer advertises in the United States.)

Many cruisegoers find themselves stuck on a ship with people who drive them nuts—from a gang of bikers holding wet T-shirt contests to a convention of proselytizing Evangelists—and come back wondering how Kathie Lee Gifford can actually think this is "fun."

The crowd you find depends partly on the clientele that that particular line draws, partly on whether a large group is aboard, and partly on the season: If you want to treat your family to a G-rated cruise, for instance, beware spring break. Less expensive ships sometimes draw a college frat crowd in a raucous mood.

HOW TO AVOID THE HORDES

Here are some tricks designed to help misanthropes on any cruise escape the hubbub:

- **Book a cabin with a private veranda.** This should resolve worries about being able to nab a secluded deck chair far from the poolside madness. You can typically opt to dine here as well.

- **Avoid buffet lines.** At breakfast and lunch, when crowded buffets are held on the pool deck, the dining room is half empty, so consider eating there instead.

- **Dodge public events.** Rick Kaplan, president of CruiseMasters, a Los Angeles agency, regularly skips the captain's cocktail party. I wish I had done so on my first Caribbean cruise, where it meant standing in line for 45 minutes just to shake the captain's hand, have my photo taken, and be quickly shooed away.

- **Don't let ship photographers invade your space.** Wherever there are crowds, official ship photographers are close at hand. State up front that you won't be buying any pictures, so they might as well save their film.

- **Avoid long disembarkation lines.** The larger the ship, the greater the number of passengers, the more buses need to be loaded, and the longer it takes to get everyone off. Savvy cruise agents advise being last in line for disembarkation rather than first. If it's between 8 and 10 AM, for instance, eat a leisurely breakfast, relax in your cabin (disregarding the order to vacate it), and get in line at 9:45. On the other hand, if your airline arrangements require an earlier exit and you did not book them through the cruise line, tell the purser you have independent flight arrangements and must disembark early. You will be among the first passengers off.

- **Ditch unpleasant dinner companions.** On most cruises, passengers request a specific seating time and table size in advance. If you are a party of two or more, ask to dine by yourselves. As seating time and table size are not guaranteed, confirm with the maitre d' upon boarding that you've gotten what you requested. If you must dine with others and you are a party of two, request a table for at least six—it will be less uncomfortable to leave a table with four other people if you decide you can't stand them than to leave a table with only one other couple. Do not wait until the second or third night to ask the maitre d' to make a switch. If all else fails, order room service (for which there is typically no charge).

from the public rooms and insulated by other cabins, and take a pair of ear plugs just in case.

- **View.** Limited-view cabins can be a good value if you want natural light and like to check the morning weather but won't be in your cabin much. Deck plans may show such obstructions as lifeboats and staircases but not other structures—winches, railings, pillars. Find out exactly what will fill your line of sight (and ask if your cabin will have a window or just a porthole).

- **Size.** If you plan to read, doze, or entertain, consider a deluxe cabin with a sitting area; if you want only a place to sleep, think small. On some ships, same-priced cabins may differ in size, but don't assume that the dimensions portrayed on deck plans are accurate.

- **Traffic.** You may find less peace and privacy in a cabin outside theaters and restaurants, near elevators and stairwells, next to the purser's office, along promenades, and across from the laundry room.

- **Access.** An athlete may want to be near the fitness center, an elderly passenger near the elevators, a parent of four near the laundry room.

Unfair Fares

It's a lamentable tale I've heard countless times: You book a cruise for hundreds of dollars less than the brochure rate and couldn't be more pleased with yourself. Then at dinner your first night onboard, you learn that all your dining companions paid even less and got better cabins. You nearly choke on your fettucine Alfredo.

How not to fall into this trap?

- **Book early.** Most cruise lines offer the largest discounts on fares bought four to six months in advance. And most promise a refund if the price goes down after you've bought your ticket. Occasionally great deals can be found on last-minute fares as well, through discount agencies trying to unload unsold cabin space.

- **Use a travel agency that does lots of business with the cruise line you're interested in.** Ask the line for names of agencies in your area. Those that send the line many passengers can get you better prices and extras such as cabin upgrades. Moreover, luxury lines often don't make the best values

The Wrong Cabin

My family and I took a cruise on the *Royal Majesty*. Before booking, I reviewed the deck plan in the brochure and noticed that next to some cabins it said "obstructed view." I told my travel agent I would not take the cruise unless I could reserve a top-grade cabin with a full view. After confirming with Majesty Cruise Line that cabin 920, a category A deluxe stateroom, would be suitable, she booked it for us. Much to my dismay, our view was blocked by a lifeboat. When I discussed the problem with the purser's office, I was told that nothing could be done. I was given the address and phone number of Majesty's passenger service supervisor and told to contact her when I got home. My phone calls were never returned. I am writing to alert other travelers before they are similarly misled.
—*Peter Tanous, Washington, DC*

Thanks for the warning. After we wrote to Majesty, it apologized and sent a paltry $100 as compensation. Tanous returned it, asking that Majesty apply the $100 to correcting its sales literature. And indeed, it did redesign the deck plan. While the brochure Tanous used pointed out only "obstructed view" staterooms, the subsequent brochure indicates "partially obstructed view" rooms as well, and cabin 920 is among them.

Because stateroom descriptions in brochures can be misleading and deck plans do not tell the whole story, it is a good idea to have your travel agent do what Tanous's agent did (unfortunately, in this case, to no avail): confirm information about cabin view, size, and location with the cruise line.

The best way to avoid a disappointing stateroom is to study the deck plan and consider these factors when choosing a cabin:

• **Motion.** The higher up you go and the farther toward the aft or bow, the worse the rolling or pitching in rough seas (the aft end often heaves less than the bow).

• **Noise.** The sound of engines in the aft, and anchor chains and bow thrusters up front, may be problematic for light sleepers. Add to the list of noisy cabins those directly under the disco, the show lounge, the kitchen, and the jogging track, and next to air-conditioning ventilator baggage-handling stations, and stewards' stations (where clattering dishes may be heard at all hours). For peace and quiet, choose a cabin available to the general public—only to former passengers and preferred travel agents. So strongly consider using an agency that belongs to a consortium that gives it access to the best deals. (For more about consortiums, ☞ How Do You Find a Good Travel Agent? *in* Chapter 4.)

There are a lot of large "800–number" cruise discount agencies around, many based in Florida. Remember that such discounters are generally better at finding the lowest fare than at matching you to the most suitable cruise. They may be more likely to steer you toward their "preferred suppliers." And some large, well-known cruise discounters have gone bust, so if you'd like to use one, check out its reputation first (☞ Chapter 4).

- **Have your travel agent look out for price breaks even after you've bought your tickets.** Although many cruise lines promise to give you a refund if the fare drops after you've paid, you usually don't get the rebate unless you ask. Some travel agencies automatically offer price breaks retroactively; in other cases, you have to find out on your own if the fare has dropped—not an easy task, because many promotions are not advertised in the paper—and request a refund. So use an agency that is properly automated and, before making your final payment, have your agent call the line one more time to check on last-minute promotions. Have your agent check again a few days before the sailing.

And by all means, whatever travel agency you use, pay with a credit card, so you can get your money back if the cruise line goes under. Insist that your agent run the charge through the cruise line's account, not the agency's.

The Importance of Insurance

I've heard innumerable tales from travelers who were forced to cancel a cruise because of an emergency and had to forfeit whopping amounts of money because they had failed to buy trip-cancellation insurance.

Travel insurance policies typically include not only trip-cancellation but also trip-interruption, trip-delay, medical, and baggage insurance. You can purchase a policy either from an insurance company or from the cruise line itself. Although insurance generally adds about 5% or 6% to the cost of a cruise, I cannot recommend it strongly enough. I also cannot be emphatic enough about reading the fine print of the policy you purchase. Many insurance buyers don't take the time to study exactly what is covered and what isn't, and policies differ dramatically. Some cover you if you need to cancel because of a medical condition that existed before you bought your coverage; others cover you only for health situations that develop after you buy the policy. Some are generous about how much they'll pay if your luggage gets lost on the way to the ship; some aren't. Some let you cancel for any reason whatsoever—including personal and business conflicts—and reimburse you in the form of a cruise credit. Others let you cancel only if you or a family member becomes ill, has an accident, or dies.

Many travel agents do not fully understand the ins and outs of travel insurance. Many don't even bring up the subject with their customers, which is downright negligent. So it's up to you to look into various policies, think about the most likely reasons you would be forced to cancel your cruise, and choose the coverage that best suits your situation (☞ Travel Insurance *in* Chapter 8).

Missing the Boat

What happens if your ship sails without you? Airline and other delays have caused many a cruise passenger to miss the boat. If you buy your air

fare from the cruise line, it is the line's responsibility to get you to the next port of call or otherwise onto the ship as soon as possible—and to absorb the extra costs involved.

But if you buy the air fare on your own or use frequent flier miles, you will be responsible for arranging transportation to the ship and for swallowing all extra costs . . . unless you bought trip insurance that covers delay.

So unless you'll save a bundle booking your own air travel, I recommend buying it through the cruise line. It typically costs no more than if you did it on your own and often costs less.

Whatever the case, you will not be reimbursed for the part of the cruise you missed unless you have bought an insurance policy that covers lost cruise days.

Missing Your Luggage

What if you arrive but your bags don't? If you are flying to the embarkation port, checked luggage can go astray on the way from the plane to the baggage carousel to the dock to your cabin.

Luggage snafus are usually not the cruise line's fault but the airline's. The airline's maximum liability for lost luggage is either $640 or $1,250, depending on whether the flight was international or domestic (☞ Lost Luggage *in* Chapter 2). The cruise line's is a mere $100. This seems stingy, considering that the formal nights on many cruises require travelers to bring along expensive clothing and accessories and that replacing them at shops onboard is a pricey proposition. Although ship stores may carry an array of sequined dresses, the selection of basic items like underwear and athletic shoes is limited. And the small credit that some lines offer for emergency purchases rarely covers all the necessities. If you buy insurance from the cruise line, it shells out more—usually between $500 and $1,000, depending on the line.

So take a carry-on bag packed with enough clothing and toiletries to last until you get to the first port of call, where the cruise line is supposed to have delayed luggage sent. (In fact, consider not checking any luggage at all. If you pack properly for a typical warm-weather cruise that is seven days or less, all you really need are playclothes and one formal and one semiformal outfit—and you can carry everything onto the plane.)

Disembarkation poses another potential luggage nightmare. Suitcases are left outside cabins on the last night, removed while you sleep, and taken to the terminal when the ship docks. If luggage is lost, damaged, or pilfered and you have not bought baggage insurance, your reimbursement will be $100 per bag.

A Far Cry from Shipshape

Although generally immaculate and well maintained, cruise ships are not always shipshape. The turmoil on the *Queen Elizabeth 2* after its $40 million renovation made headlines. Passengers boarded the ship only to discover corridors littered with chicken wire and building debris, exploding toilets, leaking cabins, and a fenced-off swimming pool. But there have been a number of less publicized instances of out-of-order ships.

How to minimize chances of ending up on a floating construction site? Ask your travel agent to find out whether the ship will be undergoing renovations close to the departure date you are considering. If the ship is scheduled to go into dry dock, avoid sailing on it the week before, when preliminary repairs may be done, and the week after, since the work may not have been completed. And keep in mind that older ships generally have more problems than newer ones.

Sanitary conditions on cruise ships are overseen by the U.S. Public Health Service. It conducts both scheduled and surprise inspections of ships in U.S. ports, focusing on proper sanitation—drinking water quality, food storage and preparation, and general cleanliness. The results of these inspections, which are conducted twice a year, are available to the public (☞ Where to Turn for Help, *below*).

As for structural safety, although the spate of shipboard disasters over the last few years—fires, groundings, collisions—have garnered quite a bit of publicity, they do not necessarily mean that cruising is unsafe. Indeed, traveling by ship is arguably safer than going by plane, train, or car.

Almost all cruise ships are registered in foreign countries—from the Bahamas to Italy to Liberia—and each is subject to the vessel inspection laws of the country of registry, some of which are more stringent than others. But the U.S. Coast Guard inspects ships calling at U.S. ports to make sure they comply with Coast Guard safety standards. It says that the mishaps that occurred on a variety of different cruise lines in 1994 and 1995 are unrelated and do not indicate a disturbing trend.

Itinerary Surprises and Skipped Ports

I paid Blyth & Company Travel, of Toronto, $3,243 for an expedition to the Antarctic on the icebreaker M.V. *Northern Ranger*. When we arrived in the Falkland Islands, we were told that because of rough weather, we could not go to Antarctica! Since the whole point of the trip was to see the only continent I haven't yet visited, it was a complete bust. Had the company planned better, I would not have had to waste so much time and money on this trip. It scheduled the expedition for March, which is very late in the Antarctic travel season. Also, the ship had already encountered great difficulties because of rough weather on its February and January trips. Shouldn't the company have known that an expedition in more hostile weather might be impossible?

—*Alice T. Merenbach, Bakersfield, California*

Other ships have completed the same itinerary in March, the company's president told us, and the "exceptionally bad" weather that the group encountered can occur at any time of the year in the Antarctic. The company's brochure stated in large print: "Due to the nature of our expedition cruises, weather, ice or government regulations may *require changes to be made to the itineraries ... In the event of unavoidable itinerary changes, passengers have no right to any refund or other compensatory considerations." Nonetheless, Merenbach and the other passengers were offered their choice of either 50% off or a $1,500 discount on a future Antarctic trip.*

Not only expedition companies but all cruise lines say they reserve the right to alter routes or eliminate stops without warning. They may do so for reasons such as inclement weather, mechanical difficulties, or civil unrest in a particular port. They usually offer a shipboard credit or a discount on a future sailing as a peace offering. If you are not satisfied with this compensation, consider settling the matter in small claims court. "Don't believe a cruise line's disclaimers," says Judge Thomas A. Dickerson, author of *Travel Law.* "The disclaimers are put in the cruise line's brochure to dissuade consumers from asserting their rights." If you arrive in small claims court with the proper documentation, he says, you will likely find a judge who will rule according to state consumer protection statutes rather than outdated maritime law. (You can sue the cruise line in small claims court only if it has a local office near you.)

Most cruise lines will not refund port taxes that passengers have paid if a port is skipped, but some do, so if it really matters to you, consider contacting passenger relations.

Shoddy Shore Excursions

Almost as frustrating as skipping a port of call is being prevented from exploring it properly. Cruise ships offer several different group tours at each port and, alas, some don't play out as advertised.

My husband and I took an Aegean cruise with Epirotiki Cruise Lines. The place I most wanted to see was the ancient Greek city of Ephesus. The Ephesus excursion, advertised as taking three and a half hours, left the port at Kuşadasi, Turkey, at 7:30 AM and reached the site at about 8. Our guide said he didn't like crowds, so we'd have to hurry. We raced through the ruins—which are famous for their sheer magnitude—

and arrived at the other end of the site at 8:30. Back in Kuşadasi by 9, we were led to a "government-approved" rug store and subjected to high-pressure sales tactics. I stayed long enough to hear the exorbitant prices and returned to the ship.

Furious, I reported the incident to the purser twice and also noted my displeasure on the cruise questionnaire. I suggested that each Ephesus tourgoer on our bus be refunded the $33 cost of the tour. Considering what it will cost me to go back to Ephesus and see it properly, I think that's the least Epirotiki could do. But I have not heard a word from them.
—*Karen E. Curran, Adamsville, Rhode Island*

Epirotiki, now Royal Olympic Cruises, eventually refunded the Currans' $66 tour fee. "Situations like this do occur, not only in the Mediterranean but throughout the world," a company spokeswoman told us. "Unfortunately, during an excursion, passengers are sometimes brought to a specific shop where they are supposedly offered the best bargains. Guides have special arrangements with the shop and, depending on their sense of responsibility, they sometimes rush people through the sites." The company said it planned to use a different guide for subsequent Ephesus excursions.

Before taking a cruise, ask your agent for a copy of the excursions brochure and research the ports so you know how you would like to spend your time there. Then, when you board, you will know exactly what to book (and can do so before it sells out).

Keep in mind that ship-arranged tours may mean being loaded onto a bus with strangers. You might prefer to rent a car for the day. Or, instead of a group excursion to, say, a public beach, you might prefer cabbing it to a lovely oceanfront resort, lunching by the pool, and lingering there for the afternoon.

Independent excursions can also be economical. On a Caribbean cruise I took with a fellow *Condé Nast Traveler* staffer, we explored Barbados by taking the ship's group sightseeing excursion in the morning and hiring a car to drive just the two of us around the other half of the island in the afternoon. Had we hired the car for the entire day, we would have spent the same amount and had more freedom. Had there been three of us, we would have saved money. In general, if you have a party of four or more, don't go with the group from the ship. Go by yourselves. You can see the same stuff, only in greater comfort and in half the time.

In far-flung lands where you want to explore on your own but you're not sure how reliable the local guides are, find out the cost of having the ship arrange private cars. That way, the cruise line takes on a certain responsibility for the quality and safety of the tour—and for making sure you're back in time.

What if an excursion turns treacherous?

While on an Amazon cruise on the *Pacific Princess,* my husband and I took the "Jungle Trek" tour. The guide succeeded in getting 21 of us lost in the jungle, in 100° weather, for 3½ hours. He spoke no English, had no compass or flare gun, and had no idea where we were. We climbed up ravines so steep that we had to slide down the other side, crossed a creek in an attempt to find our trail, and ended up in growth so thick that it was impenetrable (and the guide did not know how to use his machete to clear a path). I was dehydrated, nauseous, sweating profusely, and experiencing severe chills. I was so tired that I couldn't lift my feet, and my husband had to drag me. Several others were in the same condition or worse.

Finally, two men in the group who clearly had a better sense of direction than the guide led us back to safety. We were exhausted for the rest of the cruise. I'm horrified that Princess Cruises hired such an incompetent guide.
—*Shirley McClellan, Cincinnati, Ohio*

So were we, but Princess says that its shore excursions are run by outside tour operators and that it is "not liable for any incident which might arise from a tour." The company in charge of the Amazon excursions fired the guide and promised never to provide an inexperienced tour leader again, a Princess spokeswoman told us, adding that the cruise line made every effort to aid the lost passengers. It dispatched search boats and hired a helicopter to look for them. When they got back to the ship, Princess cleaned their clothes and made the ship's doctor available to them, both at no charge. And when McClellan later wrote to Princess asking for compensation, it offered a $500 cruise credit.

Cruise lines deny liability for mishaps on shore excursions on the assumption that they are not responsible for the actions of independent contractors. The way to protect yourself is with the proper insurance. In cases of injury or death, you can take legal action against a cruise line, but you must do it within the stated time limit and in a place specified on the cruise ticket—usually the city where the company has its U.S. headquarters.

Health Hazards

Cruise ships are typically clean and hygienic. The real problem is medical care at sea. No international or U.S. requirements govern cruise-ship medicine (at press time, at least). No agency ascertains that cruise lines hire competent doctors, that onboard infirmaries stock proper equipment and medications, and that ships follow correct procedures for medical emergencies and evacuations. The quality of care varies considerably from cruise line to cruise line and is sometimes precarious.

At about three o'clock one morning during our honeymoon cruise on Carnival's *Tropicale,* my husband became ill. He called out from the bathroom that he thought he was having a heart attack, then collapsed on the floor like a rag doll. I tried to call for help on our cabin phone, but it didn't work. I ran into the hall and down to the stewards' station. No one was there. After more searching, I found a crew member. He found the captain, and they called the doctor. By the time the doctor came to our cabin—walking, not running—Frank could not see, feel, hear, or move. The doctor examined him, administered oxygen, and took him to the infirmary.

It turned out that Frank had suffered an acute allergic reaction and not a heart attack—but I still relive the nightmare of being unable to get medical help fast when my husband's life was at stake. Afterward, the captain never inquired about his condition, and the purser brushed off our complaint about the cabin phone. When I wrote to Carnival, it said twice that it would investigate, but I never heard from the cruise line again.

—*Daron L. McDowell, Palmyra, Wisconsin*

Carnival apologized for taking a year to straighten this out— before Ombudsman intervened, the complaint had somehow slipped through the cracks and ended up unresolved in a warehouse—and finally compensated McDowell and her husband with a complimentary seven-day cruise. "Our doctors and nurses are on 24-hour call and are usually responsive in the event of an emergency," Carnival's passenger-service manager told us, adding that she had forwarded McDowell's comments about the malfunctioning telephone and crewmembers' insensitivity to those in a position to take corrective action.

There are measures you can take to prevent medical problems at sea and to minimize the damage a shipboard emergency can cause:

- **Buy travel insurance.** This is especially important if you are older or have a medical condition, because emergency evacuation from a ship and forfeiture of the rest of a cruise can cost you tens of thousands of dollars.

- **Ask the line about its medical standards and procedures before you book.** Find out whether the staff is certified in Advanced Cardiac Life Support. If you have a condition requiring a doctor with expertise in a certain field, ask in advance about the ship's doctor's training. Get answers in writing, if possible. The difficulty you face as a potential passenger trying to obtain thorough and accurate information may be an indication of the importance a cruise line places on its shipboard care.

- **Choose your cruise itinerary carefully.** That's most important if you are at risk for emergencies. Ask your doctor if it is all right for you to be far from land, or from first-world medical care, for long periods.

- **Pack enough medication to last your trip.** If you take a prescription drug or need any other medication—even occasionally—bring a supply that will last for the entire cruise, because the ship may not be able to fill your prescription. And don't pack it in checked luggage, which may get lost.

- **Carry a list of any medications you take and their dosages.** This information will help the medical staff in an emergency.

- **Bring a note from your doctor if you have a medical condition.** And alert the medical staff to your situation at the start of the cruise. Should an emergency occur, they will be better prepared to handle it. If you have a heart condition, bring a copy of your latest EKG.

- **Carry your personal doctor's phone number.**

- **If you do seek medical help, get a record of the doctor's diagnosis and treatment.** This will help later if you determine that the doctor was negligent and you pursue the matter legally.

If you think a cruise-ship doctor has committed malpractice, your chances of recourse are unfortunately slim. It is very difficult to sue because most ships' physicians are not U.S. citizens and must be sued in their home country. Such claims usually do not get far in foreign courts.

And to win, you must prove that the line was negligent—that when it hired the doctor it knew or should have known that he was not qualified. This is next to impossible to prove.

Tipping Tips

Although certain luxury lines forbid gratuities, most ships encourage them. They hand out tipping guidelines and advise passengers to place varying amounts of cash in envelopes to be handed to certain crew members. Find out in advance how much cash you will need and take the proper denominations of bills. I failed to do so on my first Caribbean sailing because the cruise line's literature had told me about its "cashless system" whereby we would charge all onboard services on a plastic card. The sorry result was that my options on tipping day were either to wait in a seemingly endless line at the cashier's desk or to waste time on St. Thomas searching for a bank.

Although cruise lines recommend tipping at the end of the trip, several frequent cruisers have told me that they receive better service when they tip the dining room staff on the first night and say that they're looking forward to a wonderful cruise. Or consider tipping half midway through the cruise, especially on long sailings.

Freighter Trips

If your idea of heaven is to spend long stretches of time at sea (months, in fact) with a deck chair and a pile of books, consider a trip by freighter. It won't blow your budget the way a luxury cruise can, and it can take you to funky ports of call— as long as you don't mind sailing with, say, canned goods.

Be warned that freighter travel is for people who don't require a casino, disco, show lounge, or many fellow passengers for entertainment (there are typically no more than 12 onboard). Amenities are usually limited to a library or lounge, a self-service bar, laundry facilities, deck space, and occasionally a pool; cabins are modest.

Most freighter travelers realize they have not signed up for a conventional cruise and don't expect conventional-cruise service. Sometimes their expectations are too high nonetheless.

My husband and I took a three-month voyage from New Orleans to the Sudan and back on a Lykes Lines freighter with 10 other passengers. We stopped in Savannah, Georgia; Durban, South Africa; Mombasa, Kenya; Aseb, Ethiopia; Port Sudan, Sudan; then returned to Durban and back to the United States.

The *Stella Lykes* was in a state of disrepair. Electricity and water supplies were problematic, and the air-conditioning never worked. The captain and most of the crew were inhospitable and uninformative. Worse, even though we had visas for the countries we visited, the captain did not allow us off the ship, except for one day in Durban and one in Mombasa. In Port Sudan, the captain obtained shore passes for his crew for the seven days we were there, but he took ours away—with no explanation—after we'd used them only two days. We felt as if we were kept under house arrest for three months. I think we're entitled to some sort of compensation.

—*Marjorie Spencer, El Centro, California*

So did Lykes Lines. Admitting that other passengers also complained about the ship's poor condition and about personality conflicts with the personnel, Lykes sent all 12 passengers a 10% refund (in the Spencers' case, $1,100). The company said it had just purchased the ship from another carrier. It was the first time the ship had carried passengers and the captain's first voyage as captain. Lykes said that passenger accommodations had since been improved and that the captain had been made "very much aware of our policy of dedication and commitment to passenger needs and satisfaction."

But Lykes added that it is not completely to blame for the infrequent shore leave. A foreign port's immigration restrictions dictate whether passengers can leave the ship and for how long. According to Lykes, immigration officers told the captain that the passengers were not allowed onshore at several stops. (The crew got shore passes because international treaties waive local immigration rules for crews.)

Travelers considering a freighter cruise should be forewarned not only about immigration restrictions but also that freighters stay in port only as long as it takes to load or unload cargo, and itineraries can change en route. A flexible schedule, an easygoing attitude, and the willingness to spend many days on the open ocean are a must.

To find the right freighter trip for you, pick up a copy of *Ford's Freighter Guide,* which lists itineraries and schedules, or call a cruise agency that specializes in freighter trips, such as Travel Tips in Flushing, New York (☎ 800/872–8584) or Freighter World Cruises in Pasadena, California (☎ 800/531–7774).

Where to Turn for Help

FINDING A TRAVEL AGENT WHO SPECIALIZES IN CRUISES

National Association of Cruise-Only Agencies
✉ 7600 Red Rd., Suite 128, Dept. CN
South Miami, FL 33143
☎ 305/663–5626
FAX 305/663–5625
For a list of cruise specialists in your vicinity, mail a request along with a self-addressed, stamped envelope.

Cruise Lines International Association
✉ 500 5th Ave., Suite 1407
New York, NY 10110
☎ 212/921–0066
FAX 212/921–0549
http://www.ten-io.com/clia/
Call CLIA-affiliated agencies and ask for a "Master Cruise Counselor." CLIA's Internet site provides a list of Master Cruise Counselors and Accredited Cruise Counselors by location.

API Travel Consultants
✉ 500 Main St., Suite 400
Fort Worth, TX 76102
☎ 817/870–0300
http://www.apitravel.com
Many agents who belong to this network of top agencies specialize in luxury cruises. Call for a referral.

CRUISE CANCELLATIONS AND FINANCIAL REIMBURSEMENTS

Federal Maritime Commission
Office of Informal Inquiries and Complaints
✉ 800 N. Capitol St. NW
Washington, DC 20573
☎ 202/523–5807
FAX 202/523–0014

The Federal Maritime Commission requires cruise lines carrying passengers from U.S. ports to be financially capable of reimbursing customers if their sailing is canceled. The Commission also requires proof of ability to pay claims arising from passenger injuries or death for which the cruise line may be liable. It cannot order a cruise line to reimburse you for a canceled cruise or to pay claims for injuries or fatal accidents but will try to assist if you are having trouble obtaining financial settlements in these areas.

VESSEL SAFETY

U.S. Coast Guard
☎ 800/368–5647 (hotline)

To complain about a safety-related matter you have observed on a cruise ship or to obtain copies of inspection reports, contact the Coast Guard Marine Inspection Office or Marine Safety Office that conducted the latest examination; call the hot line for the appropriate number. The hot line also takes requests for copies of the free consumer fact sheet, **"Ocean Cruise Ships,"** which discusses safety oversight, crewmember competency, emergency drills, terminal security, sanitation and cleanliness, and proper trash disposal.

SANITARY CONDITIONS

U.S. Public Health Service
✉ Chief of Vessel Sanitation Program
National Center for Environmental Health
1015 N. America Way, Room 107
Miami, FL 33132-2017
☎ 305/536–4307

To report unsanitary conditions, contact this office. This is also the place to send your written request for a copy of the latest sanitation inspection report for a particular ship or a copy of the "green sheets," which list all ships and their most recent scores.

TERMINAL SECURITY

To complain about security procedures or report lax security, contact the **Coast Guard Captain of the Port.** For referral to the appropriate captain, call the **Coast Guard's consumer hot line** (☏ 800/368–5647).

TO REPORT ILLEGAL GARBAGE DUMPING OR OTHER DAMAGE TO THE OCEAN ENVIRONMENT

Photograph or videotape any incidents you observe and contact:

The Coast Guard's National Response Center
☏ 800/424–8802

Center for Marine Conservation
✉ 1725 DeSales St. NW
Washington, DC 20036
☏ 202/429–5609
FAX 202/872–0619

This is the nation's leading non-profit organization dedicated to the health of the marine environment. You can report incidents anonymously, if you wish. You can also write in for a **"Cruise Passenger Kit"** ($5) that provides information on garbage dumping at sea and how to be an eco-friendly cruisegoer.

CHAPTER 6

Car Rentals

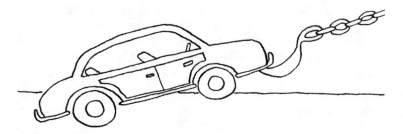

A rental car is a passport to freedom. Unconstricted by train routes and bus schedules, unjostled by herds of tourists, you can see more, at your own pace, and in your own private oasis of tranquility. What better way to explore the vast Badlands of South Dakota, go château-hopping in the Loire Valley, or wind your way along Italy's Amalfi Coast?

Unfortunately, a rental car can also be a passport to stress. And the stress begins as early as the booking process: Compact or mid-sized? Limited mileage or unlimited? Is there a drop-off fee? Does the price include taxes? What other surcharges are there? Is insurance mandatory or optional? Is it covered by my credit card?

Fussy though these details may seem, they truly matter. Your decisions on each point become part of a binding contract—a detailed catalog of terms and conditions that requires a signature and initials in three or four different boxes and is so tedious that, alas, few travelers bother to read it. If you violate the terms of the contract—say, you return the car a day early or to the wrong city, or you drive it out of a specified geographical area or let someone take the wheel who isn't signed up as an "additional driver"—you can void the contract and end up owing a small fortune.

I rented a car from Hertz in Houston, at a rate of $149 per week with unlimited mileage. Two days before the car was due, I called the Houston office and told the manager that I wished to return the car to College Station, Texas, rather than to Houston. I asked him what penalties would apply, and he said I would have to pay a $30 drop-off fee.

Upon returning the car, I charged the rental, which came to a total of $386.90, to my American Express card.

Now American Express is billing me $1,384.72 instead! Hertz says that I had to return the car to Houston in order for the $149 rate and the unlimited-mileage offer to apply. It won't recognize my $386.90 receipt and refuses to believe my version of the phone conversation with the manager because I can't prove what was said (even though I provided a phone bill showing the date and time of my call). American Express investigated the dispute, sided with Hertz, and is demanding full payment.

Had Hertz simply informed me that the original contract would be voided and a new rate applied, I would have returned the car to Houston—a mere 60 miles from College Station!

—*Chryseis Fox, College Station, Texas*

 *What a rip-off. When we asked Hertz for a response, it sent Fox an apology and issued a $997.82 refund. It said that the College Station office should have explained to her, when she was returning the car, that because she was dropping it off in a different place than was indicated on the contract, the charge would be $1,384.72. Many's the time Ombudsman has seen a seemingly harmless change in a car rental itinerary nullify the terms of the original contract.*

———

Rentals can be particularly stressful abroad, where language barriers and local laws come into play. First there's the endless queue when you arrive at the rental counter after an all-night transoceanic flight. In your sleepless condition, it's hard to think straight, much less drive straight. You begin to realize you probably can't live with the subcompact you reserved and that you'd really prefer automatic transmission to manual. Then it turns out there are four types of insurance you have to accept or decline. You realize you forgot to check whether the collision-damage coverage provided by your credit card includes theft insurance. When you mutter something about declining, the rental agent says that he'll have to put through a deposit of several thousand dollars on your credit card in case you wrap his car around a tree. But this will tie up your credit line and put a serious dent in your shopping plans. So you opt for the coverage, and after the insurance cost and the country's taxes are added to your bill, you're suddenly spending 50% more than you planned. Your shopping funds are shrinking by the minute. And, worse, you're not sure what you're signing and initialing because the contract is in a language you don't read. Never mind that you can't understand the rental agent's directions for exiting the airport. . .

Just thinking about car rentals is enough to drive up your blood pressure. All those policy exclusions and contractual loopholes. You practically have to bring a lawyer with you to the rental counter. And, unfortunately, it's the least titillating topics—collision-damage coverage, guaranteed rates, final audits, and other soporifics—that are the most important to scrutinize if you want to avoid the headaches and the gouging.

Dodging the Gouges

First of all, those lowball prices you spot in newspaper ads are often illusions. Once you get to the rental office, you may be hit with a bunch of extra charges that can send your bill skyward.

- **Taxes and surcharges.** These can come to more than 25% of the base rental rate when you combine taxes (which can reach 10% in many U.S. cities and a hair-raising 18% in Chicago) with city surcharges (ranging from $1 per rental to $3 per day) and so-called "off-airport" surcharges levied by rental offices that are near an airport but require a shuttle-bus ride to get there (a mere $3.10 per rental in Fort Lauderdale but a whopping 10% in Atlantic City).

- **Insurance.** Most car rental companies try to get you to pay about $11 to $14 per day for collision-damage coverage and two or three other types of protection. Because you may already have this coverage, either through your own auto insurance policy or your credit card, always check before you rent. Then ask the rental company for the prices of the types of coverage you don't have, and add them to your estimated budget. Warning: An "all-inclusive rate" may exclude plenty, particularly insurance. Or it may include coverage you don't need (for example, collision-damage protection provided by your credit card) but not coverage you do need (for example, liability protection not provided by your card).

- **Drop-off fees.** Renting a car in one country and dropping it off in another can cost a mint if you're not careful—so shop around. Fees vary dramatically from company to company and from region to region.

- **Fuel charges.** If you return your car with an empty tank, you may be charged a service fee to refuel it (not to mention a steep gasoline price).

- **Additional driver fees.** If you rent a car with someone else who plans to share the driving, you may have to fork over an extra $2 to $25 per day. Spouses and co-workers are often exempted, and extra-driver fees are illegal in certain states (for example, California and Nevada). You may be tempted to avoid paying the fee and simply not let it slip that there'll be a second driver. Don't. If you get into an accident or are stopped by a police officer with an unauthorized driver at the wheel, your contract will be void and your collision coverage canceled.

Extra-driver fees vary between companies, so comparison-shop. Check with the specific rental office where you plan to pick up your car as well; some franchises charge fees for spouses and co-workers, even when the chain they belong to doesn't.

- **Under-age surcharges.** Some companies won't rent to anyone under the age of 25. Those that do may impose a surcharge of up to $20 per day if renters are between 21 and 24.

As for base rental rates, it's important to press reservationists repeatedly for a better price. They may not divulge their lowest rates until you've made it clear that you're a vacationer desperate to save a few dollars rather than a business traveler with an expense account. So ask about discounts for members of organizations such as AAA and about fly-drive packages, special weekend rates, and weekly rates (which often apply to four-day rentals and are a much better deal than daily rates).

Also, when you pick up your car, don't be pressured into an upgrade unless you know what it costs and are willing to pay.

———

I reserved a large Alamo rental car—a Buick Century or Regal—at Kansas City International Airport. When I arrived, the agent suggested that with my lanky frame I might be more comfortable in a Chevrolet Caprice. I said that sounded fine and stupidly signed the contract without reading it. I have now been charged $110.34 more than the price originally quoted. The agent never mentioned that the Caprice would cost $7.99 more per day than the Buick. I know I am responsible for the extra charge, but I think it was the agent's responsibility to warn me about it.
—*Donald A. Bluhm, Milwaukee, Wisconsin*

Alamo agreed and sent Bluhm a $110.34 refund and a free-upgrade certificate. It said it had passed his criticism on to the Kansas City station manager. Maybe so, but Ombudsman rented a car from the same office a few weeks later and was also encouraged to take a car *larger and better equipped—and, consequently, more expensive—than the one reserved. (We turned it down.)*

Booking an Overseas Rental

Rule number one: Use a major company with either headquarters or a big corporate office in the United States. It's your security blanket. If something goes wrong, your chances of immediate help—provided by someone who speaks English—are better, as are your opportunities for recourse later.

Rule number two: Make your reservation before leaving home. Walk-in rates can be exorbitant, and snags are less likely if the details have been ironed out in advance and you have a confirmation number or slip.

I rented a 300D Mercedes from Hertz in Paris. Two days later, I dropped it off at the airport in Bilbao, Spain. I had had a difficult time communicating when I picked up the car; to my regret, no final cost was estimated or quoted.

A month later, I received a $7,000 bill for the two-day rental! I would just like to warn travelers to confirm all quoted rates before driving away from the rental office.

—Patrick Michael Riordan, Aptos, California

Ombudsman thanks Riordan for the good advice. Hertz eventually reduced the bill to about $5,700 by substituting a three-day rate with unlimited mileage for the original daily rate. But it would not reduce the $2,539 drop-off charge or the $149-per-day collision-damage coverage. Hertz told us its Paris office warned Riordan that the luxury car he wanted was available only through the company's "prestige service" program—its top-of-the-line pricing stratum—and suggested that he switch to a nonluxury car. Because Hertz didn't offer prestige service in Spain, it had to pay a transporter to fly to Bilbao and drive the car back to Paris. Hertz also disputed any language barrier, claiming its counter personnel speak fluent English.

If you're already abroad when you decide you want to rent a car, try to avoid exorbitant walk-in rates by arranging the rental through the company's U.S. reservation office—it's worth the price of the transoceanic call—or through your travel agent back home. Or stop into the local office of a U.S. airline and try arranging it through the airline's computer reservation system.

BEATING THE GOUGES IN EUROPE

It's a good idea to comparison-shop, since rates and perks vary significantly from agency to agency. Keep in mind, though, that there is no uniform way of classifying cars in Europe. One company's category "A" car is another company's category "B," so ask for specific car model names to be sure you're comparing apples with apples.

Weekly rates and air/car and rail/car packages are usually economical. So is a guaranteed U.S. dollar rate, if the dollar is sliding against foreign currencies. Often you pay a dollar rate in advance and receive a voucher to present to the rental office upon arrival. Be warned that although you may think you've prepaid in full, the voucher might not include payment for those delightful extra charges.

And as bad as those charges are in the United States, they're worse in Europe. Collision-damage coverage can reach $25 per day for nonluxury cars. Taxes can be as high as 25%; they exceed 20% in Belgium, Turkey, and most Scandinavian and Eastern European countries. Airport surcharges can be either a percentage of the total rental cost (9% in Switzerland, 10% in Italy) or a flat fee ($22 in the Netherlands, $18 in Copenhagen, $11 in France). Other hidden fees—some legitimate, some not—also pop up. One driver we know was charged a $6 fee in Milan to cover the cost of washing the car so it would be clean for the next renter!

Rental rates are typically highest in Scandinavia and Eastern Europe. They're typically lowest in the United Kingdom, Germany, and Switzerland. Some companies offer reasonable rates in Belgium, Ireland, the Netherlands, and Portugal. If you're planning to drive through several countries, pick up the car in the one where rates are lowest.

Keep in mind that gasoline prices in Europe can be three to four times the U.S. price.

CHOOSING THE RIGHT CAR

In the United States, some travelers in the market for a new car see renting as an excellent opportunity to audition different models. In Europe, the variety of unfamiliar models can be more of a source of frustration than fun.

A few factors to think about:

- **How much space do you need?** European cars are generally smaller than American ones. Consider the storage space, too; you may want to be able to hide all your luggage in the trunk.

- **How much power do you want?** If you plan to chug through the Alps, you may want a larger car.

- **Do you need an automatic transmission?** Cars with this feature are typically less common and more expensive than those with a stick shift and often come only mid-size or larger. I've had luck finding small, reasonably priced automatic-transmission cars through the Kemwel Group (☎ 800/678–0678) and through Auto Europe (☎ 800/223–5555).

You might find a free booklet called "Europe on Wheels" helpful. Published by Dollar Rent A Car's European operation, EuroDollar (☎ 800/800–6000), it includes pictures and descriptions of various car models (☞ Where to Turn for Help, *below*).

OTHER QUESTIONS TO ASK

- **Where can't I drive the car?** Some companies won't let you drive beyond certain geographical limits. Usually, U.S. cars cannot be driven into Mexico, and cars rented in a Western European country cannot be driven into Eastern Europe. So figure out your itinerary in advance and make sure the company permits you to go where you have planned.

- **Do I need an I.D.P.?** Some countries (the Czech Republic and Hungary, for example) require an International Driving Permit, which is a translation of your driver's license. Even where an I.D.P. is not required, it may be useful (especially in Austria, Germany, Italy, and Spain, where I.D.P.'s are required in theory but not in practice). If you get into an accident, an I.D.P. will save you angst if an officer confiscates your license; better to forfeit the temporary license than to surrender your permanent one. The American Automobile Association provides these permits for $10 each. The tourist board of the country you're visiting can tell you if one is required. Note that some countries don't allow you to drive at all, regardless of your documentation (and trust me, you won't want to).

CAR RENTALS

- **Is there an age requirement?** Some companies and countries won't let you rent a car if you're above a certain age—typically 70. Sometimes upper age limits are imposed at licensee locations but not at corporate ones. So, before renting, inquire about the particular location you'll be using, and ask whether a driving test or doctor's note confirming your medical health might allow you to bypass the rule.

- **Is the insurance mandatory or optional?** Some countries require you to purchase certain types of coverage from the rental company.

- **If I decline the optional insurance, is a deposit required?** Some rental offices put a "hold" of several thousand dollars on your credit card—even if it provides collision-damage coverage. When making your reservation, ask whether such a deposit is required and how large it will be (usually somewhere between $2,000 and the full value of the car). Because this effectively diminishes the available balance on your credit card, you may need to travel with an extra credit card or ensure that you have other means of covering travel expenses.

- **Will contracts be available in English?** Although the contracts of major U.S. rental companies are bilingual, those of smaller or foreign companies sometimes aren't.

In Berlin last year, trying to decide whether to rent a car or take the train around Germany, my wife and I comparison-shopped among car rental companies. We had almost given up on finding an affordable car when we walked into a Europcar InterRent office. The Europcar agent got us a Volkswagen Passat Variant at a special rate of $160 for five days, with unlimited *kilométrage*. We found the rental agreement difficult to decipher, but the agent spoke perfect English and seemed reliable, so we took the car.

Returning it in Aachen five days later, we were slapped with an additional $544 *kilométrage* charge because the special rate only allows for 1,500 free kilometers. We contacted the Berlin office, only to learn that the agent who had rented us the car was on vacation. I ended up having to pay for the kilometers that were supposed to be free. I still question the charge.

—*Steve Petrillo, Ventura, California*

So did National Car Rental, which handles Europcar Inter-Rent's bookings and billings in the United States. When we brought the mix-up to National's attention, it reimbursed Petrillo.

Savvy travelers accustomed to examining rental contracts may find it difficult to do so in foreign countries, where the language and format of rental agreements may be unfamiliar. One way to reduce potential confusion is to reserve the car in advance and request written confirmation of the terms and conditions of your booking.

—

Alternatively, if you know your contract is not going to be in English, take a dictionary to the rental office, or familiarize yourself with key terms such as "accept" and "decline." (I've seen quite a few renters decline insurance when they thought they were accepting it, and vice-versa.)

Finally, take advantage of preparatory information services offered by rental companies, such as Avis International's "Know Before You Go" program (☎ 800/297–4447), which can provide country-specific information such as gasoline prices and speed limits (as well as banking hours, tipping customs, addresses of country tourist offices, etc.).

When You're Late to the Rental Office

How long can you be delayed without losing your reservation? Each rental company provides some leeway, ranging from one to 24 hours. Of course, you run a higher risk of losing your rental in peak season. If you know you're going to be late, notify the rental office.

If you're picking up a car at an airport, give your flight information when booking. Some companies check the flight status of delayed customers and try to make allowances. Prepaying your reservation or guaranteeing it with a credit card should also increase your chances of getting the car.

What if you don't get there at all? At press time, a few rental agencies were charging no-shows penalties of $25 to $100, depending on the company and type of car, and others were considering adopting such a policy.

When You're on Time but the Car Is Late

If the vehicle you reserved isn't available, you'll probably get a free upgrade to a higher class of car. But what if there are no cars at all? This happens when rental companies overbook in order to compensate for the anticipated number of no-shows. And it happens most often in Florida and over holiday periods.

I reserved a car for pick-up at 5 PM from Dollar Rent a Car at Miami International Airport. When I arrived, there were many people in line ahead of me. I had an important dinner meeting in West Palm Beach and was considering hiring a taxi to get me there on time, but two rental agents assured me that my car would be ready in 20 minutes. They kept assuring me of this until, almost three hours later, I was finally given a car with an empty gas tank, which meant spending time searching for a gas station in an unfamiliar city. Had the agents been straight with me about how long it would take to get the car, I could have hired a taxi and wouldn't have missed my meeting. I hope in the future Dollar will not confirm reservations it can't honor.

—*Craig Bartley Ravenhill, Kanata, Ontario, Canada*

Dollar apologized for Ravenhill's three-hour wait and for the "unprofessional service" he encountered. It said that sometimes, particularly during holidays, renters keep cars longer than anticipated but don't notify Dollar, causing a shortage. The company gave Ravenhill a complimentary one-week rental to make up for the delay.

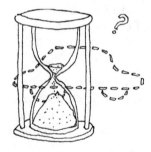

If a rental office has no car, it may promise to deliver one to your hotel later. Or it may book one for you at another agency. If you're forced to pay a higher rate as a result, the first company might refund the difference. Or it might give you a credit toward a future rental. If it does nothing, I suggest writing to customer relations to express your disappointment at the firm's insensitivity compared with other rental agencies.

When the Firm Won't Honor the "Guaranteed" Rate

Perhaps even more annoying than being forced to pay for a bunch of add-ons you didn't anticipate is having to pay a higher base rate than you were promised.

The rate isn't always guaranteed if you book a rental far in advance. At some Hertz licensee locations, for instance, rates are confirmed only 60 days before the rental. So if you make a reservation, say, three months in advance, you'll need to call back a month later to find out what it's actually going to cost.

Four months before our trip, my wife and I reserved a Hertz car, at a rate of $286 for nine days with unlimited mileage. When we arrived to pick up the car at the airport in Minot, North Dakota, the rental office refused to honor this rate, saying it does not guarantee rates for more than 60 days and that the reservationist should have told me this. Not only was I not told, but neither was my wife when she confirmed the rate 55 days before the trip and again 10 days before.

The rental agent said he would have to charge $416 plus 30¢ per mile in excess of 700 miles. Since we planned to drive 3,000 miles through the West, our bill would be about $1,106. The other rental companies at the airport had no cars available, so we really had no choice but to sign Hertz's contract. We called the company's customer-service department, but it was closed for the weekend. When we called again on Monday and Tuesday, various supervisors said they couldn't help so we decided to shorten our vacation. We returned the car five days after picking it up. When the rental agent handed me the signed American Express charge slip, I wrote $158.89 on it, representing five-ninths of the rate originally quoted.

I am outraged that we were not warned in advance that Hertz intended to bill us $1,106 instead of $286.

—*Paul B. Elis, Calabasas, California*

Hertz's rates are subject to change without notice unless they are guaranteed. Its corporate-owned locations guarantee rates 240 days before the pick-up date, while some of its franchises guarantee them only 60 days beforehand. When you book a car farther in advance than this, the reservationist is supposed to inform you that the rate being quoted is subject to change and that the company's computer will give you the best rate available on the date that the guaranteed-rate period begins.

Responding to Elis's letter, Hertz told us that it regretted if he was not properly advised by the original reservationist and that the agent who confirmed the rental should have guaranteed the rate. As a goodwill gesture, Hertz decided to let Elis's bill stand at $158.89.

If you are quoted a rate over the phone, give your credit-card number to guarantee it, and then are charged a higher rate at the rental counter, put up a fight. Raise hell on the spot, write to the company's customer-service department or, if the company has a branch in your city, sue in small claims court.

When You're Turned Down
Because of Your Driving Record

Some rental companies check the driving records of prospective renters before handing over a vehicle. The desk clerk punches your driver's license number into the computer, which pulls up data from the Department of Motor Vehicles in the state where you hold your license. The computer runs the data past the car rental company's criteria for accepting a renter—different companies have different criteria—and spits out a simple yes or no.

Only certain companies screen renters. And only renters holding licenses in certain states can be screened: at press time, California, Connecticut, Florida, Kansas, Maryland, Minnesota, New York, Ohio, Pennsylvania, South Carolina, Virginia, and Washington, D.C. (The Departments of Motor Vehicles in other states do not make driving records available to the on-line services that car rental companies use to get their data.) Reasons for rejection range from the obvious—a conviction for reckless driving, a suspended or revoked license—to the not-so-obvious—three moving violations within the last three years (including seat belt violations and speeding tickets), or operating without insurance or a valid driver's license within the past two years.

My wife and I reserved a car from Budget, to be picked up at the Fort Lauderdale airport. When we arrived, the rental agent said he could not rent it to me because the computer was showing a problem with my driver's license. I held a valid license with no points or infringements, so I said there must be a mistake. I then asked to speak to a supervisor. Finally, I was given the name of a woman in the corporate offices to call—at my own expense. I phoned her, and she pulled up my records and said I was being denied because I had been in a collision three years before. While this was true, I hadn't been at fault—the other driver had run a stop sign. Budget's representative said she could not override the computer and would not honor the reservation. Fortunately, I was able to get a car from another company, for about $35 more.

I've written to Budget several times in the last eight months and have heard nothing.

—*Harlan J. Fischer, Smithtown, New York*

It took a lot of prodding, but we finally got an answer, almost a year and a half after Fischer first wrote to us. The company didn't offer him any compensation, but it did explain its motor vehicle check system. When Budget first began screening renters in Florida, one of the rules was that it "would not rent to anyone who had had an accident involving bodily injury within the last 48 months." So Fischer's rental was denied.

Budget has changed its policies since. The accident rule has been eliminated because so many would-be renters were not at fault; and prospective customers are now warned that their records will be checked. The company has also instituted a toll-free number that you can call if you are turned down and have questions.

It's a pain in the neck that car companies check renters' records only when they arrive to pick up their vehicle. What if you're turned away and can't find a car elsewhere at the last minute? What if you find another car but must pay a much higher rate because you didn't book it in advance?

And you have little recourse if the computerized data on you is erroneous. I learned this the hard way. When an Ombudsman department staffer and I rented a car in Fort Lauderdale, the computer rejected her as an additional driver even though there was not one blip on her record. We protested, as it was important that she share the driving. The rental agent said her hands were tied, pointed to the public phone, and suggested I straighten it out with the D.M.V. Yeah, right. I'm supposed to get hold of someone in the byzantine, bungling bureaucracy known as the Manhattan D.M.V. who could actually pull up my friend's record and communicate it to the clerk in Fort Lauderdale? That's one expensive phone call.

How to avoid being turned away at the rental counter? Ask whether the company screens drivers from your state. If you want to know whether your driving record will pass the company's criteria, you can find out from T.M.L. Information Services, which provides rental agencies with D.M.V. data, for a $9.95 fee (☎ 800/388–9099).

Or just choose a rental company that doesn't screen drivers. Be warned, though, that some non-screening companies may ask you, at pick-up time, to sign a statement that you have an acceptable driving record—that you've had no violations within the past, say, two or three years. Be careful. If you sign erroneously, in the belief that your record is clear, and then have an accident, the rental company could say you violated the rental agreement, thus negating your collision coverage.

Optional Insurance: To Buy or Not to Buy?

So you've been approved as a renter and it's time to sign on the dotted line. Do you accept or decline the insurance? Checking the wrong options could cost you thousands of dollars. Some travelers waste money buying all the different types of coverage offered even if they don't need it. Others decline the coverage, mistakenly thinking they're covered by their credit card. Others know exactly what protection they have but, when they try to decline, are browbeaten by the rental agent into accepting.

THE DIFFERENT TYPES OF COVERAGE

Rental companies offer three or four types of protection:

- **Collision-damage coverage.** This protects you in case the car is stolen, lost, vandalized, or otherwise damaged.

- **Liability coverage.** This protects you in case you get into an accident that involves bodily injury or property damage to a third party who decides to sue.

- **Personal-accident insurance.** This covers you and anyone else in the car for bodily injuries caused by an accident. It may be combined with personal-effects insurance, which reimburses you for theft of or damage to baggage and other personal property.

- **Theft protection.** Available abroad, it provides coverage in case the car is stolen. In the United States, collision-damage coverage includes theft protection.

BEFORE ARRIVING AT THE RENTAL COUNTER

Check your private auto-insurance policy. Does it cover cars rented for vacation purposes—not just to replace a car being repaired? Is there a time limit? Most auto-insurance policies do not cover overseas rentals.

Also determine what insurance, if any, your credit card provides. If it provides collision-damage coverage, do the terms of your planned rental fit the credit card issuer's criteria? For instance, is the type of car you want to rent covered? Are you covered for the length of time you want to rent? Are you covered in the country in which you want to rent? Does your credit card provide liability coverage in case you injure someone? Are you covered for theft of your car? What about theft of belongings from the car?

CREDIT-CARD COVERAGE: THE COMMON PITFALLS

Don't wait until you get to the rental counter to ask these questions. Rental agents are in the business of trying to sell you their company's insurance. And there are too many different types of credit cards, each with its own different restrictions and exclusions, for the rental clerk to have any reliable information about your particular card.

I rented a Dodge Dynasty four-door sedan from National Car Rental and paid for it with my American Express Gold Card, since it provides collision-damage coverage. After driving the car a few miles, I realized that it wouldn't have enough space for my family's luggage. I returned to the rental office to ask for a car with more luggage room, and National gave me a four-door Jeep Cherokee. Unfortunately, it was stolen, and $1,000 worth of damage was done to it. But now American Express won't pay for the damage because Jeep models are excluded from its collision-damage coverage. Had I known, I would have used my Visa Gold Card, which  covers Jeep Cherokees. I think it was National's responsibility to warn me that American Express does not cover Jeeps.

—*William J. Holland, Nassau, Bahamas*

National did not agree, and neither did we. National responded that the customer is responsible for knowing what coverage his credit card or automobile insurance policy provides.

Renters planning to rely on credit card coverage should be warned that there are many restrictions and that they vary from card to card. Ask your card issuer what vehicles are excluded (often vans, minivans, utility vehicles such as Jeeps, recreational vehicles, specialty cars, and lux-

ury cars). Find out whether coverage is available only for rentals of a certain length (often the rental agreement must be limited to 15 or 30 days; sometimes the time limit varies between U.S. and overseas rentals). Find out whether there are certain parts of the world where coverage is not valid (often in Italy, Australia, and New Zealand).

And find out if your credit card provides primary or secondary coverage. If the former, your credit card company is the first to pick up the bill in the event of an accident; you don't need to file a claim first with your personal auto-insurance carrier. If the coverage is secondary, the credit card coverage kicks in only after your private auto insurance pays up to its limit.

Credit-card policies change frequently, so if you rent infrequently, call your credit-card issuer each time you reserve a car to make sure the coverage applies to the particular conditions of that booking. The rules are complicated and the exclusions substantial, so request a copy of your credit card company's written policy rather than trying to absorb it all by phone.

WHEN YOU'RE FORCED TO BUY THE RENTAL COMPANY'S COVERAGE

I prepaid for a 12-day car rental in Austria, charging it to my credit card. I did not purchase the rental company's collision-damage coverage because my Gold MasterCard provides it. I knew that if I paid with the MasterCard and declined the company's coverage, I would be protected in case of an accident.

At the Budget rental office in Linz, the agent said I was required to buy the coverage. If I didn't, he wouldn't give me the car. I argued with him for a long time, but he was inflexible. I had a MasterCard number in the United States that I could call collect if I ran into this kind of problem, but the agent wouldn't let me make the call. He would only let me speak to someone in MasterCard's Vienna office, who said he didn't know anything about the card providing coverage. I finally gave in and signed for the coverage, but I'm furious that I should have to pay $190 for something I didn't need.

—*Robert Thompson, Laurel Springs, New Jersey*

Thompson shouldn't have to, and won't. We wrote Budget, saying that we know Thompson can't prove he was forced to buy the coverage but pointing out that he used his Gold MasterCard, which would have made the purchase unnecessary. Budget wrote back that Thompson could have avoided buying the coverage by leaving a credit card deposit of $4,400. Thompson says the agent never made him aware of any such option and that he would have had no problem leaving such a deposit. Budget eventually agreed to reimburse Thompson, "in the interest of good customer relations."

How do you avoid having unnecessary coverage foisted upon you? Ask for advance written confirmation that you won't have to buy collision-damage protection and that your card's coverage will be accepted. Or, consider taking with you proof of your coverage in the form of a copy of your credit-card policy (although the legalese is hard enough to comprehend even when you speak English fluently).

If you are forced to buy protection you don't want, note on the rental contract that you took it under protest. When you get home, submit your copy of the contract to the company's customer service department, request a refund, and cross your fingers. If you were able to get a written promise that you wouldn't have to buy coverage, use that statement—in small claims court, if necessary—to get your money back.

ENSURING YOUR CLAIM WILL GET PAID

One advantage to purchasing coverage is that you can total the car if you want and then promptly wash your hands of the whole affair. If you rely on your credit-card protection, on the other hand, you may have a lot more paperwork to complete, not to mention policy loopholes to contend with. Credit card issuers like to come up with reasons for rejecting claims, so take the following precautions:

- **Put the entire rental cost on one credit card.** If you prepay with a card that provides coverage but then make any kind of additional payment not using that credit card, you won't be covered. (We've also seen claims rejected because the renter used a free-rental certificate—say, from a frequent-flier award. You receive coverage only if you use your credit card to pay for every last cent of the rental.)

- **If the car is damaged, collect all the necessary documents.** Call your credit-card company before you leave the area to find out exactly what paperwork must accompany your claim (for example, rental agreement and receipt, police report, accident report from the rental company, itemized repair bill).

- **File your claim before the deadline.** When you call the credit-card company, ask how much time you have after an accident to file your claim. Some card companies require you to file within 60 days. Others give you a year.

Although there are fewer potential headaches if you purchase coverage, filing a claim with a rental company is not always smooth sailing.

Upon renting an Avis car in Madrid, I purchased the optional insurance to cover theft of personal belongings. But when the car was vandalized and my property stolen, the Madrid Avis office rejected my claim, saying that the incident was "not considered a theft." I wrote back inquiring why it did not qualify as a theft—did they think my property was

borrowed? I also asked Avis's U.S. headquarters for help. It gave a different excuse for rejecting my claim: the insurance I bought "does not cover personal belongings stolen from the Avis car. The optional insurance that does cover stolen articles . . . is not offered in Spain." Then Avis in Madrid sent another explanation: "The terms of the policy require that the locks of the car, and specifically the boot, be forced, in order to constitute a claim." But the trunk of the car was broken into, and the lock was jammed.

The result of my 10 letters and numerous phone calls to Avis over the past year and a half? The company has now threatened legal action unless I pay up.

—*Steven A. Decker, Los Angeles, California*

What a mess. Happily, when we asked Avis exactly why Decker's claim was rejected and why he was given conflicting explanations, it sent a check for $529.45 covering the full cost of the rental. Avis in Spain wrote that even though Decker "did not demonstrate that the car was forced [open]," the company was "making an exception in view of the long time passed and the different answers he got from different Avis *correspondents." By the way, contrary to what Avis's U.S. headquarters told Decker, Avis in Spain does offer insurance for baggage and personal property stolen from a locked car.*

—

Typically, when a rental company rejects a claim, it's because the driver violated the conditions of the contract. If an accident occurs while a renter is speeding, driving under the influence, off-roading, or driving in a geographical region that is off-limits, the contract is voided—and so is the coverage.

When You Change the Return Date or Drop-Off Location

So your plans metamorphose mid-trip and you phone the rental company. A reservationist tells you that, sure, no problem, you can return the car early without penalty. Or you can drop it off in Berlin instead of Munich without paying a fee. Fat chance. We've received countless complaints from travelers who were told there would be no penalty but were then slapped with bills for hundreds of dollars.

—

My wife and I rented an Avis car in Hamburg, Germany, intending to return it in Paris and pay a $95 drop-off fee. In Paris, we called Avis to ask if we could return the car somewhere else later. The agent said we could drop the car anywhere in France for the same fee. To our dismay, when we returned it in Nice, we were charged a fee of $430. We protested, but the agent insisted it was correct. We asked for the car back so we could drive it to Paris and pay the original fee. The agent said that she had closed out the contract when she printed our bill and that if we wanted the car back, we would have to rerent it. We had no choice but to pay the charge. Although its Paris agent misled us, Avis won't give us a refund.
—*Brett Schlaman, Los Angeles, California*

Alas, Schlaman had no documentation to back up what he said the Paris agent told him. Misunderstandings are common in Europe, given the language barriers. Travelers often complain of misinformation given over the phone by rental agents, but if they have no written documentation of what they were told, companies often won't give them the benefit of the doubt.

Schlaman should have walked into the nearest Avis branch with his rental documents in hand, spoken to an agent about changing the conditions of his contract, and gotten the amount of the new drop-off fee in writing.

●

Early returns are also a problem. Say you've gotten a special seven-day rate. If you return the car a day early—or even a few hours—the weekly rate no longer applies and you may be forced to pay a much higher daily rate. If you're told by phone that there will be no penalty for changing the return date, go to the nearest company branch and ask for a written statement to that effect or a new contract.

Car Trouble

●

When I needed to rent a car in Veracruz, Mexico, I found a Thrifty Car Rental franchise called Auto Laurencio, located in a large hotel in an affluent part of town. The car I rented broke down continually on my way to Cancun. The trip took me several more days than it should have, and I had to spend one night in the car, in the jungle. I finally took what luggage I could carry and hitched a ride to Cancun. After securing a hotel room, I returned to the car to try to get it and the rest of the luggage to the hotel. It broke down again 1 mile from town and had to be pushed the rest of the way.

When I received a $980 charge for the car on my credit card statement, I refused to pay it. Thrifty said it could offer me no assistance, since it had no Veracruz franchise. When I disputed the bill through American Express, Auto Laurencio insisted on charging the full fee. Now, almost a year later, negotiations with American Express are not progressing.

—*Thom Stein, Albuquerque, New Mexico*

It's a sad story, and Ombudsman's was not the only sympathetic ear. American Express reopened the case and, although it could retrieve no money from Auto Laurencio, decided to absorb $300 of Stein's bill, as a gesture of goodwill.

Auto Laurencio, a trademark infringer, used Thrifty signs and letterhead for months before Thrifty discovered it and issued a cease and desist order. Had Stein called Thrifty's toll-free reservations number,

*which is accessible from Mexico, he would have been informed that the
company had no Veracruz franchise, and he could have reserved a car
elsewhere.*

◗

Major rental companies maintain 24-hour emergency roadside assistance
programs, and most won't charge you for mechanical failure, as long as
you haven't been using the car improperly (for example, driving on a
beach). But you may have to shoulder the costs if you lock the keys in the
car or put the wrong type of gas in the tank.

◗

I put *gasoleo* in my Avis rental car while on holiday in Portugal
last winter. The car quickly came down with severe indigestion,
coughed a few times, and belched clouds of smoke. How was I supposed to know that *gasoleo* means diesel in Portuguese? I ended up
paying $88 to have the car towed, $55 to clean the engine, and another
$49 to refuel.

At no time did Avis warn me that *gasoleo*
is not gasoline. I have since learned that
English-speaking tourists in Portugal commonly confuse the two words. To add to the
confusion, regular gas is labeled *super*.

I think Avis should have warned me, but the
company refuses to accept responsibility.
　　—*Bill Benbow, Victoria, British Columbia*

*Although Avis insisted that its Por-
tuguese sales agents tell renters which fuel to
use, it decided to issue Benbow a full refund as a gesture of goodwill. In
Spain the word for diesel fuel is also* gasoleo, *but diesel pumps are typically set apart from regular gasoline pumps, so the two fuels are not
easily confused.*

*Incidentally, Benbow declined the insurance offered in his contract, but
even if he had accepted the collision-damage waiver, it would not have
applied in this case.*

◗

If repairs are needed on the road, notify the rental company before taking
any action. Some won't reimburse you for repairs if you don't obtain

their approval first. If you break down in a remote area where it's impossible to contact the company, be sure to save all receipts for purchase of parts or labor, and make sure they state the reason for purchase.

If you get into an accident, follow the company's emergency guidelines, usually outlined in the jacket of your rental agreement, or in the glove compartment. Notify the police and the rental office immediately. If the company wants to put a hold on your credit card to cover anticipated costs, refer it to your insurance agent or credit card company.

Returning a Damaged Car

I rented a car from EuroDollar in London and declined the collision-damage coverage. During the rental, a stone from the road hit the front bumper, causing a small dent. When I returned the car, I pointed out the defect to the rental agent, who wrote, "slight dent and paintwork scratch on front bumper" on an accident damage report. I've now been charged a whopping $405.56 for the damage, and the invoice EuroDollar sent includes replacement of the bumper and repair to the left front directional signal. I think the company is taking advantage of me.

—*Dorcas Tomlinson, Portland, Oregon*

Ombudsman thought so too, and forwarded Tomlinson's complaint to EuroDollar, which sent a $160.47 refund. It also removed her refueling charge as a goodwill gesture. The replacement bumper was necessary, but Tomlinson was charged for additional repairs that were not her fault, EuroDollar told us, adding that sometimes, when several items on a car are replaced at the same time, the repairers bill EuroDollar for them on the same invoice. The company apologized and said it has taken action to prevent such a mistake from recurring.

A lot of travelers get overcharged for repairs, particularly overseas. How to avoid excessive damage costs?

- **Examine your car thoroughly.** Look it over carefully with a rental agent before accepting it and driving off.

- **Examine it again with an agent when you return it.** Don't drop it off after hours, when no one is around. If there's damage, don't just leave an explanatory note on the windshield.

- **Leave enough time for returning the car.** Some travelers can't discuss the damage with an employee because they're racing to catch a plane.

- **Don't leave without an itemized report signed by the agent.** If you have a camera, take photos of the damage as evidence.

You Get Home . . . and You're Slapped with Another Bill

You might reasonably think that the receipt you sign when you return a car represents the final amount you'll have to pay. But that would be too easy. In addition to possible damage costs and refueling fees, rental companies reserve the right to a "final audit." This means that if headquarters discovers weeks later that its rental location made a mistake and undercharged you, it will send you a bill for the extra amount.

When I rented a car from Hertz in Seville, the bill, which I paid with my American Express card, came to $298.47. Back home, my American Express statement showed that I owed $423.08. When I disputed the charge, American Express contacted Hertz, which sent a copy of the rental agreement. Hertz's copy of the contract shows a different daily rate than mine does: Hertz's total is 41,786 pesetas, and mine is 29,847. American Express then sent me a copy of a telex from Hertz in Spain saying that the amount on my credit-card statement was correct, that Hertz would not accept a charge-back, and that it considered the case closed. American Express now claims that the $423.08 charge is correct.
—*Judith Gorgone, West Newton, Massachusetts*

Well, Ombudsman wasn't at all convinced, so we contacted Hertz's headquarters, which promptly determined that Gorgone was overcharged and issued a refund. Gorgone originally booked her rental for a shorter period of time than she actually kept the car. Her original rate was for three- or four-day rentals. When she ended up keeping the car for seven days, she was offered a cheaper, seven-day rate. Later, when Hertz audited Gorgone's bill, it mistakenly charged the original rate.

Hertz told us that Gorgone should have contacted Hertz's customer-relations department in the United States, which "could have retrieved Ms. Gorgone's Spanish rental record immediately, detected the mistake, and corrected it." Ombudsman has noticed that travelers who encounter billing problems on rentals abroad are indeed typically much better off contacting the company's U.S. headquarters. Gorgone did not contact customer relations because she assumed that the telex from Hertz in Spain represented the company's final decision. In Ombudsman's opinion, even if Gorgone did not know enough to contact Hertz in the States, American Express certainly should have.

A car company that boosts your bill after the fact because it miscalculated the rental rate is guilty of deceptive business practices, says Judge Thomas A. Dickerson, author of *Travel Law,* the travel industry's standard legal reference. If a rental agency performs this type of final audit, he says, you should consider yourself defrauded and head for small claims court.

Where to Turn for Help

COMPLAINTS

American Society of Travel Agents
Consumer Affairs Department
✉ 1101 King St., Suite 200
Alexandria, VA 22314
☎ 703/706–0387
FAX 703/684–8319

There is no car rental industry organization that investigates or mediates customer disputes. However, ASTA, the largest travel industry association, does mediate complaints against member car rental companies. Save yourself time by calling first and describing your complaint; find out if your rental company is a member and whether it's worth writing to ASTA. If the company is not a member, ASTA may be able to redirect your complaint.

PAMPHLETS CONTAINING GOOD PRECAUTIONARY INFORMATION AND TRIP-PLANNING ADVICE:

"Rent Smart: A Consumer Guide to Intelligent Car Rental in the U.S.A." provides answers to commonly asked questions. It's free from Budget Rent A Car (☎ 800/736–8762).

"A Consumer's Guide to Renting a Car" will give you basic tips for U.S. rentals. Published by Alamo Rent A Car in cooperation with the National Association of Consumer Agency Administrators, it's available from

McCool Communications (✉ Box 13005, Atlanta, GA 30324; send a self-addressed Number 10 envelope with 52¢ postage).

"Are You Protected? Here Are the Facts, Plain and Simple," published by Hertz, is a good rundown of collision-damage coverage and other insurance issues. You can pick up a copy at all Hertz counters, but it's not available by phone.

"Europe on Wheels: A Guide to European Car Rentals," a comprehensive and detailed guide, includes pictures of car models, lists of traffic laws and driving conditions by country, a European road map, and other in-depth information. It's published by Dollar Rent A Car and is available at no charge from the EuroDollar Reservation Center (☎ 800/800–6000).

"Using Credit and Charge Cards Overseas" includes a section on car rentals as well as portions on shopping, lodgings, and other travel subjects. It's available from the Consumer Information Center (✉ Dept. 351C, Pueblo, CO 81009; 50¢).

INFORMATION ABOUT DEALS AND TRENDS

Consumer Reports Travel Letter (subscriptions ☎ 800/234–1970; $39 annually, $5 per back issue) is a superb overall resource for anyone who travels frequently and wants to do it economically.

CHAPTER 7

Shopping

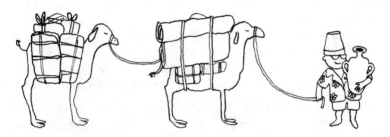

Americans who are cautious shoppers at home tend to lose all reason abroad, especially when they find what they perceive to be bargains. New Yorkers who steer clear of Times Square's crooked discount electronics stores arrive in Hong Kong and make a beeline for the shady computer and camera emporiums in Kowloon. Women who are normally too cost-conscious to approach a Ferragamo boutique arrive in Rome and act like Imelda Marcos, never considering whether the shoes are really such a bargain once tax, shipping charges, and customs duty are figured in.

Why the binging? Sometimes shoppers want to take advantage of a favorable exchange rate. Sometimes they're lured into tourist traps by irresistible sales pitches. Sometimes they seem to equate how much they bring back with how well-traveled they feel. Whatever the case, they tend not to take the usual precautions . . . and to find out too late they've been had.

A few months before her death, my mother-in-law bought what she was told were hand-carved antiques at a Singapore art gallery. She paid $16,000 for a Burmese jade holy water vase and $8,000 for a Chinese black lacquer standing screen. I sent the items to a top appraiser here in San Francisco, who determined the vase was machine-made, 20th-century jadeite, worth between $1,200 and $2,000, and that the screen was also 20th-century and worth between $400 and $600. A second appraiser corroborated the first's opinion, so I wrote to the gallery asking if it either sent the wrong items or greatly exaggerated their value. The owner responded that my mother-in-law agreed to the price, signed the receipt, and was satisfied with her purchases. He will not consider a refund. Please help.

—*Joyce Middlebrook, Sacramento, California*

Good news: The gallery was eventually persuaded to send Middlebrook a $16,000 check. We contacted the Singapore Tourist Promotion Board, which reported the case to the Consumers Association of Singapore. It informs and educates consumers about their rights and responsibilities and is "obliged to conduct investigations in any act or attempt to tarnish Singapore's image as a shopper's haven," the Tourist Promotion Board told us. Both agencies continued to press Middlebrook's claim, and eventually the gallery agreed to a full refund for the vase upon its return. The gallery would not refund the cost of the screen, however, because it claims it never represented it as an antique.

Middlebrook was lucky: Most tourist boards are not nearly as helpful or successful as Singapore's when trying to assist travelers who have been scammed.

Indeed, tourists buying goods abroad do not have nearly as much legal protection or opportunities for recourse as they are used to at home. Which is probably why 95% of the shopping fiascos I hear about concern merchants in other countries.

Caveat Emptor

First the basics:

- **Shop around before leaving home.** Know American prices for items you are considering buying overseas. Don't just assume a Burberry's raincoat will cost less in London.

- **Buy in recommended stores.** Many tourist boards publish a list of approved merchants. And many foreign cities have a local retailers' association with a code of ethics. You may be able to recognize shops that belong to such an association through special signs displayed in their windows. If no such list or signs exist, head for a top hotel and ask the concierge for advice about which stores to avoid and where to find the best bargains. Remember that any city known as a big-time shopper's paradise is also rife with rip-offs and scams.

- **Consider local bargaining etiquette.** In countries where price negotiation is the norm, get used to the local way of doing business before buying anything. Haggling tactics are different in Istanbul's Grand Bazaar than they are in Ecuador's Indian markets.

- **Ask about the store's refund policy.** If it's complicated, get it in writing.

- **Pay with a credit card if possible.** Not only is the exchange rate probably the best available, but also you'll have recourse if there is a problem with your purchase.

- **Look closely at the credit-card receipt you sign.** Make sure the store hasn't added extra digits to the price totals.

- **If you must pay cash, use automated teller machines.** ATMs typically offer a better exchange rate than banks or currency-exchange booths. Hotels and airport exchange booths offer the worst rates. ATM withdrawal fees can add up, so try to withdraw large amounts occasionally rather than small amounts frequently. Before leaving home, ask your bank whether you can use your regular password in the particular country you're going to (sometimes you punch in only the first four digits; sometimes you will need to request a new four-digit password). For a list of ATM locations in the area you're visiting, call the international electronic banking network to which your bank belongs. (For the MasterCard/Cirrus network, call ☎ 800/434–7787. For the Visa/Plus network, call ☎ 800/843–7587 for locations within the United States; for locations abroad, pick up a Visa/Plus "locator guide" at your bank, or access Visa's Worldwide Web site at http://www.visa.com.)

- **If you can carry home the merchandise, by all means do so.**

- **If you must ship your purchase, do some math first.** Make sure the total cost—including shipping charges, insurance, and customs duty—does not exceed what you would pay for the same item back home.

- **Watch while your purchases are packed and wrapped.** Make sure each item goes in.

- **Use a good shopping guidebook specific to the region.**

The Perils of Paying Cash

If you pay in cash or traveler's checks and your purchase breaks, or turns out to be unauthentic or inferior, or never arrives at all, you can most likely kiss your money good-bye.

I bought a necklace from Georgetti, an established jewelry store on Rome's Via della Vite, wiring the equivalent of $1,126 from my bank to Georgetti's. Back home, I decided the necklace wasn't quite right and wanted to exchange it for another. Georgetti promised several times to send pictures of other necklaces but never did. Finally I gave up hope and told him that I wanted to return the necklace for a refund. He agreed, so I sent it via Federal Express.

After I'd waited one month and hadn't received the refund, I began telephoning Georgetti. He kept making different excuses for why he hadn't sent the check. Finally he claimed the money had been wired to my bank but, months later, I still haven't received it.

—*Susan Reiss, New York, New York*

Reiss finally got her money back, after a frustrating tug-of-war with Georgetti. For six months he promised Ombudsman that he would send the money or assured us that he had already done so, providing false registered-air-mail tracking numbers as proof of shipment. Complaints Reiss filed with the Italian Government Travel Office and the chamber of commerce in Rome proved ineffective. So we contacted Movimento Consumatori (Consumers' Movement), a Milan-based organization that defends the rights of tourists and other consumers in 19 European countries. It threatened Georgetti with legal action, but to no avail. Only when Movimento Consumatori's lawyer walked into Georgetti's shop and demanded Reiss's money immediately, in cash, did Georgetti give in.

If you have trouble with a purchase made with cash, see if the country's U.S. tourist bureau can help. Some are more helpful than others. We give Britain, France, Germany, Hong Kong, Singapore, and Sweden gold stars. India and Italy are another story. Much depends on the particular staff member you deal with, so call and ask whether assistance is possible. If so, send a brief description of your complaint and include all documentation—invoices, credit-card receipts, the merchant's name, address, phone, and fax number.

A helpful tourist office may contact its branch nearest the store, which may write the merchant and request a solution to the problem. If the store doesn't respond, the tourist bureau usually can't do much legally, but a letter or call will often prod a merchant into action. Sometimes a tourist board can forward your complaint to a different government agency or consumer protection organization that can help.

If the tourist office proves useless and you're seething with frustration, think whether you might know someone who lives near the merchant or will be traveling to the area. Ask him or her to stop by the store and try clearing up the matter. We've seen this tactic succeed surprisingly often.

Paying with Plastic: The Perks

Far better to use a charge card or credit card. (Although the two are not exactly the same, I use the terms here interchangeably, since that's how they are often used colloquially.) If you buy something that never arrives, you're protected. Just contact your credit-card issuer and request a chargeback, or write the merchant asking for an explanation and send a copy to your credit-card issuer. Your card company must investigate the situation and, if the merchant can't prove that he sent the item, you will get your money back.

The trick here is to make sure you report non-receipt of merchandise within the time limit specified by law (60 days) or by your particular credit card (which may give you more leeway). If you make purchases abroad with a Visa card, for instance, you usually have 180 days from the posting date—the date the merchant posts the transaction—to write your card issuer and request an investigation. For goods you purchase in the United States, you usually have 120 days from the date the merchandise is supposed to arrive. (The same goes for services purchased in the United States. If you buy a cruise, for instance, and the cruise line goes bust before your sailing, you have 120 days after the scheduled sailing date to file your claim.) But the rules differ from bank to bank, so call the bank that issued your credit card and ask what the time limit is.

Whatever the limit, the sooner you file a claim, the better. Especially with American Express, which reviews complaints on a case-by-case basis and may be more likely to rule in your favor if you have been prompt and conscientious. (We've found that the case-by-case system makes American Express more likely than other card issuers to make exceptions to the rules.)

I can't stress enough how important it is, when you make a purchase overseas, to have the merchant specify on your receipt the approximate delivery date and to make sure, then and there, that date comes before your credit-card deadline for disputing a charge. If it's going to be three months before an item is delivered, and your card issuer gives you only two months to report non-receipt of merchandise, either ask the merchant to wait to post the transaction or else be prepared to dispute the charge with your credit-card issuer, as a precaution in case your merchandise never arrives.

The federal law that protects consumers using credit cards for purchases within the United States is called the Fair Credit Billing Act. If you write to your card issuer claiming a billing error, the card issuer is legally bound to take certain steps. It must acknowledge your claim in writing within 30 days of receiving it. And it must contact the merchant with whom you have a dispute and conduct a "reasonable investigation." Within two billing cycles (but no more than 90 days), your credit-card issuer must either correct the mistake or explain why the charge is believed to be correct. If your card issuer does not follow these rules precisely—if it takes, say, 35 days to acknowledge your complaint, or more than two billing cycles to resolve a claim—then the card issuer is not allowed to collect the disputed amount, up to $50, even if the bill turns out to be correct.

Paying with Plastic: The Pitfalls

In promotional brochures and television commercials, credit card companies say they will go to bat for you if something goes wrong with goods you purchase. The result is that a lot of travelers assume they

will be protected if merchandise they buy turns out to be fake, or arrives damaged, or if what arrives isn't what they bought. Wishful thinking.

If you request a chargeback for any of these reasons, your credit card issuer must contact the store and investigate. But if the merchant claims you're wrong, the credit card company may take his word over yours without digging deeper.

I bought three music boxes in Vienna with my American Express card. I had been looking for some authentically Austrian items to give as Christmas gifts, and the store manager said the music boxes were made in a village near Innsbruck. She placed a gold seal with the store's name on each one. On the train to Salzburg that night, I peeled off one of the labels and read that the merchandise was made in China.

Upon arriving in Salzburg, I mailed the music boxes back to the store and told American Express not to pay the charge, which had not yet been posted. When the $711.68 charge appeared on my monthly statement, I disputed it. Now American Express says I must pay it, because "the establishment is not willing to take any action, and there is no indication that the establishment received the merchandise." Do you think this is fair?

—*William O. Shank, Crystal Lake, Illinois*

Certainly not. But it took some doing to get American Express to agree to credit Shank's account with the $711.68. First we asked American Express why it accepted the store's claim that it never received the music boxes rather than Shank's claim that he had returned them. American Express responded by asking for proof that Shank had mailed the merchandise. He sent a copy of his receipt from the Salzburg post office. American Express then asked for proof that the merchandise had been delivered. Ombudsman pointed out that getting such documentation would be difficult, if not impossible. American Express looked into the matter again and, upon discovering that Shank is a long-standing cardmember, credited his account.

What if a merchant fails even to respond to a credit card issuer's attempts at an investigation?

A Dali lithograph that I bought for $1,520.75 at a gallery in Venice was supposed to come with a letter of authenticity. When it arrived, there was no letter, so I took it to an expert, who said that it was not a lithograph but a far less costly silk screen. I phoned the gallery, which said that the letter was on its way and that if we were not happy with the artwork, we could return it for a full refund. And MasterCard said that if I returned it and got a signed receipt, it would credit my account. The letter of authenticity never arrived, so I returned the art and sent MasterCard the receipt. MasterCard now says that it can't help me because the gallery won't respond to its letters. So I have neither the artwork nor the money I paid for it.

—*Cary Manning, Solana Beach, California*

When Ombudsman wrote to the gallery, it promptly searched its files, located the billing mistake, apologized and issued a refund. Frankly, Ombudsman is surprised that MasterCard was not able to do more for Manning. Federal regulations require that a credit card company investigate a disputed claim to the best of its ability. Considering how quickly the gallery answered our letter and how willingly it issued the refund, we wonder why MasterCard did not have more success.

Credit card companies say that their hands are often tied when dealing with merchants in foreign countries because of local laws—or the lack thereof. As Visa puts it, "The level of consumer protection for international transactions varies significantly from country to country. Prices open to negotiation, sales 'hype,' and merchant return policies are judged by different cultural standards. Except in the case of outright fraud, such standards are beyond Visa's power to regulate."

The point is that you cannot use your credit card as insurance against your own naïveté. You must treat your card as if it were cash.

In addition to having a merchant write the estimated delivery date on your receipt, you should:

- **Make sure the receipt includes a detailed description of your purchase.** If you receive the wrong thing, it will be tougher for the merchant to argue that he sent what you ordered.

- **Take a photo of the item in the store.** If you receive something different, or it arrives damaged, your case will be stronger if you have a record of what it looked like when you bought it. Of course, this may not be possible if you're buying something custom-made.

I bought three chandeliers from Mazzega SRL in Murano, Italy, with my American Express Platinum Card. They were to be custom-made, but I did not have the specifications with me. Mazzega agreed that I could send them when I got home. Back in Los Angeles two weeks later, I saw a similar chandelier for about one-fourth the price. I notified American Express's Platinum Card department, which agreed that I had the right to cancel if the goods were grossly overpriced. I immediately canceled my order.

A few months later, the merchandise arrived. I returned it, but apparently it's sitting somewhere on a pier in Murano. Mazzega says it won't accept the goods back because they had already been produced at the time I canceled. How could the store have produced a custom order without knowing the size and color I wanted?

My Platinum Card brochure states, "If a transaction is not completed as you have directed . . . we will be liable for your losses or damages." But American Express is billing me for the full amount, I have no chandeliers, and I'm out over $12,000.

—*Georgina Makabali, Los Angeles, California*

American Express wouldn't budge on this one. It said it had ful-
filled its responsibility to Makabali by investigating the case thoroughly
and that it could not fault the merchant, because Mazzega had warned
at the time of the purchase that the goods were custom-made and therefore non-returnable. As American Express sees it, Makabali purchased
the goods when she said she would send the specifications; when she
didn't, the store was right to ship the merchandise anyway, thus fulfilling
its side of the transaction. American Express also said it could not verify that the chandeliers were overpriced, because it did not know for sure
that the less expensive, "similar" chandelier was of the same quality.

We don't know what eventually happened to the chandeliers, but the
moral of the story is clear: If you buy something for $1,000 and when
you get home you find out it's worth $100, don't rely on your credit card
for help.

Avoiding Scams

ANTIQUES AND ARTWORK

Where there is great art there are great con artists. How to avoid them?

- **Stick to stores approved by the tourist board.** Or look for shops with signs in
the window indicating membership in a merchant's association with a
code of ethics.

- **Ask lots of questions about any item you're interested in buying.** If the dealer
doesn't know when it was made, where, and by whom, and doesn't offer
to find out, make for the door. Reputable dealers love to educate customers and will usually tell you more about a particular item than you
ever wanted to know.

- **Make sure the invoice gives a detailed description of the object you are purchasing.** It should include the object's age, its origin, and any flaws or repairs
done to it. For antiques, get authenticity papers. (Of course, disreputable
antiques dealers have been known to issue fake papers.)

- **Get a second opinion.** If you don't know the value of an item or whether to
trust the salesperson, some local dealers will appraise a piece for you for
a flat fee.

JEWELRY

My wife and I traveled to Bangkok to buy a sapphire for her wedding ring. We were wary, since we'd heard so much about jewelry scams in Thailand. We spent three days visiting the jewelers recommended in the Tourism Authority of Thailand (TAT) brochure. We also went to the head of the American Express customer service office in Bangkok and asked him this question: If we buy the sapphire using our American Express card, get a guarantee of authenticity from the seller, and then find out from an appraiser back home that the sapphire's value is not the amount represented on the certificate of guarantee, will American Express cancel the transaction? He assured us that it would. We asked Betty Thai Silk & Jewelers Co., Ltd., whether a sale contingent upon appraisal in the United States and subject to cancellation by American Express would be acceptable. They said yes, and we bought a $5,515 sapphire.

Back home, we found out that the stone is worth about $1,540. Many letters and phone calls to American Express led to two fruitless investigations of Betty Thai, which refuses to acknowledge the fraud or honor the guarantee. I don't know what more we could have done, as careful consumers, to protect our interests.

—*Paul Van Camp, Cardiff, California*

Neither did we, so we brought the matter up again with American Express. Although unable to retrieve one cent from Betty Thai, it ultimately decided to make up the difference between the amount Van Camp paid and the stone's actual retail value. Van Camp took every precaution advised by the TAT: Buy only at the establishments listed in the TAT brochure (they "guarantee quality at competitive prices"), comparison shop, pay by credit card, and request a certificate of authenticity.

The TAT no longer keeps a list of approved merchants, but it does record complaints filed against businesses (lately there have been no complaints about Betty Thai) and says it will mediate for travelers with disputes. There was no central organization for jewelry appraisal at the time Van Camp bought his sapphire, but today, according to the TAT, the Thai Gem Center serves as a reliable appraiser.

Heading for one of the world's great jewelry markets?

- **Shop around at home first.** Get prices for gems you're interested in from an American jeweler you trust. Don't just assume you can do better overseas.

- **Whatever the jeweler tells you about a stone you're buying, get it in writing.** The description should include the carat weight, color and clarity grades, flaws, and country of origin. This helps not only if you're sold a fake but also for clearing customs.

- **Verify your purchase locally, if possible.** Some countries have gem-testing laboratories.

ELECTRONICS

Surprised that a pastime as innocent as shopping can turn so hazardous? Well, it only gets worse. Fasten your seat belts.

Hoping to buy a video camera in Hong Kong, I described exactly what I wanted to a salesman at an electronics store on Nathan Road in Kowloon. He showed me a camera that he said suited all my needs and could be used with an adapter. We agreed on a price and he took my Visa card and gave it to the clerk. While the transaction was being authorized, he offered to spend some time in the back room showing me how to operate the camera. It soon became clear that it couldn't be used with an adapter after all. He denied having said it could, then began trying to sell me cameras more expensive than the one I'd chosen, refusing to give back my Visa card unless I bought one. He wouldn't budge when I said I'd call the police. Finally, just to get away from the store, I signed a credit card slip for a camera costing $731.53.

I disputed the charge with my Visa issuer, Bank One of Columbus, Ohio. But it won't help because my credit card slip says "I acknowledge satisfactory receipt of relative goods/services" and "no refunds." Bank One forwarded my letter to Visa International's Compliance/Enforcement Department, asking it to investigate and "take appropriate action." Ten months later, no action has been taken and the camera is sitting in my house, in its box, unopened. What should I do?

—*John Franklin, Burlington, Wisconsin*

The issue is what Franklin should not have done. Signing the credit card slip was a mistake. He should have walked out of the store without his card and immediately called Visa and canceled it. He also should have notified the police and the Hong Kong Tourist Association, whose shopper's hot line provides an avenue of recourse for victimized shoppers.

But we asked Visa International to look into the matter, and, after a lengthy review, it decided to send a full refund in exchange for the camera. "We will not allow a merchant to besmirch the good Visa name," said Michael Sherman, a company spokesman. But because Visa handles complaints like Franklin's on an individual basis, travelers should not expect it to respond so generously in all cases.

Other tips for avoiding electronics rip-offs:

- **Watch out for nosy salespeople.** If a sales clerk asks where you're from and how long you're going to be in town, be careful. He's more likely to cheat you if he knows you won't be around long enough to complain.

- **Know prices back home.** Bring along clippings of newspaper ads showing an array of prices at electronics stores near you, so you can compare them with prices you find abroad.

- **Unwrap and inspect items wrapped in plastic.** Check that all accessories listed on the box—cables, wires, adapters—are inside and that you are not charged extra for items that are supposed to be included.

- **Make sure items are repacked in front of you.** This way, merchandise cannot be switched.

- **Check your receipt before leaving the store.** It should note the names, model numbers, and serial numbers of each item you buy, the date of purchase, the form of payment, and the store's name, address, and retail license number. (If you are defrauded, a credit-card receipt or register tape alone will not be sufficient evidence.)

- **Make sure to get the manufacturer's worldwide guarantee.**

Getting Your Purchases Home

You think you can't take it with you? Think again.

Unless I'm buying from a big-name store like Harrods or Hermès, I rarely purchase more than I can lug home with me on the plane. Granted, I'm a little paranoid. But if *you* knew hundreds of travelers who never received stuff they purchased abroad, you'd be a little paranoid, too.

I bought a carpet for $240 in Selçuk, Turkey. I was unable to carry it with me, so the store's owner, Namik Simsek, agreed to send it airmail. It never arrived and he has not responded to my letters. Can you help me get the carpet or my money back?

—*Stacy Cedarholm, Portland, Oregon*

Happily, yes. Ombudsman forwarded Cedarholm's purchase certificate to the Turkish Consulate General in New York, which sent it to the Chamber of Commerce of Izmir, Turkey. It contacted Simsek, who at long last shipped the carpet. Simsek says that Cedarholm requested delayed delivery because she would not return to the United States for several months. But Cedarholm, who returned a week after buying the carpet, says she paid for airmail delivery because she needed the carpet as soon as possible.

Sometimes you can carry with you a lot more than you think you can. I hate to brag, but I myself have hauled home from Istanbul eight ceramic dinner plates, six jewelry boxes, five vases, and four mugs (no, I do not do Nautilus), and my traveling companion lugged home three huge carpets—all in our carry-ons (☞ Packing Tips *in the appendix*).

When It Absolutely, Positively, Has to Be Shipped

Of course, luggage can't be stretched to accommodate the occasional grandfather clock or chaise longue. The important point to remember when shipping goods is that merchants can inadvertently underestimate the cost. In fact, sometimes they deliberately undercharge you just to make the sale and add extra shipping fees later.

My husband and I purchased a set of china from Shops of Hungary, in the Budapest Hilton. The store assured us that the $300 shipping charge to get the china to our home would cover everything. A month later we were billed an additional $555 for extra shipping costs, customs, taxes, warehouse services, etc. Because we'd paid with our American Express card, I contacted them twice, but they said they couldn't help. I would never have made the purchase if I'd known the additional costs would amount to almost double the value of the china!

—*Amy Hudnall, Tallahassee, Florida*

After we pled Hudnall's case, American Express swallowed $300 of her bill, as a gesture of goodwill. According to American Express, Shops of Hungary should have known and should have clearly explained that the $300 charge covered shipment only to the nearest point of entry. The extra $555 charge represents the Miami-to-Tallahassee shipment.

Make sure your itemized receipt includes all shipping, handling, and insurance charges and states that these represent the total costs for door-to-door shipment. If unexpected charges appear on your credit-card statement, you will be in good shape to dispute them. Be warned, though, that when your card issuer contacts the merchant, he may respond that he can't help it if the shipping company raised its rates and he may be able to provide an itemized shipping invoice as proof. In that case you will probably have no choice but to pay the extra amount.

United Parcel Service (☎ 800/782−7892) has a list of set rates for shipments from many countries to the United States and makes this list available to customers. I recommend bringing a copy with you. If a merchant's proposed shipping charge sounds exorbitant, you'll have solid footing for negotiating a lower rate.

Or mail your parcel yourself. Especially if there's any question as to the store's reputation or efficiency. If getting to a post office is a problem, have your hotel's concierge ship it for you.

Another option: Whenever I buy souvenirs that won't fit in my luggage but would be too risky and expensive to ship, I head for the post office but, instead of mailing my new purchases—which might require hefty first-class postage and insurance charges—I mail the used guidebooks and clothing I no longer need. Because these are neither valuable nor fragile nor needed any time soon, I can economize by using second- or third-class mail.

What if your purchases are too valuable to be hauled around for the rest of your trip?

I went to a Federal Express office in Hong Kong and mailed gems with a declared wholesale value of $2,094.50. Four of us saw my husband place the goods in the Federal Express box and seal it. Then the agent said that he'd forgotten to weigh it, went into another room for a few minutes, came back with the box, and affixed the label.

The following Monday, in Missoula, Montana, I broke the seal on the package in front of the Federal Express driver and opened an empty box. I don't know how the jewels disappeared, but one possibility is that the Hong Kong agent removed them when he took them into the back room, then returned with another, empty, sealed box.

Federal Express has adeptly played the corporate shuffle with me. They offered $500, their maximum liability for lost or damaged goods. I think I deserve more than that if the jewels were stolen. If you cannot help me resolve this issue, at least I can make travelers aware of the potential risk in sending goods home from abroad via Federal Express.

—Rose Mueller, Missoula, Montana

Mueller won't get her jewels back, but after a year of persistent plodding, she reached a satisfactory settlement with Federal Express. The company told us that it had investigated the matter but would not comment on Mueller's suspicion that the jewels were removed prior to shipment. After the company offered Mueller a $1,100 settlement, she decided to take the case to court. Federal Express then made a new offer, on the condition that she not disclose the amount.

It's easy to ship valuables via Federal Express, but the company's $500 liability limit for loss of or damage to shipments is too low for very expensive jewelry, furs, artwork, manuscripts, antiques, or other high-value items.

What to do? You can still use Federal Express—or any other overnight shipping service—but, if each shipment is insured only up to $500, split the merchandise among separate packages, each with contents worth no more than $500.

Value-Added Taxes: Getting a Refund Without Getting a Headache

There is a savings strategy many American travelers in Europe don't know about or take advantage of. In fact, by not bothering to claim V.A.T. refunds, they left behind an estimated $35 million in 1995 alone.

Tourists in most European countries as well as Canada, Israel, and Singapore can often receive a refund of the government-imposed value-added tax on merchandise they buy to be taken out of the country. This means saving anywhere from 6.1% to 20% off the cost of purchases.

Trying to collect V.A.T. refunds can be either a breeze or a nightmare, and can save you either a bundle or a pittance, depending on which country you're visiting, how much you buy, which stores you choose, what method of payment you use, and whether you complete the paperwork and follow the refund procedure properly. Generally speaking, the greatest beneficiaries are big spenders—those planning to shell out upwards of $50 to $250 per store; sightseers in Canada, where taxes can be recouped not just on merchandise but also on hotel bills; and anyone who is very organized.

Next time you plan a trip, use the chart below to determine whether it's worth your while to go through the potential hassle of collecting a V.A.T. refund. Scandinavia-bound travelers, for instance, can benefit hugely, because the return on even small purchases is so high; frugal types heading for France or Belgium, on the other hand, probably wouldn't be interested.

I've listed the rebate you can expect to receive for each item you buy and the minimum amount you must spend per store to qualify (plus the dollar equivalent, as of mid-1996).

Country	V.A.T. refund (% of purchase price)	Minimum purchase amount per store in U.S. dollars	in local currency
Austria	16.7%	$100	1,000 Schillings
Belgium	17.4%	$235	7,001 Francs
Canada	7%	$73	100 Canadian Dollars
Denmark	20%	$55	301 Krone
Finland	18%	$60	250 Markka
France	17.1%	$245	2,000 Francs
Germany	13%	$35	50 Marks
Greece	11.5%–15.3%	$170	40,000 Drachmas

Hungary	9.1%–20%	$180	25,000 Forints
Ireland	17.4%		*No official minimum*
Israel	18%	$50	157 Shekels
Italy	13.8%–16%	$190	300,000 Lire
Luxembourg	13%	$100	3,000 Francs
Netherlands	14.9%	$185	301 Guilders
Norway	18.7%	$50	308 Kroner
Portugal	14.5%	$80	11,700 Escudos
Singapore	3%	$500	700 Singapore Dollars
Slovenia	4.8%–24.2%	$100	12,500 Tolar
Spain	13.8%	$125	15,000 Pesetas
Sweden	20%	$30	200 Kronor
Switzerland	6.1%	$430	500 Francs
United Kingdom	14.9%		*No official minimum*

Don't confuse the tax that is imposed on the merchant with the percentage of the price that you can retrieve. For example, if the British Tourist Authority tells you the V.A.T. is 17.5%, that means that the government applies a 17.5% tax, not that you will receive a 17.5% refund. Your refund will actually be 14.9%. (If the price of an object alone is $100, and the tax is $17.50, the total cost is $117.50. The refund you will receive is $17.50. That's 14.9% of $117.50. Got it?)

So how exactly do you collect a refund? When buying merchandise, show your passport to prove you're a foreigner and ask for a V.A.T. refund form, which the store fills out and gives to you. Upon leaving the country—or, if you are in a European Union country and are traveling to another E.U. nation, upon leaving the E.U. entirely—show your purchases to a customs officer and get the form stamped. You can mail the form back to the store, and, upon receipt, it will issue a refund, either by check or credit card.

Sounds simple enough, right? Alas, the road to a refund is paved with pitfalls. But before I go over the most common snags and how to avoid them, let me tell you about God's gift to V.A.T. refund seekers: Europe Tax-Free Shopping.

E.T.S. is a V.A.T. refund service that tries to make the whole process easier. There are other refund services, but E.T.S. is the only one that is Europe-wide and has 90,000 participating stores.

Here's the difference between the traditional process and the E.T.S. route: In affiliated stores—which display the logo "Tax-Free for Tourists"—you ask for the E.T.S. refund form, which is called a Shopping Cheque. When passing through Customs on your way out of the European Union, you present the forms you've collected to a customs officer, who inspects your merchandise and stamps the forms. You then go to an E.T.S. booth (they are at all of Europe's international airports) and pick up your refund. You can be paid in cash, by check, or by a credit to your credit card. If there is a line at the booth and you're late for a flight, you can mail the forms in the E.T.S. envelopes provided once you get home (a U.S. stamp must be affixed).

E.T.S. charges a fee of roughly 20% for this service. Highway robbery, you say? I say it's a cheap price to pay for convenience and peace of mind. It's no picnic trying to wrangle refunds out of recalcitrant foreign merchants.

Which brings me to common snags that can creep into the refund process:

- **You can't get your V.A.T. form stamped by a customs officer because none were around.** We hear this complaint from travelers who leave the E.U. by car or train, or when there is a customs strike. In the case of a strike, contact the country's U.S. consulate when you get home. (If the strike was in Italy, contact the Italian Ministry of Finance.) If you leave by car or train and fail to get the form stamped, you're sunk. So, if a refund really matters to you, either drive on a route that will take you by a customs office or, if no customs inspector comes onboard your train, get off, process the forms, and get on the next train.

- **You can't get your V.A.T. form stamped because you packed your merchandise in your checked luggage.** You usually need to pack your purchases in your carry-on (and in a way that makes them easy to get to), because suitcases typically must be checked before you go through Customs. If you must put the items in your suitcase, try to see a customs inspector before checking it. Leave extra time for this, though, and realize that some countries don't allow it.

Plenty of travelers fail to get their forms stamped simply because they were in too much of a rush at the airport to display their purchases and do the paperwork. It is often impossible to get a V.A.T. refund form stamped in the United States, so get to the airport on time.

- **The store mailed a refund check, but it is in foreign currency—and it's expensive to cash.** People often complain that the only banks that will cash the refund checks charge hefty fees that nearly cancel out the check amount. The secret is not to go to a bank but to a foreign exchange specialist such as Thomas Cook Foreign Exchange (☎ 312/993–7545 or 800/287– 7362), Ruesch International (☎ 800/424–2923 or 212/977–2700), or New York Foreign Exchange (☎ 800/346–3924 or 212/248–4700). These services will probably charge a fee of only a few dollars. They have branches around the country but also offer service by mail.

- **It's been weeks—nay, months—and the merchant hasn't sent your refund and won't respond to your letters.** Join the club. It's not unusual for V.A.T. refunds to take three to four months to arrive by mail, particularly during peak tourist season, when stores are very busy. Call the country's tourist board for help. Most tourist boards cannot legally force a merchant to pay up, but they can ask. Although some are useless, others work wonders.

The British Tourist Authority, for instance, will pursue merchants who are members of the London Tourist Board. If you've followed the V.A.T. refund process to the letter, send your documentation to the B.T.A., which will ask the London Tourist Board to contact the store on your behalf. The French Government Tourist Office, on the other hand, may suggest you write to the French equivalent of the Better Business Bureau—the Direction Départmentale de la Concurrence, de la Consommation, et de la Repression des Fraudes, which investigates consumer complaints. The German National Tourist Office will send you to the consulate. Good luck getting anywhere at all with the Italians.

When it comes to V.A.T. refunds in particular, an ounce of prevention is worth a pound of cure, so take these further precautions:

- **Before leaving home, get up-to-date V.A.T. information.** It's available from the tourist board of the country you plan to visit. Refund percentages and policies change rather frequently, and sometimes additional restrictions—too numerous to list here—apply. (In Spain, for instance, the minimum purchase amount applies not just to each store but to each individual purchase.)

- **Make sure you understand how the process works before leaving home.** It all has to be done by the book, and if you wait till you're on the road to figure it out, you may find rules and explanations written in a foreign language and salespeople who are hard to comprehend or who are misinformed.

- **Before buying anything, ask whether the store gives V.A.T. refunds.** Some do, some (usually smaller stores) don't. They are not required to by law. Also ask what is the minimum amount you must spend to qualify. Although individual countries set a standard minimum, stores do not have to comply with it and can set their own minimums instead.

- **Ask the store if it will simply deduct the tax from the price.** Many stores are willing to do this and you will avoid the hassle of getting your form stamped and mailing it. The store may make you pay in cash, though.

- **If you're paying by credit card, ask the store to credit your account upon receipt of the stamped form.** This is easier and cheaper than cashing a foreign check.

- **If the store insists on a check, ask how long it should take.** That way, you'll know when to complain if it doesn't arrive.

What if you don't want to carry your merchandise out of the country? If you want the store to ship it, you don't need to bother collecting a refund because no V.A.T. should be charged. If you want to ship it yourself, you'll have to pay the V.A.T. Give your refund form to the shipping agent with instructions to get it stamped by Customs and returned to the merchant.

Airport Duty-Free Shopping

Let's get one very confusing thing straight: "Duty-free" when used in airports means "tax-free." Travelers shopping at foreign airports before heading home can avoid paying value-added taxes on alcohol, cigarettes, and sometimes perfume and other luxury goods. But you are not exempt from paying any import duty you might owe U.S. Customs when you get home.

The idea that you're going to find unbeatable bargains and save loads of money by duty-free shopping is a myth. Airports worldwide are going to great lengths to improve their stores and other facilities, making them larger, prettier, and more user-friendly (☞ When You're Stuck at the Airport *in* Chapter 2). They're practically turning into shopping malls. But they weren't offering fabulous bargains the last time *Condé Nast Trav-*

eler checked. In our 1996 survey, we found that the best discounts were on liquor and cigarettes. As for other items available internationally—a Sony Discman, Ray-Ban sunglasses—we often found better prices in the United States.

Getting Through Customs

WHAT'S NOT ALLOWED?

We can all name products that cannot be brought into the United States: fruits, meats, vegetables, plants, seeds, illegal drugs. But prohibitions on other articles may come as something of a surprise. I've seen travelers spend hundreds of dollars on ceramics in Mexico or hand cream in the Cayman Islands only to have their acquisitions confiscated upon arrival in the United States.

Articles that are not allowed into this country include: products made from wildlife, fish, or endangered species (for example, tortoiseshell or coral jewelry, souvenirs fashioned from animal skins, creams made from sea-turtle oil); ivory (unless it is antique and comes with the proper paperwork); pirated books, records, cassettes, and computer programs; some ceramic tableware (it can contain dangerous levels of lead, especially when purchased in Mexico, China, Hong Kong, or India); certain pre-Columbian sculpture and artwork from Mexico and parts of Central and South America; certain archaeological and ethnographic material (masks, textiles) from Bolivia, El Salvador, Guatemala, Peru, and Mali.

Some medicines are also prohibited. If you require medications containing habit-forming drugs or narcotics (including cough medicines, antidepressants, stimulants), you should have all drugs properly identified, carry only as much as is reasonably required by someone with your medical condition, and have either a prescription or a written statement from your physician that the medicines are being used under a doctor's direction and are necessary for your physical well-being while traveling.

To make things even trickier, foreign countries do not allow certain articles to be taken out:

I bought a beautiful handmade Caucasian carpet while on a trip through Russia with EF Educational Tours of Cambridge, Massachusetts. The store gave me a receipt with a permission stamp stating that the carpet was new. But customs officials at the St. Petersburg airport would not let me take it out of the country unless I paid a 600% duty. I thought that such a tax was levied only on antiques. I argued with the customs inspector, but he insisted I pay. Rather than cough up the necessary $750, I left the carpet and $50 with our tour guide, who agreed to try mailing it so I wouldn't have to pay the duty. I haven't received it yet. Did I really owe such a stiff tax?

—*Kirk Johnson, Port Angeles, Washington*

Yes. "Russian customs laws and regulations are complicated and highly discretionary," explains the State Department. Russia imposes hefty export duties on a variety of items, and the 600% duty levied on Johnson was correct at the time. The good news, though, is that Johnson eventually received his rug . . . without shelling out $750. The tour guide—an employee of ASLA Eastern European Tourist Services, which helps run EF Educational Tours' Russian trips—tried mailing the carpet from the central post office in St. Petersburg, but it also demanded a 600% duty. Then he attempted to forward the rug in other people's luggage, but each time customs officials demanded the same payment. He finally sent the rug via TNT express delivery service, which cost Johnson only $190.75, plus $50 "to oil the wheels of bureaucracy."

Rugs, icons, art, antiques, and other items that may appear to have historical or cultural value are now subject to a 100% duty (at press time, at least) and may be taken out of Russia only with the prior written approval of the Ministry of Culture. Russia-bound travelers should procure a copy of the State Department's current Consular Information Sheet on Russia (☞ Where to Turn for Help in Chapter 8).

To find out exactly what is not allowed out of which foreign countries, contact their tourist bureaus or consulates. For more information about articles whose entry into the United States is prohibited or restricted, contact the Customs Service or the appropriate federal agency (☞ Where to Turn for Help, *below*).

WHAT'LL IT COST YOU?

If you are a U.S. resident, your exemption from paying duty on articles acquired abroad is usually $400. It shoots to $1,200 if you are returning directly from American Samoa, Guam, or the U.S. Virgin Islands; and to $600 if you are coming from the Netherlands or any of the following Caribbean or Central American countries: Antigua and Barbuda, Antilles, Aruba, the Bahamas, Barbados, Belize, the British Virgin Islands, Costa Rica, Dominica, the Dominican Republic, El Salvador, Grenada, Guatemala, Haiti, Honduras, Jamaica, Montserrat, Nicaragua, Panama, St. Kitts and Nevis, St. Lucia, St. Vincent and the Grenadines, Trinidad, and Tobago. But the rules change if you have traveled to more than one of these countries during the same trip or within a certain time period, so contact the Customs Service for specifics.

After the duty-free exemption, you generally pay a flat 10% duty on the next $1,000 worth of merchandise you bring back.

When itemizing your purchases on customs declaration forms, remember that customs officers have seen it all. Certain signs are tip-offs that a traveler may be fibbing on the form to avoid paying enough duty:

- **Round numbers on the declaration form, or a total that falls just under the $400 exemption.**

- **Obvious affluence.** Travelers who are well-dressed, live in a wealthy neighborhood, and are carrying expensive baggage are likely to have spent a lot of money.

- **Loads of luggage.** A couple toting four or five suitcases may be questioned.

- **No receipts.** Travelers who claim they have no receipts, or who produce handwritten receipts and say they paid cash for everything, are suspect.

To pay as little duty as possible, consider shipping purchases home as gifts to friends or relatives. Gifts of up to $200 (in retail value where shipped) can be mailed duty-free, as long as the recipient does not receive more than $200 in gift shipments in one day. On the outer wrapping of the package, write "unsolicited gift" and state the nature of the gift and its fair retail value.

And don't pay duty you don't owe: If you plan to take any foreign-made personal belongings on your trip, consider registering them at a customs office near you before departure. Overkill? Perhaps, but the Customs Service recommends it, unless you have other proof of prior possession—a receipt, insurance policy, or jeweler's appraisal. Without any document, you could be forced to pay duty on the Cartier watch you got for Christmas last year, or the Fendi coat you bought on your last trip to Italy and already paid duty on.

Where to Turn for Help

CREDIT CARDS

Federal Trade Commission
Correspondence Branch
Washington, DC 20580
Information: ☎ 202/326–2222
Complaints: ☎ 202/326–2418
http://www.ftc.gov/
This is your contact for information about U.S. consumer protection laws, or if you think a credit card issuer has violated your rights under the Fair Credit Billing Act. Its Worldwide Web site can hook you up to other consumer protection agencies such as the Better Business Bureau and the National Fraud Information Center. It also lists regional FTC offices.

Consumer Information Center
✉ Dept. 351C
Pueblo, CO 81009
A source for information about overseas shopping. It distributes the pamphlet "Using Credit and Charge Cards Overseas," available for 50¢.

VALUE-ADDED TAX REFUNDS

Europe Tax-Free Shopping
✉ 233 S. Wacker Dr., Suite 9700
Chicago, IL 60606-6502
☎ 312/382–1101
http://www.taxfree.se

CUSTOMS

U.S. Customs Service
✉ Box 7407
Franklin Station
Washington, DC 20044
☎ 202/927−5580
http://www.customs.treas.gov
Direct all general inquiries here, including information about articles whose entry into the United States is prohibited or restricted. Ask for the free pamphlet "Know Before You Go: Customs Hints for Returning Residents," which explains customs rules in great detail.

U.S. Department of Agriculture
Animal and Plant Health Inspection Service
✉ 4700 River Rd., Unit 51 (74)
Riverdale, MD 20737-1232
☎ 301/734−8645
This is your contact for information about bringing in food, plant and animal products. Or call ☎ 301/734−8633 to request a copy of the free pamphlet "Travelers' Tips: On Bringing Food, Plant, and Animal Products Into the United States."

U.S. Fish and Wildlife Service
✉ 1849 C St. NW (130WEBB)
Washington, DC 20240
☎ 703/358−1711
Call here to find out about restrictions on souvenirs made from fish, reptile, and wildlife products. Ask for a copy of the free pamphlets "Buyer Beware" and "Facts About Federal Wildlife Laws."

CHAPTER 8

Emergencies Abroad

You've lost your passport in Rome and must get it replaced overnight. You need an emergency transfer of cash after a mugging in Marrakesh. On a tour of the Far East, you get a cable that your son is ill. You break your ankle on an Amazon expedition and must be airlifted out of the jungle. How do you get the help you need in an emergency . . . without spending a fortune?

The first place some travelers turn is the nearest U.S. embassy or consulate. These State Department outposts can help with certain requests, including referring you to English-speaking physicians or arranging to have funds wired from your family, bank, or employer. Because of recent consular cutbacks, however, assistance is limited. Travelers often have better luck calling on their hotel concierge or their credit card's emergency assistance service.

Travel insurance policies generally offer the most reliable and affordable source of emergency aid. Still, there are myriad gaps in the coverage they provide.

I spent several months traveling in Tahiti, New Zealand, Fiji, Tonga, and other South Pacific islands. On Vanuatu, while crossing a brook in a forest, I fell on a rock and grazed my shin. At the hotel a couple of hours later, I washed the scratch with soap and applied alcohol and Mercurochrome. There had been no blood, and I felt fine, so I didn't worry about it. But during the night, I noticed some swelling and began to feel pains along my leg. The next morning I was dizzy and feverish. A pharmacist advised me to fly to New Caledonia to get proper medical care. By the time I got there, I was in excruciating pain. A doctor guessed that my leg had been poisoned by some sort of toxic flora—perhaps coral—covering the rock. He took me to a hospital, where I ended up spending six weeks, until I was well enough to fly home. This fiasco has cost me thousands of dollars, and The Travelers, from whom I bought medical insurance, has denied my claim. Needless to say, I'm dismayed.

—*Claude de Pontavert, New York, New York*

So were we, until we convinced the company to change its mind and reimburse $4,567.60 of de Pontavert's expenses. The policy that de Pontavert bought from The Travelers provided two types of medical coverage: one for sickness and one for injury. The company originally treated de Pontavert's file as a sickness claim. To be covered for sickness, a policy holder needed to seek emergency treatment within 12 hours of onset; because de Pontavert waited longer, the claims adjuster rejected his claim. But the company should have viewed de Pontavert's illness as an accident. The 12-hour limit does not apply to accident claims, so the company rectified its mistake.

Usually, though, it's not the travel insurance company that has goofed but the traveler who has misinterpreted the policy. If you buy insurance, take care to understand the exclusions, and follow the emergency procedures it prescribes. If you don't buy insurance, you should know the other options for coping with crises overseas. In either case, the first step is to minimize the chance of a ruined trip by taking some basic precautions before leaving home.

Preparing for Your Trip Abroad

- **Check conditions in the country you're visiting.** The State Department publishes up-to-date "consular information sheets" for almost every country. They describe health conditions, the crime and security situation, political disturbances, areas of instability, drug penalties, and unusual entry, currency, and customs regulations, and they give the locations of the country's U.S. embassy and consulates. The State Department also issues three types of travel advisories: A "Warning," which discourages travel to all or part of a country; a "Caution," which flags unusual security conditions, unstable political situations, or serious health problems; and a "Notice," which provides information on situations that do not present a big risk but could mean inconveniences or difficulties for traveling Americans.

You can listen to recordings of consular information sheets and advisories, have them faxed to you, or access them via the Internet (☞ *Where to Turn for Help, below*).

- **Find out what entry documents and health requirements are necessary.** Will you need a passport? A visa? Will you be asked to show ongoing or return transportation tickets? Will you need certificates of vaccination against yellow fever or cholera? Travel agents and airline reservationists have entry requirements listed in their computer systems, but I've seen them give out incorrect information so many times that I no longer trust just one source. Verify whatever you're told about which documents you'll need with the country's embassy or consulate in the United States, with the State Department, or with the Centers for Disease Control (☞ *Where to Turn for Help, below*).

Some countries have special requirements for children traveling alone or with only one parent, as a safeguard against kidnapping.

My young daughter and I were ticketed to fly Continental to Acapulco, but at the gate we were not allowed to board: I did not have a notarized letter of consent from my wife allowing me to take Kolby to Mexico. My travel agent had warned me that Kolby would need a passport *or* a notarized letter from her absent mother, so I had gotten her a passport. But Continental's gate personnel insisted that she needed both a passport and a visa if she had no letter. I asked if my wife could fax a notarized letter to Houston, where Kolby and I would be changing planes, but Continental refused to allow it.

I'd promised my daughter a trip, so I bought tickets for a flight to Aruba that afternoon. The last-minute Air Aruba tickets were expensive. To whom should I turn for compensation?
—*Robert L. Schweiger, Port St. Lucie, Florida*

As a compassionate gesture, Continental reimbursed Schweiger for the tickets to Aruba. According to the State Department's Mexico Desk, all children traveling to Mexico alone or with only one parent must carry a notarized letter of permission from the absent parent or parents. Continental did not let Schweiger use a faxed letter because, a company spokeswoman told us, Acapulco's immigration authorities usually won't accept one.

━●━

- **Take the right kind of money.** Your credit card will yield the best exchange rate for purchases you charge. Your ATM card will yield the best rate when you need cash. Take travelers' checks if you're going to an area where ATMs are not readily accessible, and enough foreign currency to get you from the airport to your hotel.

  Keep track of the purchases you charge to your credit card so you don't surpass your spending limit. Believe it or not, travelers have actually been arrested overseas for inadvertently exceeding their credit limit.

- **Photocopy important documents, in case they are lost or stolen.** Take the copies with you, keeping them separate from the documents. If you just can't be bothered, at least jot down important numbers—passport number, credit card numbers, travelers' checks numbers, airline ticket numbers—and keep the list in a separate place from those valuables. Leave a copy of the list at home with a relative or friend, in case you lose yours. Take duplicate passport photos as well.

- **Bring documentation for medications you are carrying.** Leave medications in their original, labeled containers. This will help you avoid hassles with customs officers, not to mention arrest for drug violations. Americans have been arrested abroad for carrying items not considered narcotics in the United States. When visiting sensitive countries, carry a letter from your doctor describing your medical condition and the prescription drugs you are taking for it.

- **Familiarize yourself with local laws.** Check the country's consular information sheet for information about local regulations that affect tourists. Some countries are particularly sensitive about tourists taking snapshots. In general, it's wise not to photograph border areas, scenes of civil disorder or other public disturbances, police and military installations and personnel, and industrial structures, including harbor, rail, and airport facilities. If you do, you could be detained or fined, or your camera and film could be confiscated. Also check a country's consular information sheet before you sell any personal belongings such as clothing, cameras, or jewelry.

Travel Insurance

SHOULD YOU BUY IT?

Sometimes the costliest emergencies occur before you ever leave home. You lay out a whopping non-refundable advance payment for a trip and then must cancel at the last minute because you've come down with pneumonia or Aunt Sally has died.

Many travelers convince themselves they don't need trip-cancellation insurance. Many don't even know it exists. Either they don't read the materials the cruise line or tour company sends them, or their travel agent never suggests this type of protection. Then, when they have to cancel, they kick themselves for being so short-sighted (or they kick their travel agent). They write a heart-breaking letter to the resort or cruise line, pleading for compassion, but their efforts are in vain. The company refuses to make their case an exception to the rule, because a refund in one case would open a Pandora's box.

Travel insurance kicks in when you have to cancel a trip or cut it short. It covers you if you become sick or injured during your trip or must be evacuated because of a serious medical emergency. It also provides protection if you miss part of your trip or incur extra expenses because you have been delayed by a certain number of hours (usually 12 or more); if your baggage is lost, stolen, or damaged; or if you require other emergency assistance such as a transfer of funds or replacement of travel documents.

The specific types and amounts of coverage you get depend on the policy you choose. And you're covered only for what is specified in the policy and for nothing else. You are usually covered if you have to cancel because of the flu or a car accident, but not if you cancel because of a business or personal conflict.

You don't need trip-cancellation insurance if you're paying very little in advance or if your prepayment is refundable. You don't need it if you're putting down a $100 deposit on a hotel room or buying a plane ticket to visit family in Florida. But if you're making a big investment and the cancellation penalties are high—say you're booking a $6,000 Baltic cruise or a two-week African safari—you should strongly consider it. You should also consider trip insurance if your regular health insurance does not cover you outside the United States (Medicare, for instance, does not). Even if your health insurance does protect you abroad, it probably doesn't cover emergency evacuations, which can cost between $10,000 and $50,000 (the more remote or undeveloped the destination, the more expensive the evacuation).

If you decide to buy insurance, check out your current coverage and then fill in the gaps. Examine not just your regular health plan but also your homeowner's insurance. Are you covered for loss of or damage to personal property while you're on the road? If not, there's more reason to take the baggage coverage that travel insurance companies offer. Do you have medical evacuation coverage through an emergency assistance program offered by your credit card? If not, make that part of your travel insurance policy as well. Even if you already have adequate medical and property insurance, you'll probably still need trip-cancellation and trip-interruption coverage, which are available only through travel insurance policies.

Shop around for the policy that suits you best by calling several different travel insurance companies (☞ Where to Turn for Help, *below*). Consider the likeliest reasons why you would be forced to cancel your trip or cut it short. Do you have a medical condition that could flare up? Do you have a sick relative? Are you heading for a somewhat dangerous part of the world where hostilities could break out or a terrorist incident could occur? Choose a policy that allows you to cancel for the reasons you are most likely to need to.

WHICH POLICY SHOULD YOU BUY?

Granted, there are few activities more tedious than poring over the fine print of insurance policies, and it's the last thing you want to spend time doing when planning a trip. Far more fun to flip through hotel brochures and shop for the right camera. The more exotic and expensive your trip, however, the more vital it is to examine insurance plans.

If you're planning a cruise or tour, the biggest decision you may need to make is whether to buy your policy from a travel insurance company or through the cruise or tour company. Cruise lines and tour operators sell policies that are tailored to their average customer. That may include you. Or it may not.

Policies change frequently, but at press time, these were some of the advantages of buying insurance through a cruise or tour company rather than from an insurance company:

- **It's cheaper.** While a policy you buy from an insurance provider usually costs $5.50 to $6.50 for every $100 of coverage, a policy purchased from a travel company may be closer to $4 or $5 for every $100. Sometimes the price is based on the length of the trip (say, $49 for a three- to four-day cruise, $59 for a five- to seven-day cruise), sometimes on the trip cost ($49 for a $1,000 trip, $59 for a $1,500 trip). Because the policy sold by the travel supplier is designed for the specific trip you're taking, the coverage and the cost may be closer to what you actually need and should pay for.

- **It's easier and more convenient.** There are no forms to fill out and no signature is required. All you have to do is say yes or no. It's very easy—and tempting—to skip looking over the written policy. Of course, if you don't scrutinize it, you risk misunderstanding exactly what you are and are not covered for.

(A few cruise lines offer a type of basic protection known as a cancellation fee waiver. Although it's not strictly insurance, it allows you to bow out of the trip for any reason whatsoever, without paying any penalty, as long as you cancel before a specified deadline—usually at least 24 to 48 hours before departure. In other words, you're covered if an office emergency arises three days before your vacation, but not if your car breaks down on your way to the airport or you come down with malaria mid-trip.)

Now for the disadvantages of buying through the cruise or tour company:

- **The company could go bankrupt or default.** In this case, you can say good-bye not only to your vacation but also to your money—you will not be covered as you would be if you had purchased your policy from an insurance company. (All the more reason, if you're buying through the tour operator or cruise line, to use a credit card: Depending on the circumstances of your purchase and the policies of your card issuer, the card may provide enough protection against potential default of the operator.)

- **You can't dictate the types of coverage or the amounts.** The coverage is less comprehensive and less tailored to your individual needs. If you buy from an insurance company, on the other hand, you can pick and choose the policy features you want. And you can opt for extras such as insurance for any purchases you make that are broken or damaged during your trip.

- **The amount of coverage may be insufficient.** You'll usually get a lower amount of coverage than if you buy from an insurance carrier. Coverage for lost, stolen, or damaged luggage, for instance, may be a very unrealistic $500 per bag.

- **You are covered only for the cruise or tour portion of your trip.** If you book an African safari but purchase your airfare separately, you won't be covered if your flight to Kenya is delayed and you miss the first two days. If you decide to spend a few extra nights in Venice after a Mediterranean cruise, you won't be covered if you break your ankle stepping into a gondola.

- **Your coverage may be secondary.** In other words, the insurance will pay only for what your own private health or homeowner's insurance doesn't cover. Say your luggage is damaged on a flight. You must first file claims with the airline and your homeowner's insurance. Only after they both pay up—which can take a good long while—will your travel insurance absorb whatever's left of your claim.

- **You generally can't waive the "pre-existing condition exclusion."** This is important, since, in my experience it's the number-one coverage exclusion that trips people up and costs them a mint. Normally, you're not covered if you must cancel a trip because of a medical condition that existed at the time you bought your policy, or for which you had received treatment within a certain number of days before you bought your policy (usually 60 to 90)—unless it's a chronic condition (such as asthma, diabetes, or high blood pressure) that has remained stable under medication and that warranted no medical consultation or changes in treatment within the specified time period. If you buy your policy from an insurance company, you can eliminate that pre-existing condition exclusion, as long as you buy the policy within a certain period of time after you make your deposit for the trip (often 7 days). Some cruise lines and tour operators that sell insurance compensate for the lack of pre-existing condition coverage in their protection by allowing you, in the event that a pre-existing condition makes it necessary for you to cancel, to apply your payment toward a future trip rather than forcing you to forfeit your payment altogether.

Buying your policy from an insurance company calls for some comparison shopping. If you decide to go that route, here are a few factors to consider:

- **Is the plan prepackaged, or can you custom-design your own coverage?** If it is a package deal, it may duplicate coverage you already have through your regular health or property insurance.

- **Can you waive the pre-existing condition exclusion?** If you have a medical condition that makes it important for you to be covered for trip cancellation or interruption, choose a policy that exempts you from the pre-existing condition clause and that allows you sufficient time between the date you make your trip deposit and the date you buy your policy to qualify for that exemption.

- **Are you covered for cancellation due to a terrorist incident?** Sometimes you're covered if the incident occurs within 30 days of your departure date, sometimes if it occurs within 10 days of your departure date. Sometimes you're not covered at all.

For a trip to Seoul, South Korea, my husband and I bought an insurance policy from Access America that covered trip cancellation for various reasons, including "a terrorist incident in a foreign city to which you are scheduled to arrive within thirty days following the incident."

On the day preceding our flight, our local newspapers and TV programs headlined riots in Seoul, the fire-bombing of the U.S. Information Service Building, and general anti-American violence. I was afraid to arrive in a city where Americans were being threatened, and I wished to postpone our vacation until the situation became stable. I phoned Access America and requested a definition of terrorism from an employee who did not know there were riots in Korea and who said that we were not covered for "civil disobedience."

Since we were reluctant to forfeit our entire prepayment for flights and accommodations in Seoul, we took the chance and went on our trip. We were rewarded with a dose of tear gas as we entered the city of Taegu.
—*Frances N. Lilienthal, San Francisco, California*

Access America's insurance does not cover civil unrest. It does cover terrorism, as defined by the State Department: "premeditated, politically motivated violence perpetrated against noncombatant targets by subnational groups or clandestine state agents, usually intended to influence an audience." The State Department did not think events in Seoul at the time qualified as terrorism or merited a travel "Warning". Many travel-insurance policies cover cancellation because of a terrorist incident. Few cover cancellation because of civil disorder.

Keep in mind that Travel Guard International offers coverage of up to $400 for trip cancellation for any reason whatsoever.

If you buy your insurance from a tour operator or cruise line, you should make separate payments for the tour and the insurance, and request an itemized invoice. Here's why:

EMERGENCIES ABROAD

When a friend and I booked a month-long "Highlights of Nepal and India" tour with Mandala Tours of Camarillo, California, we each paid an extra $89 for Mandala's "travel protection insurance." Should we be forced to cancel the tour for medical reasons, we would receive a full refund for the unused portion.

We were scheduled to fly to London and then to New Delhi. Unfortunately, I became ill and feverish on the flight to London. I was 66 years old at the time and reluctant to go to India for a month while sick. So I took the next available flight home, accompanied by my friend. I was diagnosed with a viral infection, and sent my trip-interruption claim to the insurance company. To my horror, the National Union Fire Insurance Company responded that I had no coverage: Mandala's policy had expired. So now I'm out $3,963, Mandala won't answer my letters, and National Union doesn't seem to be able to help. Can you?

—*Esther Schreiner, Silver Spring, Maryland*

Happily, yes. After Ombudsman interceded, Mandala reimbursed Schreiner and her friend, but not without putting up a struggle. When we asked Mandala's president, Dave Sharma, why he had accepted payments for an expired policy, he promised to try to send a refund. Then he said he would offer a tour credit of $2,000 each instead. When no refund or credit came, we reported the case to several government agencies, including the California Department of Insurance. It demanded an explanation from Sharma and, soon after, he sent a refund.

Meanwhile, Ombudsman had received similar complaints about insurance problems with Mandala. Allan and Sharon Heller of Westlake Village, California, said they paid Mandala for travel insurance, cut their tour short because of a medical emergency, sent National Union a $6,942 claim, and were told that they had no coverage. Sharma told us Heller never bought the insurance. Unfortunately, Heller did not have proof of payment: Unlike Schreiner, who was able to provide a canceled $89 check stating "Insurance: India trip," Heller did not pay for his insurance separately. He put the entire tour payment on his Visa card. Mandala refused to compensate Heller. Fortunately, Ombudsman explained the situation to Visa, with which Heller was disputing the nearly $7,000 worth of charges that the insurance should have covered, and Visa sent a check for $4,633.81, covering the unused land portion of his tour but not his medical expenses.

Mandala Tours is now out of business. At press time, Sharma had been arraigned in criminal court on 37 felony counts, but had failed to appear.

A few more helpful hints that apply no matter whom you buy insurance from:

- **Ask as many "what if" questions as you can dream up.** Am I covered if part of my trip is canceled due to inclement weather? Am I covered if I'm delayed due to inclement weather? What if something happens on the way to the airport and I miss my flight? What if the cruise line goes belly up before I take my cruise? What if I have a chronic medical condition that flares up and I want to go home? What if my traveling companion, who has a chronic medical condition, gets sick and wants to go home and I want to accompany her? What if my uncle back home—the one with the chronic medical condition—gets sick and needs me to come home early?

- **Don't rely on what your travel agent tells you about what's covered and what's not.** I can't tell you how many dozens of travelers have griped to me that their agent gave them the wrong information about their coverage. Read the policy yourself, and if you have questions, talk to the insurance company.

- **Don't forget to adjust your coverage if your vacation plans change.**

- **Carry a copy of your policy with you on your trip.** If a problem arises, you will need to refer to it. It will tell you what documents you need to collect on the spot, and what other requirements you must fulfill in order for your claim to be paid later.

Trouble Trying to Enter a Country

You may encounter trouble trying to enter a foreign country if you arrive without the required entry documents or if immigration or customs officials don't like what they see.

When my husband, my 25-year-old son, and I arrived at the Bermuda airport, a customs official determined that my son should be searched. Police officers strip-searched him, took his suitcase apart, found a few grains of sand in his shaving kit (Gary had taken the kit to Costa Rica the previous Christmas and had put shells in it), and decided that he was "in possession of a controlled substance," probably crack cocaine. They said they were going to send the crystals to be analyzed— a process that would take two to three days—and released him. We were to report back to the police station at 8:30 AM on Wednesday. They kept his passport, airline ticket, and immigration card.

I don't need to tell you how we felt. Our vacation was ruined before it started. On Wednesday morning the police returned Gary's documents, said the results of the drug test were negative, and meekly apologized. Bermuda has a drug problem, they explained, and, unfortunately, the innocent have to suffer with the guilty.

—*Muriel Salovon, Pepper Pike, Ohio*

Salovon's is not the first letter we have received from travelers subjected to the scrutiny of Bermuda's drug police. The Bermudan authorities recently began "rigorous training programs" for customs and immigration officials conducting drug searches, says director of tourism Gary Phillips, and "as a result the situation has greatly improved." Still, travelers should be aware that they may be delayed or inconvenienced by nonuniformed officials conducting searches. Explains Phillips, "Unless we have strict surveillance with respect to the importation of drugs, then the tranquility and friendliness of the island will be lost to what has become a growing worldwide social menace."

The U.S. consulate in Bermuda advises travelers with a medical condition requiring controlled drugs to carry a copy of the prescription with them. The consulate says that Americans searched or arrested should rest assured that Bermuda's legal system operates fairly, justly, and reasonably promptly. They should request a copy of the consulate's memorandum on Americans arrested in Bermuda, which explains their basic rights and Bermuda's legal procedures, and they should report complaints about mistreatment to the police commissioner or the department of tourism.

Safeguarding Your Passport

Sometimes local law requires you to carry your passport at all times; sometimes you need it with you in order to cash travelers' checks. At the same time, you want to make sure your passport is safe—which may dictate that you not have it on your person. How to manage this balancing act?

A friend and I were walking in Madrid when two plainclothes policemen asked to see identification. We produced driver's licenses and credit cards, but they insisted on seeing our passports. Fearing pick-pockets, we had left these in our relatives' apartment. We were taken to the police station and locked in a windowless cell for three hours, until our sister-in-law brought our passports. The police let us go but said that we had violated Spain's immigration law, which requires that aliens carry a passport at all times. Is this true? Shouldn't tourists leave passports in a safe place while sightseeing?

—*Alberto E. Lopez, Washington, DC*

Spanish law requires that tourists carry documentation of their identity and legal status, and a passport provides both. But while there have only been a few cases of U.S. citizens detained for not carrying passports, hundreds of tourists have had their passports stolen by pick-pockets, according to the State Department, which advises travelers to leave passports in a safe place and to carry a photocopy of the pages containing the identification information, photograph, and entry stamp. It assumes that although police may not always accept a photo-copy, most officers will let a tourist return to his lodgings to get his passport, rather than immediately hauling him off to jail.

Where should you put your passport to keep it safe? Do not leave it lying around in a hotel room or inside a locked rental car. The best idea is to store it in a hotel safe deposit box. If you must carry it with you, remember that one family member should not carry all the passports for the entire family.

Sometimes hotels ask you to leave your passport at the reception desk overnight so it can be checked by local police officials. This is a normal procedure; local law may require it. But if your passport is not returned the next morning, report the impoundment immediately to the local police and the nearest U.S. embassy or consulate.

What to Do if You're Robbed

Of course, there's often not much you *can* do. Which is why tourists are a prime target for petty theft. So don't carry all your eggs in one basket: Keep a small amount of money in a pouch hidden on your person.

If you are robbed and lose your credit cards, the card replacement process will be easier and faster if you've recorded your card numbers and the phone numbers of the issuers. If you haven't, perhaps your hotel took an imprint of your card when you checked in and thus has a record.

What if you're ripped off on the road?

I rented a car in Rio De Janeiro. On day two of the three-day rental, we were stopped in Lidice, a small mountain town near Rio, by four policemen who asked to see our papers and pointed out that the car's registration had expired. The police demanded that we pay a fine of about $300. We negotiated them down to $100, which was all the cash we had (they refused traveler's checks), and headed back to Rio to trade in the car immediately. We were stopped again by the police on the road from Angra dos Reis to Parati. After we argued that we planned to get rid of the car as soon as possible, they let us go. Returning the car a day early, we demanded a full refund of our three-day rental and compensation for the $100 fine. After arguing for an hour, the owner agreed merely to credit my American Express account with the cost of the unused day. I photocopied the car's outdated registration and the rental agreement and then went to the U.S. consulate to inform them about the car rental company and the police.

Now the full three-day charge has appeared on my American Express statement. In my opinion, the fact that the car's registration was invalid makes the rental contract invalid. I don't think I should have to pay for the car at all.

—*Michael Rosen, Los Angeles, California*

Neither did American Express. In the interest of maintaining good customer relations, it credited Rosen with the full rental cost. According to the Brazil Tourism Office, it is illegal for the police to demand that a fine be paid in cash on the spot. Normal fining procedure is for the police to examine the car documents, record the license plate number, and mail a notice of the fine to the offender. The police (assuming they were the police—there have been reports of impersonation) should have fined the car rental agency.

We've also heard from travelers in various parts of the world who were flagged down by nonuniformed "police officers," who claimed they were inspecting the car for drugs when, actually, they were filching the driver's personal property.

If you believe yourself to be the victim of mistreatment by highway officials abroad, write down the officers' names, badge numbers, and patrol car number and report the incident to the nearest U.S. embassy or consulate. If you don't have time to report it before leaving the country, write to the State Department's Overseas Citizens Services division.

How to Find Medical Help

How do you locate a competent, English-speaking doctor, anywhere in the world, any time of the day or night? And, if you're traveling alone and are incapacitated, how do you get your medical records from home to your doctor abroad?

There are many places to turn for a medical referral, some more reliable than others: your credit card's emergency assistance program (if it has one), your hotel's front desk, the nearest U.S. consulate . . . You can also turn to the International Association for Medical Assistance to Travelers, a non-profit volunteer organization with a list of bilingual doctors around the world who meet the association's criteria, and who agree to charge a specified fee (☞ Where to Turn for Help, *below*).

There are also organizations that help relay a patient's medical history to a foreign doctor. MedicAlert, a nonprofit group in Turlock, California, supplies members with an emblem, which they can wear on a bracelet or pendant and which gives important information about the member's medical condition—for instance, that he has diabetes or is allergic to penicillin or is taking a certain prescription drug; Medic Alert also operates a 24-hour hot line that overseas emergency technicians can call collect for more details about your medical history (☎ 800/763–3428; $35 initial fee to join, $15 annually thereafter). Life-Fax (☎ 800/487–0329 or 770/552–4140; membership $19 annually), based in Roswell, Georgia, stores medical data from a form that its members fill out. Members carry a brightly colored card with the toll-free number printed on it. Anyone helping in an emergency can call to have the data faxed.

A U.S. embassy or consulate can also collect information from home about your medical history. If you become ill or injured, it can inform your family or friends of your condition. It won't pay for your medical treatment, but it can arrange a transfer of funds.

What if you're injured and need to get home fast . . . and you haven't bought travel insurance? The U.S. embassy or consulate can arrange for you to return home on a commercial flight accompanied by a medical escort; by air ambulance; or, occasionally, by U.S. Air Force medical evacuation aircraft. Credit card companies coordinate medical evacuations as well; their emergency assistance programs are usually available to gold, platinum, and corporate card holders. American Express arranges evacuations for Green and Gold Card members, but will absorb the cost only if you hold a Platinum Card and only if you play by the rules.

Six days into a Caribbean cruise, I came down with pneumonia. When I started running a fever of 105°, the ship's doctor decided that I should be flown home and taken to a hospital as soon as possible. No air ambulances were available, so my husband and I chartered a regular jet to get me back to Austin, Texas.

We charged the plane trip to our American Express Optima account. Luckily, we had a good credit rating: the flight cost over $10,000. When I returned home, I realized that I was eligible for emergency evacuation coverage. But American Express refuses to cover me, saying I should have contacted them before being evacuated. Well, I was incapable of doing so, and my husband's last thought was to contact the credit card company!

—*Mrs. Roy H. Williams, Jr., Austin, Texas*

Unfortunately, we couldn't help this time. To take advantage of the emergency evacuation coverage provided to American Express Platinum cardholders and their spouses and dependents, the holder, or an agent acting on his behalf, must contact American Express's emergency assistance program before taking any action. American Express will verify that you need the service, help decide which hospital to deliver you to, and make all the arrangements. Similar coverage plans and travel insurance companies also require immediate notification.

What Else Can the U.S. Embassy or Consulate Do for You?

It can help your family or friends locate you if they are concerned for your welfare. In fact, if you find yourself in a country or area of civil unrest, political disturbance, or natural disaster, you should register with the U.S. embassy or consulate. If it becomes necessary for the agency to contact you in an emergency, it will know your whereabouts and can assist you better. Registration also makes it easier for you to apply for a new passport if yours is lost or stolen.

If you encounter legal trouble abroad, a U.S. consul cannot get you out of jail or pay your legal fees, but he or she can provide you with a list of local attorneys and help you find a competent one. If you are arrested, you have the right, by international agreement, to talk to a U.S. consul, who will contact the State Department's Overseas Citizens Services division. It will contact your family and can transfer money, food, and clothing from them to the prison authorities.

And if there is a death abroad?

On the third day of a Caribbean cruise, I returned from the pool to my cabin to find my 47-year-old husband, Mike, slumped in his chair, his book on the floor, his body cold, his color abnormal. The ship's doctor pronounced him dead.

The next day, in St. George's, Grenada, the ship sent for a local funeral director. He had Mike's body taken off the ship, and he demanded $5,432 before he would transport it home. I didn't have that much money with me, and the funeral director would not accept credit cards. The American embassy in Grenada wouldn't help me with funds. All the embassy would do was stamp holes in Mike's passport and forward a report of death to the State Department. Finally, I phoned a friend back home, who sent a check by overnight mail.

I was completely unprepared for this situation, and I think your readers should know the limits of what the government will do in such emergencies.

—*Cathryn Witty, Shelton, Connecticut*

It's surprising how little embassies and consulates overseas do for bereaved travelers like Witty. They prepare an official Foreign Service Report of Death and help arrange for a local burial or for the return of the remains to the United States. They arrange for the safeguarding of the deceased's personal effects and documents, prepare an inventory, and distribute the property according to instructions from family members. If the deceased was traveling alone, they locate and inform the next-of-kin and relay the necessary funds from home to cover the costs involved to the embassy or consulate. But they do not loan money to transport the body home. So, after the funeral director took charge of shipping her husband's body and the cruise line arranged for Witty's air travel home, there was not much more the U.S. embassy in Grenada could have done. Had Witty purchased an emergency assistance policy from a travel insurance or credit card company, all the funeral and shipping expenses would have been covered.

Other things consular officers *cannot* do for you: get you visas or driving permits; act as information bureaus or interpreters or law enforcement officers; search for missing luggage; call your credit card company or bank; replace stolen travelers checks; settle disputes with hotel managers; and, unless you are absolutely, positively destitute, loan you money.

The Claim Game: Making Your Insurance Pay

As black-and-white as insurance policies may seem, there's actually a big gray area that becomes visible when claims are disputed. We've seen claims denied with rather flimsy excuses.

I paid Travel Guard International $189 for travel insurance for a Southeast Asia tour. Unfortunately, while hiking in a jungle in Borneo, I tripped and smashed my face against a rock. Some tour members thought that I had broken my nose, but the doctor I was taken to disagreed. He cleaned up the injury free of charge and said I could continue the trip.

Back home, x-rays showed that my nose was indeed broken. A plastic surgeon had to break it again and reposition it. I sent Travel Guard a claim for $2,308, which it rejected because I could not prove that my initial medical treatment had occurred during the trip. I wrote back, saying that everyone in the tour group would testify that I had received treatment on the day of the accident. Travel Guard has not responded.

—*Sister Edith Dunn, Chicago, Illinois*

It did respond to Ombudsman, however, and said that Dunn's second request was somehow routed improperly to the analyst who had turned down her claim the first time. Ombudsman's letter, on the other hand, was routed to Travel Guard's top claims analyst, who decided to believe Dunn and forego sworn statements or proof that the initial medical treatment occurred on the trip. Eventually, her claim was paid. Amen.

If you have a complaint about a policy you bought or think a claim you've filed has been handled unfairly, and you don't want to hire a lawyer, seek help from the insurance commissioner in the state where you purchased the policy.

Where to Turn for Help

FOR CONSULAR INFORMATION SHEETS AND INFORMATION ON TRAVELING SAFELY

U.S. Department of State Overseas Citizens Services
✉ Bureau of Consular Affairs, Room 4811 N.S.
Washington, DC 20520
☎ 202/647–5225
http://travel.state.gov
travel-advisories-REQUEST@stolaf.edu
The State Department issues consular information sheets and travel advisories for virtually every country. It also publishes the following free pamphlets, usually available by fax, through the Internet, or electronically via the Consular Affairs Bulletin Board (if you have a computer and a modem, dial 202/647–9225). **"A Safe Trip Abroad"** gives helpful precautions you can take to minimize the chance of becoming a victim of terrorism or crime and other safety tips. **"Travel Tips for Older Americans"** contains special health, safety, and travel information for older citizens.

"Crisis Abroad—What the State Department Does" explains what can be done for you in an emergency. "Overseas Citizens Services" explains what assistance the State Department provides to Americans who die, are arrested, or experience financial or medical emergencies. "U.S. Consuls Help Americans Abroad" describes emergency and nonemergency services that consular officers provide.

IN CASE OF AN EMERGENCY

U.S. Department of State Citizens Emergency Center
✉ Washington, DC 20520
☎ 202/647–5225
☎ 202/647–4000 (after hours and on weekends)
This agency provides emergency services to Americans who are ill, injured, arrested, detained, or lost overseas. Also transmits emergency messages to their next-of-kin in the United States.

OTHER HELPFUL STATE DEPARTMENT PUBLICATIONS

Superintendent of Documents
✉ Box 371954
Pittsburgh, PA 15250-7954
☎ 202/512–1800
The Superintendent of Documents distributes several publications. "Your Trip Abroad" ($1.25) offers tips on obtaining a passport, considerations in preparing for your trip, and other sources of information. Also available are "Tips for Travelers to the Caribbean" ($1), "Tips for Travelers to Central and South America" ($1), "Tips for Travelers to Eastern Europe" ($1), "Tips for Travelers to Mexico" ($1), "Tips for Travelers to the People's Republic of China" ($1), "Tips for Travelers to Russia and the Newly Independent States" ($1), "Tips for Travelers to South Asia" ($1), "Tips for Travelers to Sub-Saharan Africa" ($1.50), and "Tips for Travelers to the Middle East and North Africa" ($1.50). Prices above are approximate; call for an up-to-date list of publications and prices and for fax information.

Inexplicably, several of the "Tips for Travelers" series are actually available free from the State Department as well.

FOR IMMIGRATION AND
VACCINATION REQUIREMENTS

"**Foreign Entry Requirements**" is a pamphlet that details entry documentation, immunizations, entrance and departure fees, etc., for all countries and lists addresses and phone numbers of embassies and consulates where visas may be obtained. It's available from the Consumer Information Center (✉ Pueblo, CO 81009; 50¢).

FOR HEALTH INFORMATION BY COUNTRY

Centers for Disease Control
☎ 404/639–2572 (hot line)
A recording gives health updates for various countries and detailed information about inoculations and food and water precautions.

The pamphlet "**Health Information for International Travel**" contains comprehensive information on international health and immunization requirements. It's $14 from the Superintendent of Documents (U.S. Government Printing Office, Washington, DC 20402, ☎ 202/512–1800); refer to document number CDC95-8280 when requesting it by mail.

FOR MEDICAL HELP OVERSEAS

International Association for Medical Assistance to Travelers
✉ 417 Center St.
Lewiston, NY 14092
☎ 716/754–4883
FAX 519/836–0102
IAMAT publishes a world directory of physicians in 550 countries who have been screened and trained in an English-speaking country. It also publishes a "**World Immunization Chart,**" which advises on immunizations for 200 countries, a "**World Malaria Risk Chart**" and the brochure "**How To Protect Yourself Against Malaria,**" and a "**World Schistomiasis Risk Chart**" and the brochure "**How To Protect Yourself Against Schistosomiasis.**" "**World Climate Charts,**" 24 charts that give seasonal clothing requirements and the sanitary conditions of water, milk, and food, are available to members who make donations of $25 or more.

EMERGENCIES ABROAD

TRAVEL INSURANCE PROVIDERS

Access America
☎ 800/284–8300

Carefree Travel Insurance
☎ 800/323–3149

GlobalCare Insurance Services
☎ 800/228–9792

Mutual of Omaha
☎ 800/770–1017

Travel Safe
☎ 800/523–8020

Travel Guard
☎ 800/826–1300

The Travelers (Travel Insured International)
☎ 800/243–3174

Appendix

The Savvy Traveler

Packing Tips

CHOOSING A SUITCASE

Expensive-looking luggage is a temptation for thieves and for customs officials on the lookout for travelers trying to bring in purchases without paying duty. Damaged or fragile-looking luggage is also a bad idea. If your bag gets mangled while in the airline's care, the airline may argue that the damage was pre-existing and deny liability.

- **Beware of loose stitching or handles attached with single rivets.** The best handles are cushioned and reinforced with metal and double rivets. Zipper teeth should run straight, especially around corners. Recessed wheels are the least likely to break or get snagged.

- **Avoid tweeds and cheap nylons.** They tear. Good canvas is sturdy but hard to keep clean. Look for nylons of at least 430 denier—top performers are Ballistic Nylon, bomb cloth, and Cordura.

CHOOSING A GARMENT BAG

Many planes have little or no closet space, so choose a bag that can be shoved into the overhead bin.

- **Avoid leather.** It's beautiful but weighty. Again, Ballistic Nylon is a good choice. It's lightweight, long-lasting, and practically slash-proof.

- **Go for a bag with a wide, padded shoulder strap.**

- **Look for compartments that are accessible from both outside and inside.** This makes it easier to find things.

WHAT TO PUT IN YOUR CARRY-ON

Pack anything you might need during the first 24 hours of your trip. This way, you'll be covered if your checked baggage gets lost. Include a change of clothes, a toiletry kit, and prescription medications. Also bring items to keep you comfortable in flight such as eyedrops, nasal spray, and a decongestant (☞ Staying Healthy and Comfortable in the Sky *in* Chapter 2).

Valuables you musn't put in checked luggage include cameras, eyeglasses, jewelry, house keys, cellular phones, computers, heirlooms, cash, travelers' checks, travel documents (passports, tickets, itineraries), important papers, perishables, and anything else expensive, fragile, or hard to replace. Do not carry aerosols, flammable substances or other hazardous materials, or anything that can be construed as a weapon (scissors, penknife).

HOW TO PACK LIGHTLY

Unless your trip requires formal attire, you can often carry everything you need onto the plane and avoid checking luggage.

- **Wear your bulkiest shoes and clothing so you don't have to pack them.**

- **Don't let overcoats, umbrellas, camera equipment, reading material, or pocketbooks take up space inside your bag.** Airlines usually don't count these as carry-ons.

- **Cut back on colors and patterned fabrics.** Pack neutrals (black is good since you can't tell if it's dirty) and just one or two primary colors, so you can mix and match. Stick to fabrics that won't wrinkle: knits, synthetics, most wools. Forget that linen was ever invented.

- **If you're a woman, think leggings.** They take up little space and can be worn day or night and in any weather. They can also be washed and hung up overnight and never need ironing. Dress them down with a sweatshirt or up with a sleek jacket and accessories.

- **Go light on items you plan to buy during your trip.** If you expect to acquire T-shirts, silk scarves, or the like, don't bring too many from home.

- **Leave expensive jewelry at home.**

HOW TO PACK SUITCASES SO YOUR CLOTHES ARRIVE WRINKLE-FREE

Pack on a hard surface so that the weight is distributed evenly and the corners are filled. Pack items snugly so that they don't shift around, with the heaviest items on the bottom and delicate ones near the top.

- Place a plastic dry-cleaning bag or tissue paper between each layer of clothing. This reduces friction and wrinkling.

- **Pack pants first.** Lay the top half of a pair of pants horizontally along the bottom of the suitcase, with the waistband in the center and the legs draped over one side. If you're packing two pairs, lay them waistband to waistband, with the legs hanging over opposite sides. Lay down a sheet of plastic or tissue paper, then place other items—sweaters, jeans, shirts—on top of the pants. Fold the pant legs back over the pile of clothing. More plastic. Then put a sweater or jacket on top to hold everything in place.

- **If you don't have plastic bags or tissue paper, fold clothes in overlapping layers so that they cushion each other.** For instance, lay pants along the bottom of the suitcase. Place the upper half of a sweater on top. Fold the bottom of the pants over the sweater, then fold the bottom of the sweater over the pants.

- **Fold shirts below the waist.** This prevents creasing them in midchest or at the belly. Leave men's shirts in their dry-cleaning packaging.

- **Fill the edges of the suitcase with lingerie, socks, accessories.** Shoes (in shoe bags, or at least plastic grocery bags) should also line the edges and can be stuffed with socks.

- **Turn a blazer or sport coat inside out before packing it or stuffing it into the overhead bin.** Hold the jacket facing you, then turn the collar and lapel away from you and put your hands inside the shoulders. Turn the left shoulder inside out. Tuck the right shoulder inside the left. The lining should be facing out. Fold in half and place in the overhead bin or in your bag, shielded with plastic.

- **If you run out of space, zip the suitcase closed and drop it on the floor.** Repeat until the contents settle.

HOW TO PACK DUFFEL BAGS SO YOUR CLOTHES ARRIVE WRINKLE-FREE

Actually, I rarely use a suitcase. What works best for me on domestic flights is to put clothes into two carry-ons. I hang delicates in one of those simple hanging bags you get when you buy a suit in a department store. (Each item is encased in its own plastic dry-cleaning bag, of course, so that if the garment bag must be squeezed into the overhead compartment nothing will get wrinkled.) Then I throw everything else—socks, underwear, pajamas, shoes, toiletries, books—into a duffel.

- **If the clothes you need to put in a duffel are casual but can get wrinkled, roll up each item of clothing like a poster.** Pack these rolls—T-shirts, shorts, jeans, and knits—into the duffel like cigarettes in a carton. Place your shoes and toiletry kit along the sides.

- **Don't fill shampoo bottles to the top.** Ditto for other bottles containing liquids. Pressure could force the containers to explode. Fill them only part way and squeeze out the excess air before closing, creating a vacuum that will help prevent leaks. Pack the bottles inside a plastic bag before placing them in your toiletry kit.

Tips on Holiday Travel

The heaviest travel times of the year are Thanksgiving weekend, the Christmas/New Year period, Easter week, and Washington's Birthday and Labor Day weekends. The busiest day of all is the Wednesday before Thanksgiving. And in winter, the problems created by the commuting hordes—long lines, flight delays, limited parking and seating at airports—are often aggravated by snowstorms. How to make holiday trips as civilized as possible?

- **Get to the airport early.** Overbooking is more common than usual. (For coping strategies, ☞ When You're Bumped from Your Flight *in* Chapter 2). Before leaving for the airport, call the airline to check for delays.

- **Avoid peak hours and days.** If you're choosing between flights, ask the airline reservationist how crowded each is. Avoid holiday blackout dates, when the lowest fares are unavailable and the planes are fullest.

- **If you think your flight may be canceled, head for a phone.** Call your airline and book a seat on the next available flight or, if another airline flies your route, call and reserve a seat on that plane. If your flight does end up being canceled, you can ask the gate agent to reticket you on the next flight or endorse your ticket to the other airline. (You'll be a step ahead of fellow displaced passengers, who will be competing for what few seats are left on other planes.) If your flight is canceled and you used a travel agent, call your agent, who can look up availability on a range of airlines quickly via computer and make a booking for you.

- **Try not to travel with valuable, breakable, or gorgeously wrapped gifts.** They can get damaged or lost in checked luggage and can get crushed in the cabin, since storage space on holiday flights is minimal. Also, security personnel may insist on unwrapping and opening them. If you must carry a fragile gift, put it in a sturdy carry-on and place it under the seat in front of you.

- **If you plan to rent a car, don't leave home without a reservation and a confirmation number.** Guarantee the rental with your credit card, especially if you're heading to Florida at Christmas (☞ When You're on Time but the Car Is Late *in* Chapter 6).

- **When planning a trip abroad, take into account that dates of national holidays differ.** Banks and stores at your destination could be closed. Also, holidays abroad may last longer than they do in the United States. Call the tourist board to find out whether any holidays will occur during your visit, and plan your itinerary accordingly. Make sure you have enough local currency to get by until the banks open and that stores will be open on the day you've allotted for gift shopping.

Index

INDEX

B

226